Children's Moral Lives

Wiley-Blackwell is an imprint of John Wiley & Sons, formed by the merger of
Wiley's global Scientific, Technical and Medical business with Blackwell Publishing.

Registered Office
John Wiley & Sons, Ltd, The Atrium, Southern Gate, Chichester, West Sussex,
PO19 8SQ, UK

Editorial Offices
350 Main Street, Malden, MA 02148-5020, USA
9600 Garsington Road, Oxford, OX4 2DQ, UK
The Atrium, Southern Gate, Chichester, West Sussex, PO19 8SQ, UK

For details of our global editorial offices, for customer services, and for information about
how to apply for permission to reuse the copyright material in this book please see our
website at www.wiley.com/wiley-blackwell.

Library of Congress Cataloging-in-Publication Data
Woods, Ruth (Ruth R.)
  Childrens moral lives : an ethnographic and psychological approach / Ruth Woods.
    pages   cm
  Includes bibliographical references and index.
    ISBN 978-1-119-97422-2 (cloth) – ISBN 978-1-119-97421-5 (pbk.)   1. Moral
development.   2. Children–Conduct of life.   3. Child psychology.   I. Title.
  BF723.M54W66 2013
  170.83–dc23
                                              2013007833
A catalogue record for this book is available from the British Library.

Cover image: © Janine Wiedel Photolibrary / Alamy
Cover design by E&P Design

Set in 10/12.5pt Plantin by SPi Publisher Services, Pondicherry, India
Printed in Malaysia by Ho Printing (M) Sdn Bhd

1   2013

Contents

Acknowledgements ix

1 Introduction: Children's Moral Experiences at School 1
1.1 Adults' Interest in Children's Morality: From
Indifference to Intervention 1
1.2 Understanding Moral Development in Culture 5
1.2.1 Theoretical approaches 5
1.2.2 The need for ethnography 9
1.2.3 But what is morality? 11
1.3 The School 13
1.3.1 Socioeconomic and ethnic composition 14
1.3.2 Values and discipline 16
1.4 The Research 18
1.4.1 Methodology 18
1.4.2 The researcher 20
1.5 Structure of the Book 21

2 What Counts as Harm?: Playful Aggression and Toughness 25
2.1 The Prevalence of Playful Aggression 25
2.2 Playful Aggression in Children's Friendships 26
2.3 Finding the Line Between Play and Harm 28
2.4 Drawing the Line Differently: Contrasting
Interpretations of Playful Aggression 31
2.4.1 Being sensitive 31
2.4.2 Girls and boys 33
2.4.3 Adults and children on playful racism 38
2.5 Crossing the Line 39
2.5.1 Demonstrating toughness 39

	2.5.2	*Using harm to demonstrate toughness*	41
	2.5.3	*Toughness, playful aggression and social class*	43
2.6	Implications for Schools		44

3	Physical Aggression: Prioritising Harm Avoidance, Reciprocity or Dominance?		47
3.1	School Rules: No Hitting		47
3.2	The Morality of Fairness, Reciprocity and Retaliation		49
	3.2.1	*Reciprocity versus harm avoidance at Woodwell Green*	51
	3.2.2	*'She has to get her own back': Zak and Faizel on reciprocity*	53
	3.2.3	*Fairness in aggressive boys' lives*	58
3.3	Hierarchy, Respect and Physical Aggression		63
	3.3.1	*Masculinity and violence*	64
	3.3.2	*'Mr Gardner said don't hit, tell a teacher, but it never worked': Paul negotiating hierarchy at Woodwell Green*	68
3.4	Implications for Schools		70

4	'Whose Game Is It?': Understanding Exclusion		75
4.1	School Rules: All Play Together		75
	4.1.1	*Children's views of exclusion*	78
	4.1.2	*Understanding exclusion on the playground*	79
4.2	Exclusion and Power		80
	4.2.1	*'Whose ball is it?' Exclusion from boys' football games*	80
	4.2.2	*Dominance struggles: 'Holly tries to take over from me as leader of the gang'*	85
4.3	Exclusion for Game Maintenance and Success		92
4.4	Exclusion Without an Excluder		95
	4.4.1	*Three's a crowd*	97
	4.4.2	*Ethnic identity and friendship*	99
	4.4.3	*Distorted perceptions*	102
4.5	Exclusion as Reciprocity		104
4.6	Implications for Schools		105
	4.6.1	*Mismatches between classroom representations and playground reality*	105
	4.6.2	*Power, status and accountability*	108

5	Loyalty in Girls' Friendships		112
5.1	Possessiveness, Loyalty and Independence		112
5.2	Loyalty in Best Friendship		114
	5.2.1	*Maria: 'I let her play with other people but why can't I play too?'*	115
	5.2.2	*Navneet: 'She's running off with Sarina'*	118
	5.2.3	*Zena: Prioritising independence and popularity*	121

		5.2.4 *Erickah: Loyalty and loneliness*	123
		5.2.5 *Multiple values: Reconciling loyalty with freedom and status*	125
	5.3	Loyalty through Sharing Enemies	127
		5.3.1 *'She'll say if you talk with Anjali I won't be your friend': Taking sides*	127
		5.3.2 *'Sarina wanted to talk to me but Anjali kept saying no': Submission and possession*	130
		5.3.3 *Toxic loyalty: Friendship through sharing enemies*	134
	5.4	What About Boys' Loyalty?	136
	5.5	Implications for Schools	138
		5.5.1 *Loyalty as availability*	140
		5.5.2 *Loyalty as sharing enemies*	141
6		Racism: A Special Type of Harm?	144
	6.1	Prioritising Prejudices: Racism versus Homophobia	144
		6.1.1 *'There is simply no room for racism at Woodwell Green'*	144
		6.1.2 *Homophobia: The silent harm*	146
	6.2	Defining Racism	150
		6.2.1 *Race, religion or language?*	150
		6.2.2 *Name-calling or discrimination?*	154
		6.2.3 *'I'm not racist but': English parents and ethnic identity*	158
	6.3	Implications for Schools	162
		6.3.1 *Racism versus homophobia*	162
		6.3.2 *Controversies in defining racism*	163
7		Guilty or Not Guilty: Interactive Struggles for Meaning	166
	7.1	Children's Willingness to Tell Tales	166
		7.1.1 *Telling tales for fun*	168
		7.1.2 *Teachers' responses to tales*	169
	7.2	Children Constructing Accountability	170
		7.2.1 *'It was by accident': The role of intention in allocating blame*	170
		7.2.2 *'He started it': Provocation and reciprocity*	178
	7.3	High Court Judges: Teachers 'Sorting it Out'	185
		7.3.1 *Deception*	185
		7.3.2 *'Getting to the bottom of it': Teachers' quest for truth*	188
		7.3.3 *Witnesses*	191
		7.3.4 *Trustworthiness: Truth-seeking or taking sides?*	193
		7.3.5 *Resolving disputes*	195

7.4   Implications for Schools   201
    7.4.1   Constructing responsibility   201
    7.4.2   Intervening effectively   203

8   Children's Moral Lives in Cultural Context   208
  8.1   Understanding Children's Interpretations and Priorities   209
    8.1.1   Interpretations   209
    8.1.2   Priorities   211
  8.2   Constructing Responsibility: The Importance of Power
    and Narrative   217
    8.2.1   Intention and provocation   218
    8.2.2   Children's narratives to adults   219
    8.2.3   Dominance and subordination   220
  8.3   Children's Moral Lives: Complex, Constrained,
    Cultural and Unique   222

References   225
Appendix   233
Index   237

Acknowledgements

I am indebted to the children, their parents and the staff of Woodwell Green for so generously and patiently allowing me to invade the playground, classrooms and staffroom of their school over a prolonged period of time. Many offered help, support and friendship, which was gratefully received. Particular thanks are due to the head teacher who was enormously helpful throughout the research.

The research I describe in this book was conducted during my PhD at Brunel University. My thanks go to the university for funding the first year of my PhD, and to the Economic and Social Research Council for funding subsequent years. I am also grateful to Christina Toren for supervising my PhD and introducing me to ethnographic research, and to friends and colleagues who encouraged and supported me during this time, and offered valuable intellectual feedback, particularly Ruth McLoughlin and Suzanne Zeedyk.

The book was partly written while I was a senior lecturer at Canterbury Christ Church University. I am grateful to the university for a period of study leave in 2010 enabling me to focus on the book. My thanks go to Wiley-Blackwell for their assistance during the writing process, and to Brigitte Lee Messenger for her thorough, calm efficiency during the final stages. Thank you also to Midrash, Sage, Taylor and Francis and Wiley-Blackwell for permitting me to republish extracts from work I have published previously:

Woods, R. 2007. Children constructing 'Englishness' and other ethnic identities at a multicultural London primary school. In *Approaches to Englishness: Differences, Diversity and Identities*, ed. C. Hart. Midrash Publishing, pp. 172–182.

Woods, R. 2008. When rewards and sanctions fail: A case study of a primary school rule-breaker. *International Journal of Qualitative Studies in Education* 21(2), 181–196 (Taylor and Francis).

Woods, R. 2009. The use of aggression in primary school boys' decisions about inclusion in and exclusion from playground football games. *British Journal of Educational Psychology* 79(2), 223–238 (Wiley-Blackwell).

Woods, R. 2010. A critique of the concept of accuracy in social information processing models of children's peer relations. *Theory and Psychology* 20(1), 5–27 (Sage).

Thanks are due also to Gillian Evans, Ruth McLoughlin, Masi Noor, Iris Oren, Nir Oren-Woods, Margaret Ross and Christina Toren who read and gave invaluable feedback on the initial book proposal and/or draft chapters. I have been spurred on by family and friends, and my husband Nir has, as always, been especially wonderful.

1

Introduction
Children's Moral Experiences at School

1.1 Adults' Interest in Children's Morality: From Indifference to Intervention

What moral issues do children encounter when they are not with adults, and how do they respond to them? This is probably a question we have all asked, whether in response to reading fiction on the topic (such as Golding's *Lord of the Flies* or Atwood's *Cat's Eye*), reflecting on our childhood memories, or fretting over our own children's well-being at school.

But it is also a question of increasing interest to teachers, educational psychologists and other professionals working with children. In the last 25 years, many Western countries have witnessed a sea change in attitudes towards pastoral care in school. Previously, adults at school tended to adopt a 'hands off' approach (Troyna and Hatcher 1992), and were generally unwilling to get involved in children's personal lives.[1] Children were discouraged from 'telling tales' to adults about their problems with peers. For example, in his classic book on children's morality, renowned Swiss psychologist Jean Piaget commented:

> Is it right to break the solidarity that holds between children in favour of adult authority? Any adult with a spark of generosity in him will answer that it is not. But there are exceptions. There are masters and parents so utterly devoid of pedagogic sense as to encourage the child to tell tales. (Piaget 1932, pp. 288–289)

Children's Moral Lives: An Ethnographic and Psychological Approach, First Edition. Ruth Woods.
© 2013 John Wiley & Sons, Ltd. Published 2013 by John Wiley & Sons, Ltd.

This is a psychological work, and it is not for us to take up a moral standpoint. And yet when it comes to foretelling character, it is perhaps worth while raising the question as to which of these two – the *petit saint* [child who tells tales] or the *chic type* [child who doesn't] – will develop into what is generally felt to be the best type of man and of the citizen? Given our existing system of education, one may safely say that there is every chance of the 'chic type' remaining one all of his life and of the 'petit saint' becoming a narrow-minded moralist whose principles will always predominate over his common humanity. (Piaget 1932, p. 293)

For Piaget, encouraging children to tell adults about their problems was a mistake because it led them to become 'narrow-minded moralists' instead of having a sense of solidarity with their peers. This aversion to listening to children and intervening in their peer relations continued until relatively recently. Thus, in the early 1990s, education researcher Peter Blatchford had this to say about adult supervision in British school playgrounds:

I just want to cite what seem to be the competing positions: a 'hands off' approach or an interventionalist approach. When one observes life in the playground one is forced to say that the status quo is undoubtedly in favour of the former position. We seem to have little stomach for intervening in any fundamental way with pupil activities in the playground. We have little desire to change behaviour or attitudes, and are more likely to contain misbehaviour in the hope that nothing untoward happens until the bell goes. (Blatchford 1993, p. 117)

However, during the 1990s, the 'hands off' attitude that Blatchford identified in the UK was gradually replaced by an obligation for adults to intervene in children's lives so as to protect them from harm. The transformation is evident in the difference between the first and second editions of Chris Kyriacou's popular textbook for trainee teachers, *Effective Teaching in Schools*. Both editions discuss personal problems that may affect pupils' well-being, but the second edition (published in 1997) places much more emphasis than the first (published in 1986) on the teacher's responsibility to intervene:

Other pupil worries and anxieties may be the result of reactions to crises at home, such as the death of a parent or marital disharmony, or may be school-based, such as being bullied or having some sort of conflict with the teacher's style of teaching. In most situations, guidance and counselling may be offered by the classroom teacher or pastoral staff. (Kyriacou 1986, p. 152)

Other pupil worries and anxieties may be the result of reactions to crises at home, such as the death of a parent or marital disharmony, or may be school-based, such as being bullied. Teachers need to be continually sensitive to problems arising from such worries, and in this respect the class teacher and form teacher are in a key position to identify a possible cause for concern. Part of the importance of a sound teacher–pupil relationship is that it allows for teachers to perceive changes in the pupils' behaviour that may be attributable to an acute worry of some sort. (Kyriacou 1997, p. 117)

The 1997 edition is much less complacent about pupils' anxieties than the first, and more explicit about the teacher's obligation to look out for and address these anxieties. Indeed, in the third edition, published in 2009, Kyriacou himself notes that pastoral care has become increasingly important in schools in recent years.

Why did this change of heart regarding adult intervention occur? I suggest that it is the result of an increasing preoccupation in the UK with children's well-being, particularly the desire to avoid harm and the risk of harm. Adults in the UK have become ever more reluctant to expose children to various sorts of potential danger, including abuse from strangers, physical injury in public playgrounds and bullying (Gill 2007). This desire to protect children may be part of a larger cultural shift in the West towards notions of childhood innocence (Burman 2008).

Adults' concerns about bullying are particularly relevant to adult intervention into children's peer relations at school. Research on bullying developed in Scandinavia, partly in response to the suicides of two young Norwegians in 1982, allegedly resulting from their experiences of being bullied. The suicides triggered widespread public concern and a promise of action from the Norwegian government (Roland 1993). An international conference about bullying in 1987, arranged by the Norwegian Ministry of Education and the European Council, nurtured interest outside Scandinavia, and within a few years researchers across the Western world were investigating bullying and evaluating anti-bullying interventions in several countries, including Australia (Tattum 1993), the Netherlands (Mooij 1993), the UK (Sharp and Smith 1993), Canada and the USA (see contributions to Espelage and Swearer 2010). Concern in some other countries developed more slowly. For instance, despite some concerns about violence in schools in the late 1990s, the Austrian government did not take active steps to reduce bullying in schools until 2007, in response to specific events there (Spiel and Strohmeier 2011). There is also evidence that concerns about bullying are increasing in South America (Romera Felix et al. 2011).

3

Researchers investigating bullying began to challenge adults' 'hands off' attitude in school. For example, Tattum (1993) criticised teachers for accepting bullying as an inevitable part of school life and for discouraging children from telling them their problems. He argued instead that:

> Children look to adults to protect them from the excesses of more aggressive peers. Adult intervention may at times be inept or even insensitive, but it can be effective if the response is early and firm. It may involve little effort for the adult but bring serious relief for the child. To do nothing is at best to give the impression that bullying is not regarded as serious and at worst to condone the abuse of a member of the school community by others. (Tattum 1993, p. 3)

In many countries, this 'call to arms' either led to or was accompanied by government action. In the UK, a report issued by government body Ofsted (the Office for Standards in Education, Children's Services and Skills) in 1993 recommended that teachers be sensitive and attentive to changes in the behaviour of their pupils, and 'aware of the need to listen to them and to be seen to be listening' (Ofsted 1993, p. 13). In British primary schools, the call for adult vigilance and intervention was supported by increases in the average number of adult supervisors on the playground at lunchtime, above and beyond increases in pupil numbers between 1990 and 1996 (Blatchford and Sumpner 1998). There were also some misgivings about increased intervention, with some education researchers concerned that it could diminish children's culture and friendships (Blatchford 1998; Boulton 1994).

In the UK, the new obligation to intervene was strengthened by public, media and political responses to child abuse. Eight-year-old Victoria Climbié died in London in 2000, following extensive abuse by her guardians. This tragic event triggered a major government initiative, *Every Child Matters* (HMSO 2003). This set out five aims for every child, one of which was 'stay safe'. As a consequence, schools were assigned responsibility for protecting children from 'maltreatment, neglect, violence and sexual exploitation' and 'bullying and discrimination' (DfES 2004, p. 5). Hence concerns about child abuse led to a more explicit articulation of the desire to prevent harm to children and promoted the importance assigned to pastoral care in school (Kyriacou 2009).

Clearly, the sea change that has taken place in the UK and elsewhere places teachers and other professionals working with children under considerable pressure to monitor children's well-being and to protect them from harm. This is a big change in child–adult dynamics from the past when children were more or less left to their own devices in the peer group. This book responds to that change by exploring the moral issues children confront in their peer relations, and how these are affected by adults' new obligations towards them. In other words, the book asks how Western children's moral experiences are influenced by the culture they are growing up in. This more general question has been a subject of intense debate among psychologists seeking to understand children's moral development.

1.2 Understanding Moral Development in Culture

1.2.1 Theoretical approaches

Psychologists hold dramatically different views regarding culture and its significance in understanding moral development. Here I summarise the claims of three of the most influential theories, before considering what this book can contribute to the debate.

Cultural psychologists argue that the morality that children develop is a function of the culture they are growing up in. Richard Shweder argues that interpretations of events by 'local guardians of the moral order' (Shweder et al. 1987, p. 73) are conveyed to children in three ways: the organisation of everyday routine practices (e.g. mealtimes, school), the language moral order guardians use to maintain those practices (e.g. commands, requests) and their emotional reactions to events (such as anger at a transgression) (Shweder and Much 1991). In this way, guardians of the moral order 'scaffold' children's moral development (Edwards 1987, p. 123). Through repeated participation in these practices, children's moral understanding is said to be 'socially produced and reproduced' (Shweder and Much 1991, p. 203). But the approach lacks a clear developmental theory of how precisely children learn from cultural participation (Miller 2006). In the absence of a more detailed account of how children respond to the interpretations conveyed to them in these various ways, the theory makes children look rather passive, their morality determined by their participation in cultural practices (Blasi 1987).

Jonathan Haidt's social intuitionist theory combines ideas taken from cultural psychology with an evolutionary model of morality. The theory posits that humans are innately prepared to see at least five domains of human experience as moral: harm/care, fairness/reciprocity, authority/respect (which Haidt sometimes calls hierarchy), purity/sanctity and in-group/loyalty (Haidt and Graham 2007; Haidt and Joseph 2004, 2008).

Each domain is said to have provided evolutionary advantages to our ancestors. For instance, the harm/care foundation encouraged them to care for young or vulnerable kin, and fairness/reciprocity supported dyadic cooperation with non-kin (Haidt and Joseph 2008).

Haidt suggests that children are initially equipotential in all five innately specified moral foundations, such that these five areas of experience are equally prone to become moralised during development (Haidt and Joseph 2008). Children's sensitivity to each of the five foundations is altered through their immersion in culture-specific custom complexes, defined as cultural practices plus the beliefs, values and rules commonly associated with them (Haidt 2001). For example, in the Indian state of Orissa, many places are structured such that certain areas are seen as more sacred and restricted than others. Children growing up in Orissa thus experience many practices associated with the moral value of purity (Shweder et al. 1987, 1997). Through participating in these practices, these children are, according to Haidt (2001), enhancing their moral concern with purity and sanctity. Children growing up elsewhere will experience different custom complexes relating to other moral foundations, and these will be enhanced accordingly. Meanwhile those foundations that are not supported by a culture's custom complex are said to attenuate. Haidt (2001) suggests that children's experiences with their peers may be particularly influential in this process of foundation modification.

According to Haidt and Joseph (2008), the innate foundations that are supported in a particular culture are not simply strengthened but are developed into moral virtues, such as kindness, loyalty, trustworthiness, courage and patience. They define a virtue as a set of skills enabling a person to readily perceive particular moral values in the events around them, and to respond appropriately to them. For example, to be kind is 'to have a perceptual sensitivity to certain features of situations, including those having to do with the well-being of others, and for one's motivations to be appropriately shaped and affected' (p. 386). Presumably, this virtue would originate in the innate foundation oriented to harm and welfare. But the innate origins of some virtues they mention (such as courage and patience) are less obvious (although Haidt and Joseph 2008 do claim that there are likely to be many more innate moral foundations than the five they identify, which might provide more plausible origins).

Children are said to acquire a moral virtue simply by being exposed to examples of that virtue within their culture. According to Haidt and Joseph (2004), such exposure comes about in two ways. Firstly, children experience a virtue through the 'everyday experience of construing, responding, and getting feedback' (p. 62), presumably whilst participating in cultural practices. Secondly, they experience virtues through 'the stories that permeate the culture' (p. 62). According to Haidt and Joseph (2008), all cultures employ stories or narratives as a form of moral education. These take various forms, from religious texts such as the parables in the New Testament of the Bible and the hadith in the Quran, to 'metanarratives' about history and world affairs, such as the 'liberal progress' narrative about Western history commonly employed by American sociologists (Smith 2003, cited by Haidt and Joseph 2008).

Both cultural psychology and social intuitionist theory, then, see culture as an important influence on moral development. They both argue that children learn the morality of their elders through participation in everyday cultural practices. In contrast, domain theory (sometimes called the social interactionist approach) is extremely wary of the notion of culture. Domain theorists' main concern is that it tends to make us think of a group of people who are basically similar, with the same beliefs and values. Instead, domain theorists argue that within any culture are people with very different perspectives, such that there will always be disagreements and struggles (whether overt or covert) about how things should be done (Turiel 2006; Wainryb 2006). For example, the perspectives of dominant and subordinate members of a social group are unlikely to be the same (Wainryb 2006). If members of a culture subscribe to various contradictory viewpoints and practices, then it does not make sense to generalise across the culture, and to do so will inevitably ignore some people within it – usually those who are most oppressed (Turiel 2006).

Domain theorists also consider the concept of culture to be too deterministic, leaving too little space for the agency of individual people within the culture (Wainryb 2006). This issue is critical to our understanding of how children learn or develop morality. According to domain theorists such as Turiel (2006), children actively construct morality rather than absorb it from their culture (although some culture advocates also claim to view children as active participants in their own development; see Edwards 1987; Haidt and Joseph 2008). Domain theorists observe that if a culture has many, varied norms and practices, then it simply does not make sense to talk of children learning, internalising or accepting them, as if they were unitary and consistent (Turiel 2006).

So domain theory rejects culture and argues instead that children actively construct their own morality during various types of social interaction (Smetana 2006; Turiel 2006), though it remains vague on exactly how these interactions inform moral development (Wainryb et al. 2005).

7

Turiel (2006) suggests that moral development occurs through children observing the intrinsic effects of particular acts (such as kicking someone leading to injury), which they receive or witness. In addition, children can also learn by observing their own and others' reactions to specific actions (Turiel 2006), such as how seriously a particular transgression is treated, and from adults' explanations and reasoning about transgressions (Smetana 2006). All of these are thought to provide children with information about the nature and consequences of particular actions, such that they learn their moral significance.

Turiel (2006) also suggests that conflicts and struggles are important, especially those between peers, which are more likely to address moral issues (by which domain theorists mean issues concerning justice, welfare and/or rights) than adult–child conflicts are (Smetana 2006). Non-conflictual interactions between siblings or friends are also seen as important, providing opportunities to discuss emotions and inner states, which could in turn influence children's moral development (Smetana 2006).

Finally, domain theorists consider power differences important for moral development. Wainryb (2006) argues that people occupying dominant and subordinate positions in a society are likely to have different experiences, and to develop different goals and interests as a result. Those in subordinate positions frequently oppose and resist their subordination, and Wainryb (2006) suggests that these experiences could influence moral development.

So domain theorists join cultural psychologists and social intuitionists in the belief that children's everyday interactions with other people (both peers and adults) are sources of moral development, especially interactions around transgressions. All three theories see language as important; cultural psychologists note its use by guardians of the moral order to manage children's participation, social intuitionists argue for the importance of narratives as a form of moral education, and domain theorists claim that children learn from adults' explanations and reasoning.

Where domain theory differs from the other two theories is that it does not see these sources of moral development as varying systemically between cultural groups. Thus, while cultural psychologists speak of adults conveying their (culture-specific) *interpretations* of events to children, domain theorists see only adults providing (objectively more or less accurate) *information* about these same events.

Recent cultural trends towards harm avoidance and adult intervention have implications for teachers' everyday interactions with children, for the language they use in those interactions, and for children's interactions with each other. So all three theories would predict that the trends I have identified will affect children's moral development. The question, of course, is how. I suggest that one of the best ways to answer this question is through ethnographic research.

1.2.2   The need for ethnography

Despite a large body of research on moral development, surprisingly little is known about children's actual day-to-day experiences of moral issues. The reason for this is that most research on children's moral development takes the form of interviews conducted by researchers with individual children, usually about hypothetical scenarios made up by the researcher (Goodwin 2006). Such research does not tell us much about children's own experiences of moral issues, for several reasons.

Firstly, the scenarios that children are interviewed about are usually made up by the researcher. Thus, children's reasoning about these scenarios does not tell us which moral issues they confront in their own lives. Secondly, the described scenarios inevitably fix some aspects of the situation that might in real life be contested, such as who initiated an exchange of punching or who was present at the time. They are thus oversimplified compared with children's experience of real moral events. Thirdly, the scenarios researchers use are hypothetical, whereas in their everyday lives, children usually experience moral events that matter to them, because they, or someone they care about (a friend or sibling perhaps), are directly involved (Haidt 2001). Fourthly, children are usually interviewed in school by an unfamiliar adult researcher. The child does not know whether she can trust the researcher (for example, not to tell a teacher if she says something that contravenes school regulations), and so may restrict what she tells him or her. Finally, the interview method tells us what a child *says* about moral issues, but not what he or she actually *does* in a specific situation (Goodwin 2006).

Some researchers have interviewed children about their own moral experiences, rather than about hypothetical scenarios. These studies have provided important insights into children's moral lives, for example highlighting differences in children's perceptions of moral events depending on whether they are perpetrator or victim (Wainryb et al. 2005). However, such research is still limited by an absence of trust between researcher and child, and the lack of evidence of how children actually behave in moral situations.

There are also some observational studies recording events on the school playground and how children react to them (e.g. Nucci and Nucci 1982; Turiel 2008). As with interviewing children about their own experiences, such research can tell us about what moral issues children encounter in the playground. However, the focus of such research has been to establish whether children respond differently to moral and non-moral events (a question that is of great interest to domain theorists). Researchers coded particular aspects of the observed events in order to produce quantitative data amenable to statistical analysis. This was an appropriate way to address the question the researchers were interested in, but it does not provide much detail of the events or how the children involved experienced them.

To reveal children's moral lives as they actually unfold, the researcher needs to spend an enormous amount of time hanging about with children, participating in their lives as far as possible as a peer rather than an adult, gaining their trust, and hence gaining access to children's own moral dilemmas and struggles in the playground. The researcher can then write detailed notes describing children's moral encounters and how they respond to them. This method, borrowed from anthropology, is called participant observation, and the written descriptions of people's lives that it yields are called ethnography. These descriptions have the potential to reveal the moral issues that children face, the interactions they have around those issues, and the connections (if any) between these and wider cultural discourses. The cultural trend towards adult intervention probably makes participant observation with children easier than it used to be because it normalises the researcher's interest in children's lives, rendering his or her presence less bizarre to the children than it might have been to previous generations.

Other researchers have used participant observation to produce fascinating accounts of children's lives in and out of school (see, for example, Evans 2006; Ferguson 2000; Hey 1997). However, none of these books focus on children's experiences of morality. A little research on children's morality using participant observation and/or other qualitative methodologies is starting to appear (Evaldsson 2007; Theobald and Danby in press), but so far researchers have not applied their findings directly to psychological theories of moral development, or used these theories to inform their analyses.

This book has two aims. First and foremost, it is an ethnographic account of the moral lives of primary school children growing up in the UK at a time when adults are far more concerned than in the past about avoiding harm and far more willing to intervene in children's affairs. Secondly, and at the same time, the book contributes to academic theorising about children's moral development by addressing the question of whether, and how, children's moral experiences are affected by the culture they are growing up in.

1.2.3 But what is morality?

Before introducing the research itself, it is worth pausing a moment to consider what the term 'moral' actually means. Defining morality is an area of controversy in its own right, and the different theories I introduced above employ contrasting definitions. Domain theory has the strictest criteria, defining morality as those obligations, norms and values that are perceived as generalisable (across different settings), inalterable and independent of rules or authority sanctions (Smetana 2006). Domain theorists argue that only obligations concerning welfare, justice and rights meet these criteria. All other obligations are considered to be matters either of personal preference (such as one's choice of friends; Nucci 1981) or of social convention (including sex-role customs, etiquette, school rules and religious rules; Turiel et al. 1987). There is some evidence to support this distinction. Researchers asked participants whether specific obligations were generalisable, inalterable and independent of rules and authority. They found that both adults and young children, from various cultures, judged only norms concerning welfare, justice or rights to meet these criteria (Smetana 1981; Song et al. 1987).

Cultural psychologists and social intuitionists have attacked domain theory's definition of morality, arguing that welfare, justice and rights represent the moral values only of liberal Westerners. On the basis of cross-cultural evidence comparing interview responses of Indian and American adults and children, Shweder et al. (1997) argued that there are in fact three sets of values that can be considered moral: an ethic of autonomy (which covers rights, justice, harm avoidance and freedom), an ethic of community (which includes the values of respect, loyalty, duty and interdependence) and an ethic of divinity (incorporating the values of purity and sanctity). These are said to exist to varying degrees in different cultures, with the first dominating in the USA, where most research on moral development has been carried out.

Social intuitionists developed cultural psychology's critique of domain theory and its definition of morality. In an influential study, Haidt et al. (1993) presented Americans and Brazilians of high and low socioeconomic status with a range of scenarios describing 'victimless yet offensive actions' (p. 613) relating to the values of respect and sanctity (such as eating a pet dog that had been killed by a car and cleaning a toilet with a national flag). Since these actions had no implications for welfare, justice or rights, they should, according to domain theory, be seen as non-moral. However, most interviewees saw the acts as universally wrong (even if carried out in a country where the acts were customary) and deserving of punishment or being stopped. The only participants who judged the acts to be acceptable were American university students. Haidt et al. (1993) thus argued with cultural psychologists that domain theory's definition of morality as concerning only welfare, justice and rights was inadequate, describing only the moral values of a liberal Western academic elite (Haidt and Joseph 2008). However, the research did not ask participants about alterability or rule independence, so we cannot know whether these obligations really were seen as moral by participants according to all of domain theory's stringent criteria.

Jonathan Haidt went on to extend Shweder's account of morality to include at least five domains: harm/care, fairness/reciprocity, authority/ respect, purity/sanctity and in-group/loyalty (all of which are, according to Haidt and Joseph 2004, evolutionarily prepared). Haidt's criteria for what makes these domains moral are looser than domain theory's. Haidt (2001) and Haidt and Joseph (2008) define as moral those obligations, norms and values that are willingly applied by members of a social group to everyone within that group (or belonging to a particular category within it), and transgressions of which are punished (e.g. through ostracism or criticism). Unlike domain theory, this definition does not involve generalisability (since a moral judgement is simply the application of societal norms to specific members of that society, and not necessarily to those outside it), and says nothing about perceived alterability and rule dependence. This definition would seem to mean that morality is defined by a culture's (or subculture's) majority or powerful elite, raising questions regarding the status of values held by minorities or subordinates.

This book describes a range of values and obligations that were important to children, focusing on harm avoidance, justice, status, loyalty and toughness. All three theories agree that harm avoidance and justice are moral issues. However, status, loyalty and justice fall outside domain theory's definition of moral. Status and loyalty qualify as moral according to the definitions offered by cultural psychologists and social intuitionists, falling under Shweder's ethic of community and Haidt's authority/ respect and in-group/loyalty domains. They also met their criteria in that they were norms that prevailed among the children, who considered them important and penalised those who did not conform to them. Children also penalised those who did not orient to the value of toughness, but this value is harder to fit into the domains proposed by Shweder and Haidt.

Since different theories classify the values differently from one another, in this book I refer to obligations and values without specifying whether these are moral or not. My own view is that all the main values I describe

12

can be considered moral in that they were important norms to which children held each other to account. But by avoiding the word moral in the main chapters, I acknowledge the controversy that surrounds this definition and leave readers to draw their own conclusions about which values qualify as moral.

1.3 The School

The children whose lives are described in this book all attended Woodwell Green, a large British primary school situated on the outskirts of Woodwell, a town in West London serving a multicultural community.[2] It was a highly successful school, evaluated very positively by UK government department Ofsted.

The school had three classes in each of the seven year groups, each class containing approximately 25 to 30 children. The youngest children were in reception (aged 4 to 5 years), from which they moved through year 1 (aged 5 and 6 years) and subsequent year groups until they completed year 6 (aged 10 and 11 years), when they moved to secondary school. Reception and years 1 and 2 were called 'infants', while years 3 to 6 were the 'juniors'. Infants and juniors had little contact with one another, usually attending different assemblies and playing in separate playgrounds. In addition, the school included a nursery, which took children aged 3 and 4 years on a part-time basis. In this book I focus on the full-time pupils in reception and above.

The school underwent high levels of migration throughout the research period, as families moved to and from the area. For example, over the 18 months I spent with one class, seven children in it left the school and seven joined. Teacher turnover was also high, with over 50 per cent of the staff at the time of my research having been at the school for fewer than four years, partly because housing in London was so expensive. Apart from teachers, most staff (teaching assistants, caretakers, cleaners, playground supervisors, playleaders at the after-school club) lived locally. Most staff were female, and many (but not teachers) were mothers of Woodwell Green children.

The school day began a little before 9:00 with registration in class, sometimes followed by an assembly. Mornings were mostly taken up with maths and literacy, broken by a 20-minute break called 'playtime'. Lunchtime lasted just over an hour, after which the register was taken again, followed by more lessons, and school finished soon after three o'clock in the afternoon.

Morning playtime and lunch were the periods in which children spent most time with peers, without direct adult supervision, and much of the data I describe in this book were gained during these periods. Usually, children played outside in the playground for both playtime and lunchtime, having their lunch in the canteen. In poor weather, 'wet play' was declared and children stayed in their classrooms, except for going to the canteen to eat lunch. During playtime, children were supervised by teachers and support staff, on a rotational basis. At lunchtime, supervision was provided by staff employed explicitly for this purpose. In the book I call them 'playground supervisors', but children usually called them 'dinner ladies'. Generally, teachers and playground supervisors did not get involved in children's interactions during break and lunchtime unless they believed there to be a problem, whether through direct observation (of children fighting, for example), or because a child approached the adult to request intervention.

1.3.1 Socioeconomic and ethnic composition

Multiculturalism
Most children at Woodwell Green came from ethnic minority backgrounds and were bilingual. Around 1 in 14 was a refugee or asylum seeker, with significant numbers coming from Somalia at the time of the research. According to school records, the religious makeup of the school at the time of the research was 27 per cent Sikh, 26 per cent Muslim, 22 per cent Christian, 11 per cent Hindu, 13 per cent non-religious and 2 per cent other, unknown or refused. As for home language, English was most common (34 per cent), closely followed by Punjabi (32 per cent), then Somali (8 per cent) and Urdu (8 per cent), and a number of others including Farsi, Bengali, Gujarati, Arabic and Hindi (18 per cent in total). Children of Indian ethnicity made up the biggest proportion of the school (38 per cent), followed by English (25 per cent), then Somali (8 per cent) and Pakistani (8 per cent), with the remaining 21 per cent including mixed race, Arab, Afghani and Bangladeshi. Ethnic, linguistic and religious categories did not map neatly onto one another. For example, of the children who had Indian ethnicity on their school record, some were Sikh, some Hindu, and a few were Christian or Muslim.

The categories used on school records are not neutral representations of ethnicity, which is a constructed category reflecting local and national concerns. For example, some ethnic labels map onto countries (Indian, Pakistani, Somali), others onto politically differentiated parts of countries

(English, Scottish, Welsh), and still others onto larger regions incorporating several countries (Black African, Arab). These variations can be partly understood in terms of how many children of each ethnicity were present at the school. For instance, most African children were classified simply as 'Black African' but, because there had been an influx of Somali families in recent years, 'Somali' had been given its own label. Note also that only the 'Black African' label explicitly declares a racial aspect to the ethnic categorisation (raising the question of what ethnicity white South Africans, for example, would be labelled), which may nevertheless be implicit in other categories.

Labels given to children were also sometimes contested by parents, school staff and children. For instance, parents and the school administrator responsible for entering data on children's ethnicities occasionally disagreed on the ethnicity that should be assigned. This might happen for a child whose grandparents were from India but whose parents grew up in Afghanistan: is the child's ethnicity Indian or Afghani? I also found that some children who according to school records were Christian told me that they were not religious, and vice versa.

What these examples indicate is that ethnic, religious and linguistic labels are complex products of social processes rather than objective information. Nevertheless, they do often map meaningfully onto children's identity and experience, sometimes in ways that relate to the moral issues they face (racism being the most obvious example; see Chapter 6). For all the major case studies described in this book, I report children's ethnicity and religion according to school records.

Nevertheless, in this book, I argue that only some of children's moral tensions and disputes are influenced by ethnicity or religion. More commonly, children's moral experiences cut across ethnic and religious lines. This claim is supported by my fieldnotes (as we will see in the coming chapters) and also by statistical analyses of the answers children gave to questions I asked them about hypothetical scenarios. I draw on four such scenarios during the book, concerning physical aggression (Chapter 3), exclusion (Chapter 4), possessiveness (Chapter 5) and intention (Chapter 7). I conducted statistical analyses looking for relationships between children's ethnicity or religion on the one hand, and their assignment of blame to particular protagonists and reporting of similar own experience on the other. Virtually all of my 18 analyses found no relationship.[3] I have nevertheless included an appendix providing information on ethnicity and religion for all children, for interested readers.

Social class

The school was situated in an economically and socially deprived area. At the time of the research, 30 per cent of its pupils were registered for free school meals (compared with a national average of 20 per cent), and this discounts the significant level of suspected under-reporting. The local area had a high crime rate, linked to drugs and anti-social behaviour by local youths.

It is, however, an oversimplification to say that the school served a working-class community. The reason for this is that English families had come, over a relatively short period, to constitute one of several minorities in the area, the largest of which was a thriving Indian Sikh community. While this community could probably be considered working class in terms of income and occupation, it tended to differ from typical English working-class communities in its attitude to education. According to Evans (2006), English working-class parents of course want their children to do well at school, but tend to adopt a 'hands off' attitude, handing the responsibility for educating their child over to the school. In contrast, English middle-class parents tend to be much more involved in their child's education, which they see as part of their parenting role. In this, many Indian Sikh parents (and parents from some other ethnic minorities in the area) more closely resembled the English middle class than working class. I lost count of the number of Indian (and some others, but rarely English) children at Woodwell Green who told me (usually in confidence) that their parents sent them for extra tuition in the evenings and at weekends, often with the aim of preparing them for the test that could win them a place at a secondary grammar school. This valuing of education has been observed elsewhere in the UK among South Asian parents from India, Bangladesh and Pakistan (Bhatti 1999).

As with children's ethnic and religious identities, assigning children at Woodwell Green the label 'working class' oversimplifies things, but does nevertheless tell us something useful about the general community they are growing up in. I argue in several places in this book that children's moral encounters are related to their experiences of growing up in a relatively poor and deprived urban area which was in the past more straightforwardly 'working class'.

1.3.2   *Values and discipline*

School rules: Harm avoidance

Like any other British primary school, Woodwell Green enforced a host of rules regarding children's behaviour. At the start of the school year, the teacher and children in each class together drew up a list of rules and signed an agreement to abide by them. Despite all classes developing them separately, the resulting lists of rules on classroom walls were extremely similar across the school. Most rules were aimed at creating a quiet, orderly environment in which teachers could teach. Typical rules were to work hard, to listen to the teacher and to each other, and to take care of school property.[4]

In addition to such rules, all classrooms also featured a rule that expressed cultural concerns with children's well-being and harm avoidance: 'We never hurt each other on the inside or the outside'. This rule, which focused on children's relationships with one another, encompassed both physically harmful actions, like hitting, kicking, throwing objects and so on, and psychological harm, resulting for instance from verbal abuse, rumour-spreading and exclusion ('hurting on the inside'). Thus, the cultural concern with protecting children from harm, described earlier in this chapter, found its way into every classroom at Woodwell Green. As we will see in this book, it set the scene for children's moral lives by making harm avoidance the most important value in children's peer relations.

Enforcing school rules: Discipline

In the past, corporal punishment was widely used in British schools to enforce school rules. This ended in UK state schools in 1987, thanks to legislation by the European Court and Commission of Human Rights, which was set up after the Second World War (Parker-Jenkins 1999). It was replaced by a model of discipline based on Skinner's psychological theory of behaviourism, which uses reinforcement (rewards) to encourage desirable behaviour, and punishment (sanctions) to reduce undesirable behaviour (Davis and Florian 2004; Parker-Jenkins 1999).

Rewards used at Woodwell Green included praise, writing a child's name 'on the happy face' (a smiling face drawn by the teacher on the whiteboard), and stickers and certificates given out in assembly. In addition, children could receive house points or class points (or their equivalent, 'putting a marble in the jar', for younger children) for good behaviour. Once a certain number of class points was gained (or once the jar was full of marbles), the whole class was rewarded with (for example) extra play, a party or a favoured activity such as physical education or cookery. All junior children were members of a house, and members of the house with the most points at the end of a specified period also received a reward.

As for sanctions, unless the child's behaviour was a serious transgression (such as hitting another child), children in all age groups were first given a warning for misbehaviour, explicitly stated by the teacher or conveyed by a stern look or writing the child's name on the board (often 'under the sad face'). If they broke the rules soon after this a more severe sanction would usually be applied, such as being sent to sit outside the staff room or in another classroom, staying inside for part of playtime or lunchtime, writing lines, or parents being contacted. Many of these rewards and sanctions are recommended by government department Ofsted; see, for example, Ofsted (1993). Teachers also encouraged conformity to school rules via other means such as lectures about behaviour and comparisons with other classes.

Many teachers at Woodwell Green combined rewards and sanctions with the concept of choice. Their aim in doing so was to inculcate in children a sense of responsibility for their own actions. When a child disobeyed a rule, the teacher would ask him or her to choose between continuing to disobey and facing a sanction, or obeying the rule and evading the sanction. For example, when a boy wandered around the classroom in the middle of a lesson, his teacher said, 'You choose to lose your play time if you don't stay in your seat'. Some teachers spoke with children about the 'good choice' and the 'bad choice' they could take in specific situations. Teachers presented such choices as having inevitable outcomes that in fact only followed because of the teacher's own decisions (which were of course based upon the class's rules).

Teachers mainly used discipline to enforce rules relating to classroom management and their ability to teach, such as rewarding children who worked hard and reprimanding those who chatted when they were supposed to be listening. However, they did sometimes employ the discipline system to manage children's behaviour towards each other, particularly in the playground. For instance, I witnessed a teacher promising class points for children who asked lonely peers to play with them, and often saw children being chastised and punished for harming one another (as we will see in later chapters).

1.4 The Research

1.4.1 Methodology

The research reported in this book was conducted in the early 2000s. The main method used was participant observation, whereby a solo researcher spends long periods of time (usually at least a year) with the people under investigation, seeking to live like them as far as possible, and writing detailed fieldnotes about their everyday life (Van Maanen 1996).

I attended one year 4 class (of 8- and 9-year-olds) for two days a week for the entire school year. I also spent one day a week in reception (4- and 5-year-olds), year 1 (5- and 6-year-olds), year 3 (7- and 8-year-olds) and year 6 (10- and 11-year-olds) for approximately eight weeks each. On three or four days a week, I joined children in the playground and canteen over playtime and lunchtime. I attended the after-school club (which ran from 15:15 to 18:00) approximately twice a week, and also frequented school discos, Christmas bazaars, summer fetes, football matches, several class trips and local events. For the first three months of the following school year, I continued participant observation during playtime and lunchtime and at the after-school club.

In addition to participant observation, I also used questionnaires and individual and group interviews to investigate children's perspectives more systematically. Some of these asked children to name their best friends, in order to provide data on children's popularity and friendship networks. Others asked children's opinions on hypothetical versions of the various moral disputes and problems that I often saw on the playground, such as acts of physical aggression, exclusion and possessiveness. Children's responses sometimes aided my understanding of what I was seeing first hand on the playground, and also enabled me to gain a general sense of how common these problems, and particular perspectives on them, were among Woodwell Green children. In addition, I interviewed children in the year 4 class I spent most time with about a range of other topics, including racism and their perceptions of school discipline (some of these interviews took place when the children had moved into year 5).

Throughout the book, when I refer to particular children, I provide their year group. Because my research lasted for more than one school year, particular children may be described as being in two different year groups. This is purely a reflection of precisely when during my research the incident being described occurred.

I gained consent from teachers and children involved in the research, and from children's parents. I told children that my research was about trying to understand their lives from their point of view. It is difficult, however, for children to understand the ongoing nature of ethnographic research, so where possible, at the end of the research, I told them which incidents I wanted to write about, and only did so with their agreement. In almost all cases, children and adults alike generously agreed to my writing about them, although occasionally they disagreed with my descriptions; I have noted any such disagreements in the chapters that follow. To ensure participants' confidentiality, pseudonyms have been used.

I gathered all my data at one school, raising the issue of how representative my findings are of children growing up in other places. I have tried to gauge this in two ways. One is to give detailed information about how children's moral experiences arose out of their relationships with each other and with adults, and out of the material and cultural conditions of their lives. If children elsewhere have similar relationships and backgrounds, then we can expect that similar issues might arise for them. In particular, I try to take into account how children's social class and ethnic and religious identity might inform their experiences. The second way I have attempted to gauge the generality of my findings is to draw on research by others, which can be revealing of the extent to which children struggle with similar issues elsewhere.

1.4.2   The researcher

I carried out the research for this book during my PhD. The question I was most interested in at the time was how best to theorise the relationship between 'the individual' (particularly the child) and 'culture' (particularly how it is 'acquired' by children). I saw morality and moral development as a topic through which that question could be considered. During the research, I realised that there had been a huge change in attitudes towards adult intervention since I was a child at school, and became intrigued by the implications of this change for children's experiences. Hence, this book was born.

Carrying out participant observation research with children is exciting, rewarding and, at times, very stressful. One common problem is the tension between adult and (honorary) child roles in school (Thorne 1993). Sometimes this dual role drew suspicion or condemnation from adults. Consider the following extract from my fieldnotes, describing a parents' evening at the school during which I met the mother of Simran, a year 4 girl with whom I had spent a lot of time:

> I have been chatting to Simran's mum about cookbooks, and agree to lend her some of mine. She then tells me that Simran sometimes pretends to be me at home. Simran smiles. 'This is me,' she says, writing 'Miss Wood' on the whiteboard. We joke about her misspelling my name, and then she opens my bag and starts looking through it. Her mum tells her off. 'She's your teacher, not your friend.' 'She *is* my friend,' Simran replies. Her mum tells me that Simran is too informal with me. Feeling awkward, I smile and say, 'Yes, I suppose she is a bit.'

In this extract, my success as a researcher in establishing a trusting, peer-like relationship with Simran was met with disapproval by Simran's mother, who clearly expected a more hierarchical relationship between children and adults in school. But it was not only other adults who challenged my dual role at Woodwell Green; I also struggled with it. If a teacher joked with me about the children, I was drawn into an adult role and felt a sense of betrayal towards the children, while if I chatted with children in class or failed to report or reprimand a child for breaking a school rule, I sometimes felt guilty about not fulfilling adult obligations. These anxieties were particularly acute in situations where I thought a child might be harmed. Sometimes, I switched to adult mode without even thinking (for example, to break up a fight). In other situations, particularly when documenting girls' interactions, where harm rarely took a physical form, it was more difficult to know how to act. Essentially, I was struggling over whether to prioritise my desire to document children's lives or my desire to intervene in them and prevent harm.

Even when I tried not to intervene in an adult way, my presence did of course have an impact on what happened between the children, as will become obvious in the chapters that follow. What I was striving for was not to have no impact at all, but, as far as possible, to have the kind of impact a child has on a peer, rather than the effect of an adult on a child. Unless data collection is completely covert, any researcher studying human psychology or social life will have an impact on the people he or she studies. We have to accept this fact, work with it and, where possible, use it to our advantage. For example, in Chapter 3, I consider what we can learn from observing differences in how boys at Woodwell Green behaved in front of different audiences, including myself (see also Evans 2006 for an excellent example of how a researcher can use his or her own impact on participants as a source of data).

1.5   Structure of the Book

Chapters 2 to 6 examine how the school's injunction not to harm was experienced by the children of Woodwell Green. Each chapter looks at why children did not always conform to this rule, arguing that this is because they had other concerns or values that they sometimes prioritised over harm avoidance, or because they interpreted the situation differently from adults and did not see the behaviour in question as harmful. At the end of each chapter, I consider implications for practitioners; theoretical implications are saved for Chapter 8.

Chapter 2 focuses on children's acts of playful aggression (both verbal and physical), and shows that differences in how these were interpreted led to misunderstandings and disputes about whether an act was harmful. These differences were not random and could usually be understood with reference to the prior relationship between children, membership of certain categories (adult–child, girl–boy) or the tendencies of particular children. The Chapter also argues that playful aggression was an important way that children could demonstrate toughness and explores how this value challenged the value of harm avoidance condoned by teachers.

Continuing the theme of toughness, Chapter 3 asks why, despite school rules, some boys persisted in physical aggression. I argue that as well as the principle of harm avoidance promoted by the school, aggressive boys had two other considerations, which they sometimes prioritised. One was the value of justice, according to which it is right and fair to hit back if you are provoked, provided that the retaliatory hit is in proportion to the original offence. The other was hierarchy and status, which were produced partly through boys' acts of violence against one another.

Chapter 4 asks why, despite adults' admonishments, children routinely excluded particular peers from their play. It argues that adults' advice against exclusion did not always have the desired effect because acts of exclusion were often more complex than teachers acknowledged. In particular, the chapter highlights three complicating factors: (1) Most children in a group deferred to one child to make decisions about who could play. Thus most children did not view themselves as actively excluding other children, even if they allowed their group leader to do so in their name. (2) Exclusion sometimes arose not through the stereotypical image of a group deliberately telling a lone peer s/he cannot play, but through more indirect and sometimes benevolent processes such as game stability, competitiveness and differential access to desired knowledge and abilities. (3) Children sometimes used exclusion as a means of enforcing other values that were important to them, such as justice.

Chapter 5 explores children's notions of loyalty. The head teacher of the school was concerned that some children (particularly girls) were excessively possessive of one another, and recommended that children should be free to associate with whomever they wished. This chapter looks at how this advice conflicted with children's expectations of loyalty from their friends. I describe two different aspects of loyalty: the commitment to always be available to play with a particular friend, and the commitment to share that friend's enemies. I show how these concepts of loyalty were expressed differently by girls and boys, and how girls' expectations of loyalty often clashed not only with official school rhetoric regarding freedom and indiscriminate inclusion, but also with their competing desires for popularity and status.

Chapter 6 focuses on a form of harm that was assigned particular importance at Woodwell Green: racism. I show how the school prioritised this form of harm over others, such as homophobia. I also reveal disagreements within the school community about what counted as racism. For instance, I describe tensions that existed between some teachers and parents based on their contrasting definitions of racism, tolerance and ethnic identity. I consider how different definitions of racism had repercussions for how children experienced, and adults dealt with, harmful acts.

Chapter 7 considers the implications for children of the nascent adult obligation to intervene in their affairs. I describe how, in seeking to understand and resolve children's disputes, teachers have come to take up a judge-like role, calling witnesses, making judgements about truth and trustworthiness and meting out punishments. Through detailed examples, I show that children's and adults' interpretations of such disputes are often made not in a calm, detached manner but in a heated, disputed setting, in which language (such as claims about intention) and reputation (of accusing, accused and witnessing children) are important contributors to adults' decisions about blame. Finally, the chapter provides a glimpse of what children's moral lives might look like without adult intervention, by exploring how children resolve their disputes by themselves.

To conclude, Chapter 8 considers what the preceding chapters tell us about this book's two main questions: what do children's moral lives look like in contemporary Britain? And how are their experiences (and those of other children) informed by the cultural context they are growing up in?

Notes

1. A similar attitude has been noted in some non-Western societies too. For example, Fijians and Luo-speaking Kenyans were reluctant to respond to a child's complaint about another child (Edwards 1987; Toren 1990).
2. The names of the school, the area and all the people I write about in this book are pseudonyms.
3. The analyses concerning ethnicity included Indian, English and Pakistani children. Those on religion included Christian, Sikh and Muslim children. There were insufficient numbers of other ethnic and religious groups in my sample to include them in the analyses. Each analysis involved over 100 children, spanning year 1 (5- and 6-year-olds) to year 6 (10- and 11-year-olds). I used

four χ^2 tests of association to look for a relationship between children's ethnicities and their allocation of blame to specific protagonists in the exclusion and possessiveness scenarios. Another three χ^2 tests were carried out on the relationship between children's ethnicities and whether they reported an experience similar to each of the three scenarios. Two one-way ANOVAs looked for relationships between children's ethnicity and their approval of hitting in the physical aggression scenario, plus their attention to intention in another scenario. In addition to these nine tests exploring ethnicity, nine further identical tests were conducted using children's religion as an independent variable instead of ethnicity.

Since I conducted so many analyses, and since these were not hypothesis-led, I divided the significance level by the number of analyses (giving a significance level of .003). No analyses even approached significance at this level. Indeed, only one analysis gave rise to a p value below .05. This was for the relationship between children's ethnicity and whether they reported having had an experience similar to the physical aggression scenario ($\chi^2(2)=7.550$, $p=.023$ (two-tailed)). Comparisons of expected and actual counts indicate that compared with the English and Pakistani children, relatively few Indian children claimed to have experienced a situation similar to the scenario. This is an interesting result worthy of further research, but in the context of 17 other (non-significant) exploratory tests, not much can be made of the result here.

The overall lack of significant relationships between ethnicity/religion and children's responses to my scenarios does not mean that children's religious and ethnic background had no impact on their moral development. Rather, the results suggest either that children's religious and ethnic experiences are usually not relevant to the moral issues they face with their peers, or that they are relevant, but in some way or to some degree that I have not been able to detect with my questions and analyses.

4. Such rules would be seen as conventional rather than moral by domain theory, but may be conceived as (at least potentially) moral by social intuitionists and cultural psychologists. For instance, rules prescribing that children listen to the teacher could be seen as respect for authority and hierarchy.

2

What Counts as Harm?
Playful Aggression and Toughness

2.1 The Prevalence of Playful Aggression

In Chapter 1, I noted that on the wall of every classroom at Woodwell Green was a rule stating that children should not harm one another. I argued that this rule emanates from adults' growing concern in the UK and elsewhere that children should be protected from harm of all kinds. The application of this rule in practice was complicated by the widespread use by children of playful aggression, both verbal and physical. Most children at the school, including those who behaved perfectly in the classroom, enjoyed intense, rapid, noisy, playfully aggressive exchanges with their friends: shouting, screaming, insulting or teasing one another, swearing (in English or Punjabi), laughing loudly, and jostling, pushing, chasing or tickling each other. Also very common, mostly among boys, was playful physical aggression, or play fighting, which was officially banned at Woodwell Green (as it is at many schools in the UK [Gill 2007] and elsewhere [Goodwin 2006]). Here are examples, all involving year 4 children (8- and 9-year-olds), unless otherwise stated:

1. On the playground, James [year 3 boy] and Sarina are teasing each other. Sarina starts to hang onto my waist, laughing hysterically, leaning around me to shout insults at James, who darts towards her to shout something back. All the time the two are grinning. I catch the following exchange. James [threatening tone]: 'I'm gonna come round your house!' Sarina: 'I'm gonna lock the door. I'm gonna come round

Children's Moral Lives: An Ethnographic and Psychological Approach, First Edition. Ruth Woods.
© 2013 John Wiley & Sons, Ltd. Published 2013 by John Wiley & Sons, Ltd.

your house!' James: 'You don't know where I live.' Sarina [clutching ever tighter to me, still laughing]: 'I do, in a pigsty!' James [lurches towards her with fists raised threateningly, but still has a grin on his face]: 'What did you say?' Sarina: 'And you eat poo!' This banter continues, and they start to playfully push each other.

2. Lining up at the end of lunch break, Idris and Farhan are playfully arguing about what the score was in the football [soccer] match they have just participated in. They shove each other and then, with hands on each other's shoulders and arms straight, they push hard against each other. They are leaning so hard that when Amar, grinning, runs up and crashes into the side of them, Farhan falls right over. He jumps up, and next minute a whole cluster of boys is tripping and headlocking each other, laughing all the while.

3. Standing behind Kiran, Farah holds her open drink carton over her head and squeezes it gently. I give a mild warning look, but it's too late, drops spill out onto Kiran's hair and Farah's mouth changes to an 'O'. Kiran doesn't feel it straight away so I tell her what happened. 'Farah!' she snaps. Farah apologises, but she's laughing as well. I dab some water from my water bottle on to make it less sticky. Kiran complains to a canteen supervisor who doesn't seem to be listening. 'I hate you Farah,' Kiran says venomously. 'I wanna punch you,' says Farah. 'See, I'm gonna punch you,' she says, pulling a fist up and in slow motion bringing it really close to Kiran's forehead. They both sound serious but have smiles playing at the corners of their mouths.

What these extracts have in common is that they all include behaviours which, out of context, most of us would agree are aggressive and harmful. Yet the children in these extracts did not seem to be harmed; in fact they seemed to relish these interactions as an enjoyable way of interacting with their friends.

2.2   Playful Aggression in Children's Friendships

Playful aggression was an important medium through which Woodwell Green children carried out their friendships. Consider the following extract, which involves three boys who all named each other as friends in interviews with me.

During a year 4 school trip to a botanical garden, an old woman walking past comments that Mohamed is handsome. The other boys tease him mercilessly for this. At one point, when Zak and Faizel are teasing him, he falls silent and starts to look sullen. 'Don't go in a mood, we're only joking,' says Zak. 'On the next school trip you'll be winding me and Faizel up.' This seems to work and the three continue walking and talking together.

When Mohamed began to take offence at his friends' teasing, Zak reminded him that it was what friends do; 'On the next school trip you'll be winding me and Faizel up.' The role of playful aggression in friendship was also apparent when I interviewed the boys' classmate Farhan about his friendships. I had just asked him why he liked Mohamed, and instead of answering the question directly, Farhan launched into a detailed account of a play fight. 'Once yeah at my birthday there was Muslims versus Sikhs for the Tag Team Championships,' he opened. His rapid account told of a wrestling competition he and his friends held in his bedroom: three Sikhs against three Muslims. He explained enthusiastically how each boy went out, until just he, on the Muslim team, and his best friend Amandeep, on the Sikh team, remained. Amandeep pinned Farhan, and 'By mistake I kicked him in the face and I was like sorry Amandeep, sorry Amandeep'. But Farhan said that Amandeep 'went mad' until Farhan 'punched his nuts'. Amandeep collapsed groaning, and got stuck in the gap between two beds, so Farhan won. 'This birthday we're gonna have a proper wrestling match with metal posts!' he exclaimed.

The accuracy of Farhan's heroic account is not important here. What is relevant is that he obviously saw play fighting as a legitimate and valuable aspect of his friendships with other boys. In particular, according to his account at least, he and his best friend fought enthusiastically, but this did not entail a break in their friendship. A similar example comes from Amandeep, during his interview about friendships. He had named Faizel as someone he liked, and when I asked why, he immediately replied, 'I just had a fight with him in class!' He explained that Faizel scribbled over his work, so he did the same back, and then they fought, one grabbing the other's neck. I asked Amandeep when he thought that he and Faizel would 'make up' from their 'fight'. He looked surprised and said, 'We were just playing about'.

So for Zak, Amandeep and Farhan, playful fights and banter between friends were constitutive of friendship, even when there was some level of physical injury. There is evidence that playful aggression is an important component of social competence elsewhere too. Tholander and Aronsson (2002) describe how the social standing of children attending urban Swedish junior schools was, to a large extent, predicated on their ability to respond skilfully to teasing.

However, the same act may be understood quite differently if it takes place between children without a prior friendly relationship. Consider the following extracts, which also involve Mohamed. The first took place in Mohamed's year 4 classroom, the second a week later, on the playground.

1. Faizel comments that he and Mohamed have got the same shirt. Mohamed notes that Faizel's is lighter than his, and Faizel replies grinning that it's because Mohamed's is dirtier than his. Mohamed replies that Faizel's face is dirtier than his, and they both giggle.
2. Some children find a dead bird at the edge of the playground. A playground supervisor is concerned that Mohamed may have touched it, and she and I exhort him to wash his hands. Kiran, who is by my side, shouts something antagonistically about Mohamed being dirty. Mohamed retorts angrily that he's not dirty. 'I hate you,' he says, his face contorted with anger. 'I hate you,' Kiran shouts back, head strained forward.

In individual interviews, both Mohamed and Kiran named each other as someone in their class whom they did *not* like. It is hardly surprising, then, that when Kiran used essentially the same insult as Mohamed's friend Faizel had, Mohamed responded not with smiles and banter but with genuine anger. This example illustrates how differently the same action can be interpreted, depending on the prior relationship between the children concerned (Blatchford 1998).

2.3   Finding the Line Between Play and Harm

If playful aggression was an important component of friendship at Woodwell Green, then children who were not competent at it were at a disadvantage, effectively excluded from these friendship-enforcing interactions and marginalised in the peer group. So newcomers who joined the school from places where playful aggression was not important (or at least, not in the form practised at Woodwell Green) had to learn to aggress playfully. This was quite a difficult challenge, since the closer to cruelty children get in their playfulness (but without going over the line), the more thrilling the interaction is (Blatchford 1998).

I was such a newcomer. My own schooling (mostly at middle-class rural schools) did not prepare me for playful aggression at Woodwell Green, and consequently I often found it extremely difficult to interpret children's aggressive exchanges. Similarly, Thorne (1993) notes that her tendency to interpret play fighting amongst American working-class boys as genuine aggression was the result of her own status as an upper-middle-class woman. These extracts, involving year 4 children, are typical:

1. As I walk past Paul and Amandeep in the classroom, I hear them teasing each other. Amandeep repeats short adamant phrases of Punjabi to Paul, and tells me that Paul is copying his work. I ask a girl sitting nearby what he's saying [she speaks Urdu, which is sufficiently similar to Punjabi to enable her to understand]. She informs me that Amandeep told Paul to stop looking at his work. The two continue to tease one another, with children nearby listening in and smiling. In high spirits, Amandeep tells me that Paul said a 'really rude swear word' to him. I ask what he said, and he explains that Paul said an 'Indian swear word' to Amandeep. 'Do you two not get on?' I ask, puzzled. 'No, we're friends!' Amandeep says in a surprised tone.
2. Amandeep and his best friend Farhan run past me in the playground shouting at each other and occasionally hitting each other. I watch them, trying to work out if it's real or pretend. One calls to me, 'We're not joking!' 'I thought you were joking,' I say. 'We are joking,' one of them replies, and they continue with the skirmish.

I was not the only one to struggle with children's playful insults and fights. Maria moved to the UK from Pakistan, joining Woodwell Green in February, halfway through year 4. Like me, she was clearly not used to the banter and teasing that was the mainstay of children's interactions at her new school. At first she was quiet and polite, did not swear and did not participate in banter. This interaction, recorded in the classroom in early May, is typical:

The children have been set work, and I help Kiran and Maria with theirs. Maria and I chat a little, and Kiran says sharply to Maria, 'Can't you just stop talking?' Maria is the only child in the class writing in pen rather than pencil [because she has beautiful handwriting]. Kiran and a couple of other children complain that this is unfair, and Maria replies that she asked the teacher. Sohaib comes up to her a couple of times and says smiling that her writing is ugly, and 'That girl's annoying'. He also says that Simran thinks she 'talks funny'. 'Miss, why are they *jealous*?' says Maria in a loud, slightly superior sounding voice. 'You're *jealous*,' Simran mocks, imitating Maria's Pakistani accent, and the children sitting either side of her laugh.

After about three months at Woodwell Green, Maria began to change. The first sign I saw was only a week after the extract above. On the playground, in front of Sohaib, she told me that Sohaib called her, and all the other girls, 'a b-i-t-c-h'. However, she told me that she didn't mind because Sohaib had also said it to her tough and aggressive classmate, Anjali. Sohaib, listening, smirked and laughed. It was the first time I saw Maria really take Sohaib's playful aggression in her stride. The following month, Maria was trying out playful aggression for herself:

> I am sitting on a bench with several year 4 girls when Maria comes over. She tries to sit by me, but Ayesha won't move over. So Maria sits on my knee for a while, and also paces around. She is noisy and rude, telling people to shut up, screaming, and entering into Sohaib's rude teasing dialogues which she used to try to avoid. Within earshot of Maria, Zena comments that when Maria was new she was really quiet and good but now she's 'a bit rude'. Harpreet confirms, 'Maria's getting really naughty now, she's gone a bit bad.' 'She's gone silly,' Simran agrees, and Maria laughs and plays up even more, screaming when she's sitting on my knee and half deafening me. She says a rhyme with 'fuck off' at the end, with a certain relish, and some of the girls laugh. A couple say to me, in a tone mixing mild condemnation with amusement, 'She said the F word!'

The girls responded to Maria's newly found boisterousness with a mixture of amusement and disapproval, suggesting that she was not yet an expert at this style of interaction, her rudeness being too indiscriminate and annoying. With time, Maria calmed down a little, and my perception was that she became more skilled and confident at banter with her peers. For example, in October, having moved into year 5, I witnessed Maria holding her own in a game of skipping with Zena and Sohaib:

> Zena and Sohaib both claim that it's their turn next. They pull at the rope, and Maria says she'll do a dip [a rhyme designed to select one person from a group]. Hanging onto the middle of the rope while the other two struggle boisterously, she chants, 'Ip dip dog shit fucking bastard silly git!' Zena wins the dip, and she laughs loudly into Sohaib's face and pulls the rope off him. But then she starts to do a different skipping rhyme which the others don't want to do. Maria pulls the rope off her saying that it's her turn and she starts to skip.

Maria adapted well from the politeness of her former school to the boisterousness and banter of Woodwell Green. In doing so, she gradually transformed herself into a skilled participant in this locally important form of interaction, and became proficient at interpreting the playful aggression of her friends. However, her task was complicated still further by the fact that her friends differed somewhat in where each of them drew the line between play and harm.

2.4 Drawing the Line Differently: Contrasting Interpretations of Playful Aggression

2.4.1 Being sensitive

Some children coped better with playful aggression than others. Sohaib usually played with a group of girls in his class whom he constantly teased and insulted. These extracts illustrate how differently his classmates responded to his teasing:

1. In the playground, Sarah opens up her lunchbox to show me what she's got. Sohaib keeps pushing it to the edge of the bench, trying to knock it onto the floor. He almost succeeds a couple of times, and Sarah has to grab it as it half falls. Sohaib also says, 'I hate you' to Sarah, and 'I hate her,' about Sarah to Simran and me. He calls her 'fat cow' and various other names, taking no notice of Sarah's complaints to me and my requests and demands that he stop. Simran occasionally defends Sarah, and Sohaib insults her when she does. Sarah complains to me repeatedly, and then changes tack for a while and starts insulting him back, smiling as she does so. Sohaib, grinning, keeps up the barrage of insults. Then Anjali approaches with two other girls, and Sohaib calls her a bitch. Anjali retorts immediately and he changes his mind, instead insulting another girl who is not present.

2. I am hanging out with a group of year 4 girls, plus Sohaib, in the playground. Wearing a teasing smile, Sohaib seems to be taunting Erickah, although I can't hear exactly what he says. Erickah complains to me that Sohaib is being horrible to her, so I tell him to stop. Ignoring me, he teases, 'Erickah cried, Erickah cried!' Erickah is standing quietly beside me. 'Don't take any notice Erickah,' I say. Sohaib won't let up, dancing about and repeating the same phrase, and Kiran starts to laugh, pointing her finger right into Erickah's face. I criticise her for doing this. 'Sorry but Sohaib's making me laugh!' she says and starts to laugh again. Then Erickah snuggles into my side and starts to cry, her head bowed and away from Kiran and Sohaib. 'She's crying,' exclaims Kiran, putting her arm around Erickah. I tell Sohaib to go away and come back only when he is willing to apologise. 'He's still smiling!' exclaims Anjali. He moves away a little but continues smirking.

3. In the playground, Simran is combing and tying up Harpreet's hair, while Amrita does the same for Anjali. Sohaib takes Simran's bag and hits Amrita with it. Then he calls Anjali a bitch. Pointing first at Anjali then at Harpreet, he says, 'Buy one bitch get one free!' Most of us can't help but laugh, including Anjali, but Harpreet's face doesn't change

31

and she says nothing. 'Why are they bitches?' I ask. 'They just are. She looks like a bitch,' Sohaib says pointing at Harpreet, who continues to ignore him. Then Sohaib manages to open a nearby classroom door and runs inside. Farah [Pakistani Muslim] pulls out Harpreet's hair-band. 'She keeps opening my hair!' Harpreet complains. Harpreet pulls out one of Farah's hairbands, which I redo for her. Farah pulls out Harpreet's band again. Harpreet makes a move to chase her and she runs off laughing, with Simran calling, 'You [inaudible] shit!' after her. A couple of the girls say they've never heard Simran say that before. Harpreet sticks her middle finger up at Farah's fleeing behind. 'Mrs Timms [a playground supervisor] is there!' someone says. 'I don't care,' Harpreet says quietly. A few minutes later the whistle goes for end of lunchtime. As Farah walks with me to the line, she calls, 'Buy one get one free, *Harpreet*!'

Erickah is most visibly upset by Sohaib's teasing, while Sarah complains to me and tries to banter back, Harpreet ignores him, and Anjali banters back and laughs at Sohaib's insults. These differences in response are probably not all down to stable differences in the children who are on the receiving end of Sohaib's attacks. There are many other possible factors, including how new the children were to the school, and what else had happened to them on that day. Nevertheless, some children do seem to be more susceptible than others to being hurt by banter and teasing. One such child was Harpreet, an Indian Sikh girl in Sohaib's class. She was extremely well behaved in the classroom and often praised by her teachers. She was also popular amongst her peers, named by 13 of her classmates in interviews during year 4 as someone they liked. My field-notes reveal one reason for her popularity: she was very prosocial, frequently inviting children to join in whatever game she was playing, approaching and including new children, and offering to look after upset or injured peers. However, her responses to banter were varied, as the following extracts reveal.

1. Harpreet and Farah approach me in the playground to tell me that Harpreet has made up a new 'dipping rhyme' [to select one child from a group]: 'Ip dip fucking shit, fucking bastard, fucking git!' Harpreet says that Farah's real name is cow. 'Your real name is *stupid* cow!' Farah retorts, and they laugh.
2. I join Simran, Harpreet and a few other children in the playground. Harpreet is practising a dance with two other children. Someone comments that they are doing it wrong, and Simran says there is supposed to be more jumping around. The onlookers chat while

Harpreet and the other dancers discuss the moves. There is some more teasing from the onlookers. Simran calls, 'Hurry up!' and suddenly Harpreet's face falls and she stalks off. One of the girls goes after her, and the others say that Harpreet is always getting upset when people joke with her. Upset at Harpreet's reaction, Simran goes to speak with her but returns more distressed, reporting that the girl with Harpreet told her to go away.

In the first extract, Harpreet seemed to be enjoying the banter with Farah. In the second extract, however, she was offended by Simran's 'Hurry up!' and her peers told me that this was a typical response. During an interview, when I asked Simran who, if anyone, she argued with most often at school, she named Harpreet, who she said argued with others too. For example, she said that if Sohaib pushed Harpreet, she would get upset and say, 'I'm telling on you'. 'She gets the wrong idea,' she explained. Anjali also commented in an interview that Harpreet sometimes took her jokes seriously. Harpreet's sensitivity to teasing was not a consequence of having a bad relationship with those who teased her; she and Simran both named each other as friends in interviews. It would seem that although sometimes she did banter quite happily, Harpreet was more prone than some of her peers to being harmed by banter and teasing.

2.4.2   Girls and boys

As well as differences existing between individual children, boys and girls also sometimes differed in their interpretations of playful aggression. Specifically, when they played together, girls sometimes interpreted as harmful acts that boys claimed were playful. Here is an example from the playground, involving children in year 5 (aged 9 and 10 years):

Amandeep and Paul have been playing a game with some of the girls, including Harpreet and Sarina, stealing items of clothing from each other. Sarina runs up to tell me that Harpreet's crying. I go over to Harpreet, who is sitting with her legs bent in front of her, head bowed and weeping. I ask her what's wrong but she doesn't reply. Sarina has gone to tell a playground supervisor, and when she returns I ask her what happened. She says that Paul was mean to Harpreet and hurt her. Amandeep drifts over. When he sees that Harpreet is upset, he laughs incredulously, and says that Paul was only playing about. Sarina tells me that he grabbed Harpreet and squeezed her round the waist. But Amandeep laughs again and says that Paul only touched her arms. Shortly afterwards, the whistle goes for the end of playtime. Sarina walks Harpreet, still crying, to the line ready to go into class. Paul is further up the line, darting about and laughing. Gesturing to Maria, he laughs, 'She said don't hurt my sister!'[1] I tell him to apologise. 'I didn't do anything!' he exclaims.

In this incident, Harpreet was apparently injured by Paul, yet Paul and Amandeep protested that he did nothing to harm her. This might be just another example of Harpreet's sensitivity compared to her peers, but note that in the extract above, both Sarina and Maria came to Harpreet's defence and accused Paul, who was defended by Amandeep, the other boy playing. In other words, the girls closed ranks in accusing the boys of harm, while the boys closed ranks in claiming that the act had been playful and not harmful. This suggests that gender was a salient aspect of their interpretation of playful physical aggression.

A few weeks later, Harpreet's classmates Faizel and Zak told me in an interview that girls were overly sensitive to boys' actions. They were telling me why they did not like one of their classmates, Joshua:

ZAK: This what happened yeah, Zena yeah, I don't know if she got hit by Mohamed.
FAIZEL: She didn't yeah, he just touched her shoulder.
ZAK: Miss the thing about girls yeah, you just touch them and they go running to the teacher.

Two days after this interview, the children's teacher, Mrs Samson, held 'circle time' with her class, because she was concerned about the level of aggression among boys in their football [soccer] games. It was intended as an opportunity for children to express grievances and solve problems in a safe space. After some ice breakers, she put them into groups and gave each group a hypothetical scenario, telling them, 'You can act out, first of all a poor behaviour choice to solve that problem. Then you'll do a better way of dealing with that problem, and how you'll go about solving it.' One of the cards read, 'It is Friday. The girls have the large goals but the boys want to use them instead.'[2] This card was given to four girls. For a 'poor behaviour choice', they acted out a scenario in which two boys prevented two girls from playing, telling them, 'Girls can't play football, boys play football'. In their alternative, improved version, they ended with the boys agreeing to leave the girls to play. This led to the following discussion:

Harpreet says, 'Miss normally girls are a bit scared of boys cos they come and boss them around sometimes. After a while we just say let's go, cos boys are stronger than girls.' 'Does that happen to you?' Mrs Samson asks.

34

'Miss it happens to us,' Harpreet replies, continuing that that very day, Anil's [a boy in this class] cousin had told them to go away, and had hit Harpreet. Some of the boys are derisive, and Anil calls out, 'He's only in year 3!' Mrs Samson says that nobody's criticising his cousin and so there's no need to be defensive, and Anil quietens down. Mrs Samson asks three other girls if they have similar problems, and they all say they haven't. The children briefly discuss the issue of how many days the girls should be given priority in having the best pitch on the playground, with the girls complaining that the one day allocated to them is unfair. Then the following exchange occurs:

SIMRAN: Miss they're trying to take advantage of us.
MRS SAMSON: Why?
SIMRAN: Miss because of the goals. We do let them play but
FARAH: [interrupts] Miss we don't mind them playing but they're
                 too rough. [Mrs Samson stops Farah and turns back to
                 Simran.]
SIMRAN: We do let them play but they're too rough.
AMANDEEP: Miss, it's not our fault if we play rough, cos it's just like,
                 boys, cos if you try and hit it lightly you just hit it hard so
                 it's not our fault if we're rough.
SANDEEP: Miss I know what Amandeep's trying to say. We don't try
                 to, we're not rough but other people think we're rough
                 because sometimes we kick it really hard and if it hit them
                 it could hurt someone really badly.

Simran, Farah and Harpreet all expressed the view that the boys were rough and that this created problems when they played football together. Meanwhile, Anil, Amandeep and Sandeep challenged their interpretation, arguing that they did not intentionally cause harm, and thus were not actually rough (Sandeep) or could not help being rough (Amandeep). The problem at this point looked rather intractable, and indeed the very next day, I witnessed a clash of interpretations when some of the children were playing netball during lunch break.

The children gather around the net and take turns to try shooting. It's quite boisterous, with children standing under the net and jiggling the post when others try to shoot, Faizel boasting that he's winning, and Simran sneaking up behind Faizel and pushing him when he's about to take a shot. He turns and chases her, she grabs his arms, laughing, and he pushes her. Soon after, Zena says something I can't hear to Faizel, he pushes her and she falls over. She immediately starts crying. Faizel looks distressed and alarmed as Zena falls, and I tell him gently to apologise. 'I didn't mean to, sorry,' he says quietly, but I don't think she heard. Zena gets up and walks away, brushing herself down. I say that I don't think Faizel did it on purpose, but she retorts forcefully that he did. Later in the lunch break, I see Zena again and repeat that I saw Faizel's face and could see that he didn't mean to hurt her, but she insists, 'He did, he went like this!' gesturing a shoving motion.

In Chapter 3, we will see that Faizel was not afraid of deliberately harming other children, in his efforts to maintain dominance on the playground. In this incident, Faizel's alarmed reaction when Zena fell suggests that his push was playful, and he did not mean to harm her. Yet Zena saw him as having deliberately pushed her over, and would not be persuaded otherwise.

Why, in all these examples, did girls tend to interpret as genuinely aggressive acts that boys saw as playful? One possible reason is that boys had more experience of playful physical aggression than girls did. While both boys and girls engaged in playful verbal aggression (which had a physical component but was not centred on physical interaction), most of the playful physical aggression I observed took place between boys. Moreover, there is evidence that across different cultures, boys play fight more than girls do (Pellegrini and Blatchford 2000; Power 2000). Girls and boys do not usually play together very often at this age (Maccoby 1990). When I asked each of the 30 children in this class (then in year 4) to name their friends, one said she had none, 18 named only same-sex peers, eight named one opposite-sex and several same-sex friends, and only three named more than one opposite-sex friend. So there were not many opportunities for girls to experience boys' play fighting.

Another likely contributor to girls' and boys' contrasting interpretations is the perceptions they had about the opposite sex. In individual interviews, I asked children their views about playing with same- and opposite-sex peers. Many made negative stereotyped claims about the opposite sex. Here are some examples:

Girls on why they don't like playing with boys
Harpreet: 'Miss, because they're [girls] kind and they're helpful. Boys are also kind and helpful, but they don't take responsibility, cos whenever Sohaib plays with us, he pushes me and pulls my hair.'

Sarina: 'Boys are like rough, right, and girls are more sensible. But Sandeep and Amandeep are like sensible, but sometimes they be naughty.'

Navneet: 'Because boys are boo and girls are yes, cos boys are fighting and girls are not, and girls are pretty and boys are not.'

Simran: 'Boys are always naughty and get into trouble. Girls sometimes get into trouble but not as much, and boys fight and girls don't.'

Boys on why they don't like playing with girls

Farhan: 'Because I hate girls!' I ask why. 'Because they're stupid, idiot and dumb and thick and gay.'[3]

Soraj: 'If you play with girls, that's girls' stuff like Barbie.' I suggest that playing with Barbie might be fun. He looks at me as if I'm mad. 'No, it's Barbie,' he says. 'But why don't you like Barbie?' I push. He shrugs. 'It's for babies. Boys play wrestling, Playstation, WWF, Pinball, games, and going on the computer.' 'Don't girls like going on the computer?' I ask. 'No, they hate it,' he says decisively.

Zak: 'The girls!' he says disdainfully. 'They might be boring! They don't play football [soccer]! Miss I never played a girl in my life.' I ask if a girl played football would he play with her. He says that no girls in year 4 play football, but there is one in year 6. I ask if he'd play with her. 'She's in year 6!' he says. I ask if he would if she was in year 4. 'Yeah.'

Amar: 'Because we play more games than girls, like more sports, because I'm good at sports. Girls just play teachers, stuff like that. That's what my sister does.'

The girls describe the boys as rough, naughty and fighting. The boys criticise the girls for the games they play, and call them 'stupid' and 'boring'. Such polarised views of the opposite sex have been found among working- and middle-class children in both the UK and the USA (Adler and Adler 1998; Connolly 1998). These assumptions make both girls and boys prone to interpreting acts by members of the opposite sex negatively, and girls' preconceptions certainly lend themselves to interpretations of boys as deliberately harming them.

It is worth noting, though, that these differences, and the accompanying misunderstandings between boys and girls, do not seem to be inevitable. Evaldsson (2004) found in her study of working-class boys and girls of diverse ethnic backgrounds in Sweden that cross-sex interactions in physically active games can also take a more humorous form, in which misunderstandings about playfulness are rare.

These examples of children interpreting the same act differently, as either playful and harmless, or serious and harmful, demonstrate what a minefield teachers must negotiate whenever they attempt to prevent harm from befalling children on the receiving end of (playfully) aggressive behaviours. In all these cases, they must make a judgement about whether to accept the interpretation of the hurt party (that the act was genuinely harmful) or that of the perpetrator (that it was just some fun). Not only that, but teachers also sometimes differed from children altogether in their interpretations of playful aggression.

2.4.3   Adults and children on playful racism

Differences in interpretation of playful aggression existed not only between individual children, but also between children and adults. In particular, when children adopted racist terms and used them jokily to each other, alarm bells went off for teachers, because racism was an extremely hot topic at Woodwell Green (see Chapter 6). Here are two extracts illustrating this phenomenon among year 4 children.

1. Miss Chahal, who is leaning on Faizel's desk, notices Mohamed calling something in Urdu to Faizel across the class. She calls Mohamed up and asks him what he said. 'I was only joking,' he repeats several times. Miss Chahal eventually says that if he doesn't answer, he'll get a detention. He mutters something in Urdu, which Miss Chahal later tells me means 'fat black dog'.[4] Miss Chahal tells him off. Mohamed protests that they all say it to each other and they're only joking, adding that Amar [who, like Mohamed and Faizel, is Pakistani Muslim] says it to him. So Miss Chahal calls Amar up. She asks the three boys if they mind being called that, and they shrug and say they don't mind. She tells them they need to be careful using such language as someone might take it the wrong way and accuse them of racism. Mohamed pipes up that Zak was pulling a face and gesturing at him. Miss Chahal asks me if I saw and I say that I didn't. She tells Zak off. The class is getting noisy and Miss Chahal snaps, 'One minute!'[5] Hassan gasps loudly. 'Who did that?' asks Miss Chahal. 'Hassan,' call several children. 'Hassan, five minutes!' I am finding the whole thing amusing and can't help smiling. Miss Chahal catches my eye and I start to laugh, covering my mouth. Faizel is smiling and Miss Chahal points this out. Then she and the other boys all start to laugh, and she sends them back to their seats.

2. The class have just finished a dress rehearsal for their assembly and are still in their costumes. Best friends Amandeep [Indian Sikh] and Farhan [Pakistani Muslim] are both wearing Asian clothes, and as we head from the hall back to the classroom, they walk with their arms around each other's shoulders chanting, 'We're the Asian boys!' 'Cos he's a Paki and I'm Indian,' Amandeep says to me, and Farhan says something similar using the same terms. They are laughing and acting cool. Later, in the staffroom, a year 3 teacher is telling other teachers that she heard an Asian boy call a black girl a Paki. She sent them to the head teacher, but was amused at the misuse of labels. I tell them about what Amandeep and Farhan had said. Miss Chahal, their class

teacher, is there too and she looks disapproving at Amandeep's use of 'Paki'. Worried that I might get him into trouble, I reassure her that Farhan was using the term too.

In these extracts, adults struggled with children's playful use of racist insults 'fat black dog' and 'Paki'. In the first case, the boys convinced their teacher that they were playing and were not harmed by the insult. Nevertheless, Miss Chahal warned them that they were prone to being misunderstood. In the second extract, despite knowing that they were good friends, Miss Chahal showed misgivings about Amandeep's use of the word 'Paki' to refer to Farhan. These extracts indicate that even when insults take place within friendships and with no evidence of harm taking place, they may in certain cases be seen as problematic and harmful. We will see in Chapter 6 that racism was considered a particularly serious type of harm at Woodwell Green. No wonder, then, that teachers, obligated to protect children from harm, seemed almost incapable of interpreting racist verbal aggression as playful.

2.5 Crossing the Line

2.5.1 Demonstrating toughness

We have seen that playful aggression was an important element of children's friendships at Woodwell Green. Children were mostly skilful at teasing, insulting, bantering with and physically attacking friends in a manner that went close to genuine harm, but stopped short of it. Outside of friendship, however, children sometimes deliberately crossed the line from play to serious aggression. This was particularly obvious to me when I watched children of different ages bantering together. Many children took pleasure in teasing those younger than them, and this teasing usually seemed more antagonistic than good-natured. But the victims responded very differently; some were careful not to get involved, while others gave (at least) as good as they got. These varying responses are exemplified in the following extracts, all involving girls in year 4 (8 and 9 years old) and year 6 (10 and 11 years old) in the playground.

1. Amira, Priyanka and Nadia [year 6] approach the bench where I am standing chatting with some year 4 girls. They stand on the bench, climb onto the back of it, and jump off. Simran and Zena [year 4] have a go at doing this as well. Then Simran and Priyanka exchange a few insults antagonistically. Several other year 6 girls come up. Simran asks

one of them confrontationally, 'What's that on your neck? Is it a burn?' The girl looks self-conscious, and replies that it's a birth mark.

2. I am with Anjali and her friends Amrita and Louise [all year 4] in the playground. Amira, Priyanka, Nadia and another year 6 girl come up to tell me something about a dance I am helping them put together. While they tell me, they climb on the bench, stand on the back, lean on me, and jump off. Anjali and the year 6 girls start to insult one another. Anjali says something to Priyanka that I don't hear, and Priyanka says something back in Punjabi. 'She swore at me!' Anjali exclaims. 'I don't care if you tell cos I'll just say you said something first,' retorts Priyanka. They call each other 'cow' and other insults, and it is fairly fraught. Anjali's friends, Amrita and Louise, don't join in. Eventually, the year 6 girls move to the next bench and chat together.

3. I approach year 6 girls Amira, Nadia, Priyanka and one other girl about the dance we are producing, when Zena and five other year 4 girls approach. The year 6 girls tell the year 4 girls to go away, but they remain. The year 6 girls say that Zena's only a little girl, and Zena replies that she's not little. 'You're not old enough to hear about the dance,' Amira says. 'Yes I am, I'm –' Zena pauses, then launches into a long number in the millions. 'You have to be between ten and thirteen to listen,' Amira retorts. Still the year 4 girls remain, while I discuss dance practice arrangements with the year 6 girls. Then Amira shakes Nadia, who is perched on a railing about two metres above concrete. 'Don't do that Amira, she might fall off!' I exclaim. 'So, I don't care,' Amira replies. One of the year 6 girls comments that Nadia and Zena look like sisters. Nadia walks off, and Amira and Priyanka begin to tease Zena. 'How can we be sisters, I'm in year 4 and she's in year 6!' Zena exclaims. Amira laughs and tries to persuade her to say that again, but she refuses. So Amira imitates her, exaggerating her slight accent.

    Zena starts to look fed up so I beckon her as I walk away. She follows me, as do most of the other year 4 girls. 'Don't take any notice, Nadia's really good at dancing anyway,' I comfort her. Zena immediately turns to Amira and Priyanka, saying, 'Nadia's a better dancer than you anyway, so *I'm* better than you are as well.' 'I didn't say that!' I quickly tell Amira and Priyanka. They continue teasing. Nadia returns and tries to make them stop, but Priyanka carries on, her arm round Nadia's shoulder and half wrapped round her throat. Nadia is smiling good humouredly but not actually laughing. Zena retorts, 'How can we be sisters? She's Muslim and I'm a Christian.' This silences them briefly. 'Are you Muslim?' I ask Nadia. She nods. 'You could be stepsisters,' someone suggests. 'How can we be stepsisters? I haven't got a stepmother or father,' retorts Zena. 'You have,' someone says. This continues, and Zena begins to look fed up again. I tell the year 6 girls to stop otherwise I won't practise the dance with them.

In extract 1, Simran but not Zena was prepared to take on the year 6 girls, and in extract 2, Anjali readily responded to Priyanka's insults, while Amrita and Louise remained quiet. In extract 3, Zena made some effort to retaliate to the older girls' teasing, but also showed signs of being distressed by it. So only Simran and Anjali in these extracts really took on the older girls and retaliated with aggressive insults of their own. It is not that Zena, Amrita and Louise were incapable of banter; all three bantered skilfully with their friends. But only Simran and Anjali dared to cross the line from playful to genuine aggression, in order to stand up for themselves against older children. In doing so, they demonstrated that they were tougher than their peers, and a force to be reckoned with on the playground.

2.5.2   Using harm to demonstrate toughness

Anjali (ethnicity recorded on school records as 'other ethnic group', and her religion Christian) was particularly tough. I saw her cry only once during my fieldwork, near the start of year 4, during a dispute with a classmate. Generally, though, she seemed more able to both give and take hard knocks than most of her peers. We saw earlier that she could handle insults from classmate Sohaib and from older girls. In addition, she was amused and buoyant about getting told off by her teacher, despite the fact that she was extremely invested in educational achievement (telling me in an interview that she wanted to be friends with Simran partly because Simran was clever and 'I wanna keep up with her. Don't tell! Her intelligence, I wanna keep that up'). In contrast, some of the other girls in her class were afraid of getting told off, and even cried when they were chastised. The mother of one of Anjali's more sensitive classmates commented to me approvingly that Anjali was tough, noting that this would benefit her in secondary school, and wishing that her own daughter was more like that. Anjali's year 4 teacher also noted Anjali's toughness approvingly, which she said reminded her of herself when she was younger.

Anjali demonstrated her toughness not only by withstanding harm, but also by meting it out to others. When Harpreet's gloves got stained with custard, Anjali blamed classmate Navneet. 'No,' said Navneet. 'Yes,' countered Anjali. 'No.' 'Yes.' 'No.' '*Yes!*' Anjali said forcefully, leaning into Navneet's face. Navneet did not reply, and so Anjali's version of events was the one that stuck. She was also assertive and sometimes offensive in her interactions with me, daring to do and say things that others did not. For example, she sometimes told, rather than asked, me to come to her in the classroom; she often criticised my appearance, exhorting me to wear makeup and more fashionable clothes; and she repeatedly requested that I draw a picture just for her. Other children only rarely dared to do any of these things. Through these means, I experienced a little of the stress that some of Anjali's more sensitive peers faced in their interactions with her (see Chapter 5).

Anjali thus showed signs of valuing harm as a means of demonstrating her own toughness and resilience, and of developing and testing these qualities in other children. Of course, she was not the only child at Woodwell Green to do so. Here is an example involving children in year 3 (7 and 8 years old):

> In the playground, Ethan runs up to me, looking stressed, complaining that Jack keeps pushing him, and something I don't catch about his girl-friend, a girl in their class called Laura. I suggest that Ethan moves away, but he says he's involved in a football game so he can't. Then Jack grabs Laura and holds her firmly from behind. She acts as though she wants to escape, but she's not trying very hard. When Ethan sees, he runs fast towards them, leaping as he crashes Jack out of the way, releasing Laura. Jack starts to chase Ethan. Laura turns to her friend and they grin and laugh in nervous excitement. The boys are both running at full speed, and as Ethan starts to tire, he begins to cry and he looks terrified. 'Run to me,' I shout to him, and he eventually heads nearer, but not right to me. He is still crying as Jack grabs him round the neck, but as the two slow to stand-still, Jack says, grinning, 'Why you crying, I'm not gonna hurt a mate!' He repeats this a couple of times. Ethan stops crying but still looks very stressed. He doesn't say anything, but jogs back to the football game he was playing. Jack walks over to Laura and her friend and chats with them.

In this incident, Jack claimed to be playful, while behaving quite aggressively. Ethan showed signs of interpreting the behaviour as genuinely aggressive, but his interpretation was challenged by Jack's claim that he's 'not gonna hurt a mate' (although in interviews at the end of year 3, Jack and Ethan did not name each other as friends). In taking play fighting to the brink of acceptability, Jack was doing more than having fun: he was also demonstrating toughness, and testing that of Ethan. Ethan failed that test by responding fearfully, and this allowed Jack to assert his dominance over Ethan by once more approaching his girlfriend, Laura – this time unchallenged by Ethan.

Children who value the production of toughness through harm challenged the school's position that all harm is wrong by placing some harm in a positive light. One way to define toughness is as the ability to withstand harmful actions without actually being harmed (at least not in the long term) by them. According to this definition, a certain amount of harm is a desirable and good thing, enabling one to develop and demonstrate one's resilience. This is obviously in tension with the school's official rule asserting that hurting one another is never acceptable.

2.5.3   Toughness, playful aggression and social class

The value that Anjali and others at Woodwell Green assigned to toughness is probably related to the fact that the school was in an urban, working-class area. To survive and thrive amidst poverty and crime requires some toughness. It is also likely that working-class children use more playful aggression in their interactions with one another than middle-class children do. I noted earlier in the chapter that my own mostly rural, middle-class schooling did not prepare me for the playful aggression so pervasive at Woodwell Green.

Several studies have documented playful aggression among working-class children. Play fighting and 'piss-taking' were widespread among the British working-class boys studied by Willis (1977). Evans (2006) found that teasing and swearing were valued among working-class people in Bermondsey (south-east London) as a way of ensuring that children are kept down to earth. Evaldsson (2002) found that working-class boys in Sweden used gossip to construct crying and sulking as weak and deviant behaviours (for boys). White working-class girls in a harsh rural setting in the USA also valued toughness and the ability to express opinions and resentments (Brown 1998).

The prevalence of teasing may also derive from the large proportion of children of Indian ethnicity at Woodwell Green. Many of these children were strongly influenced by Bollywood films and, possibly, by British Asian comedies such as *The Kumars at Number 42*, both of which often involved banter and teasing. Children of Indian ethnicity sometimes bantered in Punjabi, or in English with an Indian accent, adding gestures that were reminiscent of characters in particular Bollywood films. Thus, wider community values and influences are likely to have informed the value that children placed on playful aggression and toughness.

My suggestion that cultural influences inform children's playful aggression does not mean that playful aggression will be absent in some communities. Play fighting has been observed in several quite different cultures (Fry 1988; Pellegrini 2003; Whiting and Whiting 1975), suggesting that children, particularly boys (Pellegrini and Blatchford 2000; Power 2000), are predisposed to play fight. Still, cultural factors can affect the extent to which that predisposition is expressed. Fry (1988) compared levels of playful and serious physical aggression among children in La Paz and San Andres, two Zapotec-speaking communities in Oaxaca, Mexico. These communities were similar in many respects, but there was much more violence in San Andres than in La Paz. Fry (1988) found that children in San Andres carried out significantly more playful and serious aggression than those in La Paz, presumably because of the more violent community in which they were growing up.

So we might expect playful physical aggression to be less common in middle-class settings, which tend to be less physically violent, but it will probably still exist. What about the prevalence of playful *verbal* aggression? The difficulties faced by some new children at Woodwell Green, like Maria, suggest that it is not universal (at least not in the form practised at Woodwell Green). Studies describe playful verbal aggression among Aboriginal and white Australian working-class children (Davies 1982), teenage white working-class girls in northern England (Griffiths 1995) and among teenage black working-class boys in the USA (Lefever 1981). However, Ayoub and Barnett (1965) found playful verbal aggression among white middle- and upper-class American boys, and Goodwin (2006) describes an example of middle-class girls playfully insulting each other at a Californian school (although it is not clear whether this was a common occurrence). So playful verbal aggression is not an exclusively working-class phenomenon. Nevertheless, it may be less common in middle-class schools. For example, middle-class girls experience pressure to be 'nice', a value that may inhibit playful verbal aggression (Brown 1998; Hey 1997).

2.6 Implications for Schools

This chapter has demonstrated that at some schools at least, children enjoy playfully teasing, insulting and physically attacking their peers. At Woodwell Green, such behaviours were an important aspect of children's friendships; children who did not know how to conduct playful aggression (like Maria) were effectively excluded from many interactions. Playful aggression complicates schools' apparently straightforward edict, 'Do not hurt one another on the inside or the outside', because different members of the school community are prone to interpret the same act differently from each other, such that some perceive harm, and others perceive play. We saw that individual children differed in where they drew the line, and girls and boys also tended to differ in their interpretations of playful physical aggression. Teachers and children also sometimes differed from each other, at least when it came to racism, perceived by teachers to be so serious that playful use was impossible. There is evidence that teachers and children may differ systematically in their interpretations of play fighting as well (Boulton 1993b).

So a single act may be both playful and harmful, depending on one's perspective. Adjudicating adults will be faced with a situation in which some children claim to have been harmed while others claim not to have inflicted harm, and find themselves genuinely unable to establish which party is 'right'. In such a situation, an adjudicating adult must assess instead whether the claim of harm is *reasonable*. In other words, adults need to ask themselves whether a playful act is automatically wrong if it harms the recipient, or whether they should also consider whether the recipient is being too sensitive.

In evaluating the playfulness and harmfulness of an aggressive act, adults will inevitably be informed by the extent to which they value toughness because, as we have seen, this value involves seeing some harm as legitimate, even desirable, if it demonstrates or develops a person's ability to withstand adversity. Since this value may be associated with working-class communities, adults are likely to be influenced by their own social class backgrounds in making judgements about the acceptability of specific acts. Being aware of this may help them to better understand their own visceral reactions to children's aggressive actions, and to judge their seriousness.

Like many other schools, Woodwell Green banned all play fighting, although as we have seen, many children defied this rule. But some teachers went one step further in their efforts to prevent children from harming one another and tried to prevent children from having any physical contact with one another at all (for example, see the extracts at the start of Chapters 3 and 4). Yet children's friendships are typically physical, lively and invasive. The very physical nature of children's interactions is evident in this chapter – not only in play fighting among boys, but also in girls' banter, which often involved jostling and pushing. It has also been noted elsewhere, for example among American working-class children of various ethnicities (Ferguson 2000; Thorne 1993). Efforts to prevent harm by instructing children not to touch one another seem unrealistic and may negate crucial aspects of their friendship and play.

I suggested that playful and genuine aggression lie on a continuum, with the line between them being drawn in different places by different people. We saw how some children were willing to cross the line to assert themselves and demonstrate toughness. For boys, this often involved serious physical aggression, which is the focus of the next chapter.

Notes

1. Maria and Harpreet were not family. It is likely that Maria was borrowing an idiom commonly used by Muslim children at Woodwell Green, that all Muslim children are brothers and sisters. See Woods (2005) for a description of this phenomenon. I occasionally heard children of other religions using the idiom to refer to their own relationships with other children. Maria was Christian and Harpreet was Sikh.
2. There were two football pitches on the junior playground, one (the most desirable) with large goals, the other with smaller goals. Since there were always many more than two groups of children wanting to play football, the school instituted a rule designating the large goals to a different year group each day. Thus years 3 to 6 had one day each of Monday to Thursday, and Friday used to be a free for all. When some of the girls, including Harpreet, Zena and Simran, got into playing football (following the release of British film *Bend it like Beckham*), the teachers decided to allocate Friday as the girls' day. However, boys from the girls' classes often joined in the girls' games and/or watched them, offering advice and getting involved in disputes.
3. Children's use of the word 'gay' as an insult is examined in Chapter 6.
4. Miss Chahal spoke Punjabi, which is sufficiently similar to Urdu to enable understanding.
5. This meant that all the children would have to stay in the classroom for one minute at the start of playtime. See Chapter 1 for more on discipline methods used at Woodwell Green.

3

Physical Aggression
Prioritising Harm Avoidance, Reciprocity or Dominance?

3.1 School Rules: No Hitting

School staff at Woodwell Green were strongly committed to a 'no hitting' policy, and physical aggression was treated as wrong in all situations, regardless of whether it was provoked. Children were urged not to hit back, but instead to report physical aggression to an adult – which was, as we saw in Chapter 1, what they were encouraged to do for all of their playground problems. In this, the school was similar to many others, such as the American West Coast elementary school studied by Ferguson (2000). All intentional harming of one another's bodies, such as hitting, kicking, punching and throwing stones, was banned, as were games seen to encourage such behaviour (including play fighting, wrestling and rugby).

Along with racism, physical aggression was perhaps the behaviour most consistently discouraged and penalised at the school. For example, at an assembly attended by years 3 to 6 (7- to 11-year-olds), the head teacher drew attention to the fact that some boys had, the previous day, been caught throwing stones at each other. He emphasised the harm that could result from this, and warned that if a child was caught even with a stone in their hand, a letter would be sent to their parents (one of the most serious consequences for wrongdoing). The head teacher acknowledged that the children involved felt angry, but argued that to give in to the anger with aggression was to be like an animal. He contrasted this

Children's Moral Lives: An Ethnographic and Psychological Approach, First Edition. Ruth Woods.
© 2013 John Wiley & Sons, Ltd. Published 2013 by John Wiley & Sons, Ltd.

with stopping, thinking and realising that 'If I hit him, he'll hit me and I'll hit him and it'll never end'. Finally, he emphasised that even if the other person hit first, a child would still get into trouble for hitting. The same themes are evident in this extract from a year 1 classroom of 5- and 6-year-olds.

It is the period directly after lunch, and Miss Hart is discussing with the children an incident that took place that lunchtime, in which Mahdi bit Navjot, and Karan kicked Mahdi's head, during a game of 'karate'. Miss Hart says that they're not to play karate; 'We need to play nice games in the playground.' She says they mustn't kick or hit or punch each other. 'Do we need to even touch each other?' 'Noo,' chorus several children. After further discussion of the biting incident, Miss Hart reiterates that if someone hits them, they mustn't hit back, but should instead tell a teacher. Adam raises his hand. 'I can still remember from Leon in reception – not actually in reception, in nursery – and he kept kicking me, and I told every time he did that.' 'Adam, you did the right thing. You must tell a teacher, you mustn't hit them back yourself,' replies Miss Hart approvingly. Zain, one of the boys who was playing karate, puts his hand up, and when picked he says, 'I'm gonna try and be good'. Miss Hart says she's pleased to hear it. Then Gagandeep says, 'One day when I was in the playground, a boy in reception hit me'. Miss Hart asks if he told the teacher, and he says yes. She asks if the teacher sorted it out, and the boy stopped. Gagandeep replies that the boy kept on hitting him every day. Miss Hart asks whether the teacher sorted it out in the end, and he says yes. After a couple of other children have spoken, Sophie says, 'You know when I was in nursery, yeah, this boy kicked me in the face'. Miss Hart comments on the fact that this event has stuck in Sophie's mind and says, 'It doesn't feel nice, does it Sophie?' Sophie shakes her head. Miss Hart says that they should remember how it feels so that they don't do it to others.

After this incident, Miss Hart told me that she particularly wanted the children to think about how it feels to be the recipient of a hurtful action. Both the year 1 and the head teacher pointed out the harm that results from hitting, and both were adamant that children should not retaliate if they were hit (although note that Gagandeep's account questions the efficacy of telling a teacher instead – an issue discussed later in this chapter). Thus, the school assigned moral right firmly on the side of non-aggression. Hitting was presented as wrong because it harms the recipient; it is animalistic, less than human; and it escalates, rather than solves, the dispute. From this angle, physical aggression is unequivocally wrong and cannot be justified on moral grounds.

3.2 The Morality of Fairness, Reciprocity and Retaliation

Despite the negative portrayal of physical aggression as morally wrong, researchers have shown that some children do see retaliatory physical aggression as appropriate if it is a fair and proportionate response to a provocation. Astor (1994) asked children aged 8 to 12 years old attending inner-city schools in San Francisco about hypothetical scenarios involving provoked and unprovoked acts of physical aggression. Half of the children in each age group were physically aggressive (according to records kept by school staff). All children considered the unprovoked aggression wrong, usually justifying their answer with reference to the physical welfare of the victim and/or the wrongful intent of the perpetrator. However, aggressive and unaggressive children responded very differently to the stories about *provoked* aggression. When told a story in which child A called child B names, and child B hit child A, 80 per cent of the aggressive children approved of this retaliatory act, compared with only 28 per cent of the unaggressive children (a statistically significant difference). All the children justified their answer with reference to the value of welfare or harm avoidance. Unaggressive children who disapproved of hitting back tended to focus on the physical harm to the victim, while aggressive children who approved of hitting back focused on the psychological harm caused by name-calling to the perpetrator. Astor (1994, 1998) argued that the aggressive children condoned hitting as a form of reciprocal justice.

The principle of reciprocal justice does not only appeal to aggressive children. Smetana et al. (2003) interviewed American working- and middle-class children aged 6 and 8 years about hypothetical incidents of provoked and unprovoked physical aggression. The children generally agreed that both acts of aggression were wrong, and would still be wrong even if authority figures did not condemn them. In other words, most children in this study saw hitting as morally wrong, according to criteria specified by domain theory (see Chapter 1). However, children were more forgiving of the provoked than the unprovoked aggression. They rated the unprovoked hit as more deserving of punishment than the provoked hit, and the younger children also saw the unprovoked hit as more serious. When justifying their answers, they used what the authors consider moral reasons (harm to victim, unfairness of aggressive act) significantly more often, and pragmatic reasons (will get hitter into trouble, better to tell a teacher) significantly less often, for unprovoked than provoked aggression. Thus, although most children condemned hitting in both circumstances, they displayed some sympathy for those who hit back. Blatchford (1998) notes that this alternative moral code of reciprocity is widespread in British schools:

> As many teachers will recognise, there can appear to be two very different moral codes operating in schools. School policies on behaviour have as an aim the reduction of aggression, and the setting in place of non-retaliatory solutions to conflict. Yet, out of the classroom, pupils can appear driven to respond in kind to aggression or threat. This out-of-classroom moral code seems to have at its heart a strong sense of reciprocity, and a sensitivity to any perception that they have been slighted or humiliated. (p. 157)

From a cross-cultural perspective, this orientation to the principle of justice, fairness or reciprocity is unsurprising. Drawing on anthropological evidence, Fry (2006) argues that proportionate reciprocity, of both good and bad acts, is a key feature of morality in all cultures, but that it does not manifest in the same way in all of them. For example, in 54 per cent of societies sampled in the Standard Cross-Cultural Sample, representing all major regions of the world, it is legitimate for a relative to avenge a homicide victim by killing the perpetrator or a close relative of the perpetrator (Ericksen and Horton 1992, cited in Fry 2006). Fry argues that this aspect of reciprocal justice is not universal because it is related to the way a society is organised. He draws on Service's (1971, cited in Fry 2006) division of societies into four basic types of social organisation: bands (nomadic or semi-nomadic, egalitarian); tribes (sedentary, quite egalitarian); chiefdoms (social hierarchy); and states (social hierarchy, centralised political power, economic specialisation, bureaucracy). Fry argues that proportionate retaliation becomes less common as one moves through the four categories, because administration of justice shifts with societal complexity from the individual, to kin groups, to public officials. The result is that in states, 'Should a citizen take the law into his or her own hands, the state judicial system treats such acts of self-redress as new crimes, not as the legitimate administration of justice' (Fry 2006, p. 411).

This is exactly the situation we see at Woodwell Green. Teachers consider themselves the administrators of justice, requesting that children refer acts of hitting to them, rather than reciprocating; and they treat children's own efforts to reciprocate as new crimes worthy of punishment in their own right (recall the head teacher's warning that all acts of hitting are wrong regardless of whether they were provoked). So the school's position on physical aggression is that of the society writ small, with teachers placed in

50

the position of judges – a phenomenon examined further in Chapter 7. In this context, the value of not harming is celebrated over the value of reciprocity, which is barely acknowledged in official school rhetoric on physical aggression. Do the children share the school's official position?

3.2.1   Reciprocity versus harm avoidance at Woodwell Green

Towards the end of my fieldwork, I carried out interviews with 142 children in years 1 to 6 (age range of 5 to 11 years), about a variety of hypothetical scenarios, describing disputes I often witnessed on the playground. One involved physical aggression and read as follows: 'Some children are playing football. Jenny says she scored a goal, but Priya says it didn't go in because she saved it. The two girls start to shout at each other, calling each other a liar, and some of the children crowd round to watch. Then Jenny hits Priya.' (Half the children heard this scenario, the other half heard an identical one involving Hamzah and Ben, respectively, rather than Jenny and Priya. In my discussion of this scenario, I refer only to the female version for simplicity.)

The first questions children were asked were, 'Do you think Jenny was right or wrong to hit Priya? Why?' The overwhelming majority (136 of 142) responded that Jenny was wrong. Here is a summary of the reasons they gave (including only those reasons provided by 10 per cent or more of the children giving this answer):

- The hit harms Priya. (23 children)
- The argument was not a good reason to have a fight. (21 children)
- It would have been better to take a penalty (or similar). (18 children)
- Generic statements that 'you don't hit' or shouldn't hit. (18 children)
- Jenny should have told the teacher instead. (16 children)
- Jenny will get into trouble, or Priya will tell the teacher. (14 children)

The most popular reason children gave for why Jenny should not have made an initial hit referred to harm to Priya, and this is in line with previous research in the USA (Astor 1994; Smetana et al. 2003). However, interestingly, the second most popular reason given against the initial hit was that the preceding events were not a sufficiently good reason for hitting. This suggests that for these children, *other* preceding events *would* have constituted a reasonable provocation for physical aggression. In other words, we see here quite widespread support for retaliatory hitting in certain circumstances.

Children were then asked, 'Do you think Priya should hit Jenny back? Why?' The majority (128 of 142 children) said she should not. Reasons for not hitting back, mentioned by over 10 per cent of these children, are listed below.

- It would be better to tell a teacher. (56 children)
- If Priya hit back, she would get into trouble. (34 children)
- Hitting back would prolong the dispute or invite retaliation. (24 children)

As Smetana et al. (2003) found, even those children who did not think that Priya should hit back nevertheless seemed to demonstrate some sympathy for reciprocal justice because their reasons for why she should not hit back were largely pragmatic (better to tell a teacher; Priya would get into trouble). Less than 10 per cent of children mentioned harm to Jenny as a reason for Priya not to hit. Thus, their reasons again suggest some support for reciprocal justice. This support was even clearer among the 14 children who told me that Priya should hit Jenny back. Here are the reasons they gave:

- 'Cos he hit him.' (year 1 girl)
- 'Because they said they wanted a turn.' (year 1 girl)
- 'Jenny hit Priya, so Priya should hit Jenny back.' (year 1 boy)
- 'Because Jenny hit her.' (year 1 boy)
- 'Because Hamzah hit him.' (year 1 boy)
- 'Because she hit Priya.' (year 2 girl)
- 'He hit him back first.' (year 2 girl)
- 'Ben has to punch him in the face and Hamzah has to kick him.' (year 2 boy)
- 'She done it to her.' (year 3 boy)
- 'Hamzah hit Ben.' (year 3 girl)
- 'Priya feels angry, feels like hitting her and calling her bad names.' (year 5 girl)
- 'Cos Jenny hit her.' (year 5 boy)
- 'Self defence.' (year 5 boy)
- 'Defend himself, because Hamzah might hit him again.' (year 6 boy)

Overwhelmingly, the most common reason given is reciprocity: 'She done it to her,' in the words of a boy in year 3. How is this view maintained despite the strong school injunction against physical aggression of all kinds? I consider this question via a case study of Zak and Faizel, two boys whose fortunes I followed throughout year 4 and part of year 5. Zak and Faizel were in year 5 when I interviewed them about the hypothetical vignette involving Jenny and Priya. Both said that Priya should hit Jenny back. For Faizel, this was 'Cos Jenny hit her', and for Zak, 'Self defence'. Their support for reciprocal physical aggression is explored further below.

3.2.2 'She has to get her own back': Zak and Faizel on reciprocity

I first met Zak (Somali Muslim) and Faizel (Pakistani Muslim) at the start of year 4, when they were 8 years old. As we saw in Chapter 2, the two boys were friends, naming each other as someone they liked in more than one interview with me. Both were dedicated fans of London football team Arsenal, and were almost always to be found playing football in the playground during break times at school.

There is evidence that both boys were sometimes physically aggressive. In interviews in year 4, Faizel was named by four classmates as someone with whom they argued or fought, and Zak was named by two (mean of boys in the class was 1.2). In year 5, six children named each boy as someone who frequently got into arguments or fights (mean of boys in the class who were participating in the research was 5.5). Zak was seen as both physically and verbally aggressive by his year 5 teacher, who saw Faizel as verbally aggressive, but not particularly physically aggressive. Their year 5 teacher also agreed to note for me all incidents in which a child in her class complained to her about other children over seven consecutive days. She recorded six incidents, with Zak involved in two (swearing at boys in another class, getting into a fight with boys in another class), and Faizel in four (the two that Zak was involved in, plus fighting with a boy in another class who swore at him, and spitting back at another boy). These data indicate that Faizel and Zak were both willing to physically aggress against other children in the playground. Both were among the six children named by their year 5 teacher as those in the class she reprimanded most often. (The only contradictory data are that one of Faizel's classmates, Farhan, told me in an interview that Faizel did not get into fights.)

At times, Zak in particular demonstrated that he was aware of, and sympathetic towards, the value of harm avoidance promoted by the school. In an interview I conducted with him and his friend Idris when they were in year 4, I asked their views on the US invasion of Afghanistan that followed the September 11 terrorist attacks in the USA in 2001.

Idris suggested that it was 'fair' that America attacked Afghanistan, in retaliation for the September 11 attacks. However, Zak noted that this line of thought meant that the attacks could perpetuate, making an analogy with the playground, where 'Someone hits me so I hit them so they hit me so I hit them'. Later, in year 5, Zak again showed support for the school policy of not hitting back. The following exchange took place during an interview I conducted with him and Faizel about their class rules, rewards and consequences (see Chapter 1 for an explanation of these terms):

ZAK: Miss can I tell you one thing about consequences?

RW: Yeah, go on.

ZAK: Miss, children never learn by if children go to the quiet table, exit the room or speak to mum and dad [all consequences used by the teacher when children disobeyed school rules], shall I tell you why?

RW: Yeah, go on.

ZAK: Miss if you don't give them consequences yeah, Miss they'll start to like the teacher yeah, and start to get better. That's what happened in Miss Hall's class [when Zak was in year 2] cos she never used to give us consequences. She used to say what's good about fighting? Nothing's good about fighting! And I never got in any fights when I was in year 2.

RW: But don't you like fighting?

ZAK: Miss when someone punches you, you're still angry yeah, but you still gonna remember what your teacher told you. Cos you learned your lesson, from last time.

Zak argued that if a teacher did not give him consequences, he would start to like and listen to them, and learn not to fight, a view he reiterated in year 6, asserting that if teachers talked with transgressing children about what they had done wrong, 'the good side comes through'. He thus expressed sympathy on several occasions with the value of harm avoidance promoted by teachers, and with the idea of obedience to school authority figures. Nevertheless, more often Zak and Faizel seemed to prioritise reciprocal justice over harm avoidance. Here are their responses to my questions about the hypothetical vignette in which Jenny hit Priya.

Interview with Faizel

RW: Do you think Jenny was right or wrong to hit Priya?

FAIZEL: [pause] Right [laughs]. Cos Priya would, Priya is lying cos, she just, she's lying cos Priya's team are probably losing and Jenny's winning so she was probably lying and annoying Jenny so that's why Jenny hit her.

54

RW: Do you think Priya should hit Jenny back?

FAIZEL: Yeah.

RW: Why?

FAIZEL: Cos Jenny hit her.

RW: Okay, how do you think Jenny's feeling?

FAIZEL: Angry. And upset cos she knows she's gonna get told off.

RW: And how do you think Priya's feeling?

FAIZEL: She's feeling, she's feeling hurt.

RW: What do you think will happen next?

FAIZEL: More and more people are going to start to crowd in and going to start a fight.

RW: Then what will happen?

FAIZEL: And then they started to shout, and Priya's friends will be saying go on Priya, and Jenny's friends will be saying go on Jenny, and then the teacher will come and take them both in.

RW: What would have been the best way to sort this out? Is it the same as what you just said, or different?

FAIZEL: Er, Priya should've just gone and told the teacher.

Interview with Zak

RW: Do you think Jenny was right or wrong to hit Priya?

ZAK: Wrong cos Miss it's only a game! If someone's gonna kill you you have to fight for your life yeah but Jenny, it's just a little football game, it's just one little goal. Can't she just have a penalty, that's the way we sort it out.

RW: Do you think Priya should hit Jenny back?

ZAK: *Yes.* Self defence.

RW: How do you think Jenny is feeling?

ZAK: She'll be feeling proud of herself, she'll be feeling good, but part of her brain will be feeling good, part of her brain will be feeling bad. Part of her brain will be thinking, 'Wicked, I got my own back', and part of her brain will be thinking, 'Oh no I'm gonna get in big trouble'. But the next thing that Jenny knows she's got hit by Priya too.

RW: How do you think Priya is feeling?

ZAK: Miss she can't stop herself, she has to hit.

RW: Why can't she stop herself?

ZAK: She has to hit, she has to get her own back. But Miss, if she's a good student yeah, she won't hit her back, she'll tell Miss.

RW: Is that better or worse than hitting her?

ZAK: Miss it depends, if she's a good girl she'll tell Miss, if she's a bad girl … Miss if she smacks her back that'll be *good*. Cos Miss you know Jenny, Jenny's quite thick, Priya's gonna say you smacked me first,

55

you're gonna be in most trouble, but don't tell of me and I won't tell of you for the smacking, just tell everything else.[1]

RW: Do people do that quite a lot, so they won't get in trouble?

ZAK: Not quite a lot, sometimes.

RW: What's the best way to sort this out? Is it the same as what you just said, or different?

ZAK: Just say it's a penalty.

RW: Can they do that after Jenny's hit Priya though?

ZAK: No, Priya smack her back, tell her to get off the football pitch, Jenny for a red card, Priya got a red card. Then they get sent to the head teacher, and when they're waiting, when they're waiting outside the office, Priya says you're gonna be in deep trouble, so don't tell of me for the smacking, and I won't tell of you, and Jenny says okay.

For Faizel, Jenny was right to hit in retaliation for what he perceived as Priya's deception, and Priya should hit back simply 'Cos Jenny hit her'. Zak, on the other hand, considered the initial hit to be unjustified in the circumstances: 'it's just a little football game, it's just one little goal'. In condemning the initial hit, he did not refer to the principle of harm avoidance but rather to the principle of reciprocity, suggesting that the hit was disproportionate. Like Faizel, he claimed that Priya should hit back, saying that 'she has to get her own back'. Both boys thus prioritised reciprocal justice over harm avoidance.

Both, however, did show awareness of the contrasting stance taken by the school. This was apparent in Faizel's interview when I asked what would have been the best course of action to take. He replied, 'Priya should've just gone and told the teacher', which is of course the official course of action recommended by the school and justified with reference to harm avoidance. It was even clearer in Zak's interview, when he made an intriguing distinction between 'good girls' who tell the teacher and 'bad girls' who hit back. However, from Zak's point of view, it is not that telling the teacher is a better thing to do than hitting back; each is appropriate to the type of girl. Zak therefore articulated two different values: reciprocity for 'bad' children like him, and school-condoned harm avoidance for 'good' children.

On several other occasions, Zak and Faizel defended retaliatory physical aggression to me. For example, in a joint interview when they were in year 5, I asked them what they thought of their classroom rule, 'We never hurt anyone on the inside or the outside'. 'If someone punches you, what do you do, just back off or something?' Zak asked critically. 'So you think you should hit back?' I asked. 'Yeah. That's fair, that's fair,' he replied.

Faizel articulated the same view in a group interview I conducted with him, Zak and their classmates, Idris and Amar, later in year 5. I had just asked the boys, 'If someone hit you, what would you do, and why?' Faizel replied, 'If someone hit you, I would, I would say get lost yeah and I would hit them back and started a fight, Miss and then I'll probably hit 'em and he, it depends who it is Miss, and most likely they'll probably go and cry to the teacher'. He went on to explain, 'The reason I will do that Miss, cos he's annoying me Miss, even if I tell the teacher Miss he might get a little detention Miss, what's that gonna do? Miss detentions are twenny [twenty] minutes'. Faizel finished his justification for hitting back by commenting that contrary to what their teacher, Mrs Samson, said, 'Two wrongs do make a right Miss though'. Thus Faizel justified physical aggression with the principle of reciprocity: hitting back was a more equal retaliation than telling a teacher, and in addition, hitting followed by hitting back was an acceptable course of events. Later in the same interview, I asked the boys what the word 'fair' meant. 'Miss, if someone hits you, and you hit them back, that's fair,' he replied.

Zak also evoked the principle of reciprocity in this group interview when I asked what he would do if someone hit him. He told me that if he was hit by a boy (though not by a girl), he would hit back rather than tell a teacher. 'Why wouldn't it help to tell a teacher?' I asked. 'Because, because what the hell can the teachers do, they're gonna just gonna say walk away, how can you walk away when someone hits you? Walk away. Yeah right, all the pain inside's gonna tell you to walk away, I don't think so Miss.' In this rhetorically powerful statement, Zak argued in favour of taking playground aggression into his own hands rather than letting a teacher resolve the situation and mete out consequences. He clearly articulated the drive to give back what is given to you, which is at the heart of the concept of reciprocal justice.

The principle of reciprocity revolves around a clear distinction between harmful acts that are unprovoked (and hence require retaliation) and harmful acts that are retaliations to provocations (which should in theory end the exchange). Faizel, Zak and their friends repeatedly alluded to the crucial difference between provocation and retaliation during this same group interview. Amar explained, 'Miss, if someone hit me, yeah, Miss, um I'll probably hit them back because um this, because they start like hitting me for no reason, start pushing me around'. Amar's use of 'for no reason' clearly framed the harmful act as unprovoked and hence demanding retaliation.

Faizel challenged Amar's assumption of non-provocation, interrupting to ask twice, 'What if it was for a reason?' But Amar did not respond to Faizel's challenge, and shortly afterwards Zak also used the phrase 'for no reason' when, during a passionate defence of hitting back, he acted out asking the head teacher, 'What would you do if someone kicks you for no reason, yeah or punches you or anything yeah'.

A little later in the discussion, Idris responded to Faizel's challenge by distinguishing between provoked, justified and unprovoked, unjustified hits: 'Miss do you know what? If someone hits me, I'll um, [inaudible] just hit them back because um, because Miss, because Miss, cos Miss there's no point like hitting me for no, if they hit me for no reason, I will hit them back but if it's for a reason Miss like, Miss I, I'll, Miss I wouldn't hit them back but I [inaudible] like I maybe deserve it. But Miss if they if they don't hit me for no reason I don't think I deserve anything I've got to hit them back.'

According to Idris, he was only justified in hitting back if he had been hit 'for no reason'. If, on the other hand, he was hit as a retaliation for some prior act of harm he had committed, then he said he would not hit back because 'I maybe deserve it'. Idris spelled out what was implicit in the other boys' accounts: It is appropriate to retaliate to a provocation, but it is not appropriate to retaliate to what was itself a (reasonable) retaliation. Reciprocity of harm, according to this account, is a two-way exchange: provocation followed by proportionate retaliation.[2]

3.2.3 Fairness in aggressive boys' lives

Zak's and Faizel's commitment to reciprocal justice suggests that fairness was very important to them. This is not surprising; we will see repeatedly in this book that reciprocity and justice were important concerns to the children of Woodwell Green, and other research suggests that this value is widely held by children in various cultures (Edwards 1987; Piaget 1932).

Of course, in many situations at school, fairness was important to teachers as well; for example, in ensuring that no one cheated in a test, or that everyone should have access to the football pitches during playtime. In such situations, teachers prioritised justice over other values, including welfare. For instance, one would be surprised if a teacher allowed a child who was upset at the difficulty of a test to copy their neighbour, in order to alleviate their distress. However, when it came to children's peer relations, teachers generally prioritised welfare over fairness (although see Chapter 7 for signs that teachers found fairness difficult to ignore). Thus, while Zak and Faizel prioritised justice over welfare in instances of provoked physical aggression, their teachers prioritised welfare over justice.

Zak's and Faizel's valuing of fairness and reciprocity was not confined to physical aggression. They and their friends applied the principle to several other areas of school life. One was gift giving. It was not common for children to bring presents for each other into school, but occasionally classroom activities provided opportunities for gift exchange. When their year 4 class made egg-shaped Easter cards, most of the boys decorated their eggs with the names and kit colours of football teams. When Mohamed, a keen Arsenal supporter, showed me his egg, I asked why he had decorated it with Manchester United colours. He explained that he was making it for Faizel, who was making an Arsenal card for him.

Another realm in which fairness and reciprocity were important to boys was playground football games, from ensuring 'fair teams' (i.e. the same number of players in both teams) to efforts to avoid bias when interpreting events in the game (such as whether a particular tackle was a foul). Here is a typical example, this time involving boys who were watching girls in their class playing football against another class in their year:

> After 5B's third goal, 5S girls Simran and Maria stand silently glaring at their classmate Harpreet in goal, who shrugs. She and Simran swap for a while, but after a few minutes Harpreet goes back in goal. Then there is a flurry at the other end. I couldn't see what happened, but the 5S girls come running up the pitch cheering, while the 5B goalie stands in goal at the other end looking annoyed. The 5B girls talk briefly with Abdi, the 5B boy who is referee, and then run up the pitch telling the 5S girls it's a goal kick [instead of a goal].[3] Faizel [5S] comes onto the pitch and starts arguing with the referee. Other 5S boys are shouting and getting annoyed too. Zak comes over to me and I ask him what happened. He complains hotly, 'You know that boy Abdi, he's cheating cos he's in 5B and he wants them to win'. I ask how he cheated. 'Simran scored a goal, and he's saying it's a goal kick.' I ask why. 'Cos he's in 5B, he wants them to win that's why.'

Faizel's and Zak's concerns with fairness are obvious here. They were also apparent in an interview in year 5, when the two boys complained about Yusuf, a boy they played football with, who they saw as biased in favour of his own team:

> ZAK: This is what happens in a normal fight yeah. Miss, Yusuf took a shot yeah, I was the goalkeeper and I went like this, look. [He stands up and shows me how he reached for the ball.] And I went like this [lunges to one side], I tucked my foot, I done it by purpose to save it. I say it should be a corner and he says it's a goal kick yeah.[4]

RW: Were you and Yusuf on the same team?

ZAK: Yeah.

RW: What happened then?

ZAK: Miss then I said he's gonna have a fight. Mohamed, who's in Faizel's team [playing against Zak and Yusuf's team], sticks up for Yusuf [Mohamed's cousin] yeah.

RW: Did they start hitting people?

ZAK: Yeah. Just cos I was being fair yeah, and he wanted a goal kick. He's a cheat.

FAIZEL: Yes he does, he always cheats yeah.

According to Faizel and Zak, Zak argued for a corner (advantage to the other team), while Yusuf argued for a goal kick (advantage to their team). Zak's explanation was that he was 'being fair' while Yusuf was 'a cheat', and Faizel agreed. In the same interview, Faizel described an occasion on which Mohamed, his friend and (on this occasion) team mate, argued that they should have a penalty, and he told Mohamed to accept that it was 'a fair goal' scored by the other team. Thus, both boys saw themselves as fair even when this went against the interests of their own team.

The boys also spoke of fairness in ensuring that everyone in the team had an opportunity to be involved in the game. Faizel had just told me that he was usually the captain for their class, 5S, which generally played against 5B. I asked why he was the captain, and Zak replied, 'Miss because if I say to him can I take right free kicks, he lets me take right free kicks, if I wanna take a penalty he lets me take a penalty, he's fair'. Two of his classmates told me the same of Faizel but another classmate, Idris, told me in an interview in year 4 that he disliked Faizel, 'Just because it's his ball, like when we play football, if it's his ball he don't let no one take free kicks, penalties, throw-outs'. He continued, 'If someone moans at Faizel and he's their friend he'll let him, but he won't let me'. This view contradicts the one I have set out here, of Faizel as someone who values and promotes fairness, reminding us that there may have been times when Faizel prioritised other concerns.

There was another, very different domain to which boys applied concepts of fairness, and which contributed to their resistance to the school's harm avoidance rule: the behaviour of their teachers. Faizel and Zak were both adamant that many of their teachers were unfair and biased against them, and they used this claim to support their argument for taking playground justice into their own hands, rather than telling a teacher (see Woods 2008 for more on their concerns). For example, the following group interview took place when Zak, Faizel and their class-mates Mohamed and Amar had been in year 5 for about a month. I asked them which teachers they preferred to tell problems to and which they did not get on with, and they immediately began to talk about teachers being biased against them.

ZAK: Miss I don't trust Mrs Samson [their class teacher] cos she don't trust us, what I mean is like Miss she knows us lot are bad yeah so she sends us straight to Mr Gardner [head teacher] so I'd rather just have a fight.

MOHAMED: Miss fights always come in football.

RW: [to Zak] So who would you rather tell?

ZAK: Miss if it's just a little thing like someone push me then I won't say anything but if it's like someone being racist then I will, but the reason I don't tell Mrs Samson is cos she just sends me to Mr Gardner and I don't trust Mr Gardner.[5]

RW: Why not?

ZAK: Cos Miss, Miss he's unfair. Miss just because, you know people that never done nothing yeah, he's gonna say send a letter home, just cos I done stuff in the past yeah, he thinks I'm gonna do it in the present and in the future.

Zak said the same of the deputy head, then, after an interruption, continued: 'Miss I got more. Miss I only trust myself, I trust my friends, I trust Faizel and Mohamed and Amar, and I trust Farhan a bit cos I tell him my secrets.' 'Why do you only trust your friends?' I asked. 'Miss because, Miss cos they were like encouraging me, or if I'm doing a good thing they'll encourage me, if I do a bad thing they'll stop it,' Zak explained. When I asked him for examples, Zak said that taking a penalty was a good thing, while fighting was a bad thing, adding, 'I stopped Mohamed today at fighting because he was fighting today with Ali. I was trying to stop him'. He said that this can sometimes get him into trouble because adults think he is involved in the fight: 'Miss because I'm stopping it right, you know the teachers, they always think I've done the wrong thing.'

So Zak described his peer relations as characterised by trust, while his teachers are suspicious of him and therefore treat him unfairly. Interestingly, two of his well-behaved classmates expressed the same view in a separate interview in year 5. I had asked why some children got into trouble more often than others. Simran replied, 'Miss this is an honest comment. Miss you know the ones who are the really really

61

bad ones, the teachers always look upon them, they look at them'. Sandeep agreed: 'Miss, cos the teacher, when they get told off once the teacher's always looking at them.'

At a later group interview with Zak, Faizel and their classmates Amar and Idris, the boys expressed similar concerns. I had just asked the boys what they thought the word 'fair' meant. Faizel commented provocatively, 'I don't think they [the teachers] know what fair means. They should look it up in the dictionary'. He proceeded to argue, 'Miss some teachers are sexist', claiming that 'Miss if, if a girl was to swear at anyone yeah Miss, they would always just get away with it Miss'. His classmate Amar offered an example: 'Miss you know like if we like swear at a like a girl, Miss just pretend like I sweared at a girl, I sweared at a girl and she started swearing at me, and we [inaudible] that's not fair, cos we're the one that gets told off, because, because the girl, Miss you're like, you're like a teacher, you're a girl innit [isn't it], and you believe girls, you can't, you don't believe boys.'

According to Zak, Faizel and their friends, their teachers were prejudiced against them on the basis of their reputations and their gender. They also argued on other occasions that some teachers were racist, a topic that is discussed further in Chapter 6. I did not collect the kind of data needed to test their claims, but they are certainly plausible. For one thing, it makes intuitive sense that a teacher striving to manage a classroom would watch children he or she believes to be disruptive more closely than other children. In addition, there is psychological evidence that all of us judge others on the basis of their reputations. Hymel et al. (1990) reviewed evidence that both children and adults interpret the same act differently depending on who performed it, and concluded that 'social behavior is perceived in a biased fashion as a function of prior attitudes and beliefs about the actor' (p. 158). Finally, I did gather a small amount of evidence demonstrating that teachers can be biased (though not evidence of how common such biases were). One teacher told me that although she tried to be consistent, she found it hard not to treat children differently depending on how much she liked them. And I witnessed another teacher making an assumption in the playground about Jack Thompson, a boy with a reputation for being disruptive.

> I am chatting with a teacher who is on playground duty for playtime. Year 3 girl Jane approaches with a couple of other girls and tells the teacher that Jack threw his drink over her. 'Jack Thompson!' the teacher exclaims, before adding, 'Which Jack?' But her initial guess was right; 'Thompson,' says one girl, 'In year 3,' says another. 'Wait till I get my hands on him,' she says.

The teacher's assumption about which 'Jack' Jane referred to was probably not based only on reputation, because Jack Thompson was the only Jack in Jane's class. However, her assumption may still have been informed by Jack's reputation, as she seems to recognise when she retreats from her original assumption to ask 'Which Jack?'

I do not have the data to assess how regularly teachers made such assumptions, but aggressive boys like Zak and Faizel felt that it was often enough for them not to trust their teachers. When they were in year 6, I told Zak and Faizel I wanted to write that they felt that teachers were biased against them. Both eagerly told me more recent examples, suggesting that this issue was enduring. Zak summed it up: 'Miss, trusting teachers is a very big thing Miss. You don't trust your teachers and they don't trust you.' Thus, these boys did not trust the very people they were supposed to turn to, to resolve playground disputes fairly. No wonder, then, that they preferred to take matters into their own hands using reciprocal justice, rather than embrace the school's edict to tell a teacher.

3.3   Hierarchy, Respect and Physical Aggression

We have seen that, despite the school's efforts, aggressive boys like Faizel and Zak prioritised fairness over harm avoidance, partly because they did not see telling a teacher (which is how the school advocated that children avoided harm) as effective. In fact, the situation was more complex than this. Above I described how Zak argued that if teachers ceased to punish him, he would start to like the teacher and stop being physically aggressive. When he told me this, I challenged him by suggesting, 'But you two [Zak and Faizel] are powerful in the playground partly because you sometimes hit other boys'. Zak acknowledged this, saying, 'Miss if you want respect you have to earn it'. For boys at Woodwell Green, physical aggression invoked not only a tension between the values of welfare (and obedience to authority) on the one hand, and justice on the other. It also invoked concerns with hierarchy in the peer group (Woods 2009). Hierarchies have been widely documented in children's peer groups, in that children in various settings have been found to rank themselves in relation to particular values. These values might vary between children in different settings, but the preoccupation with status and hierarchy is common to all (Goodwin and Kyratzis 2011).

3.3.1   Masculinity and violence

We saw in Chapter 2 that toughness was widely valued by children at Woodwell Green, but that this toughness typically took a different form for boys and girls. The pressure to use physical aggression to stand up for oneself is likely to be greater for boys than for girls, because of widespread associations between physical aggression and ideals of masculinity. During my research, I asked 140 children to narrate (years 1 to 4) or write (years 5 and 6) a story about children in the school playground. Thirty-four of the 68 boys (50 per cent) included acts of physical aggression in their stories, compared with only 18 of the 72 girls (25 per cent). Throughout my research I found that boys at the school relished telling each other and me about violent incidents they had witnessed or been involved in, from playground fights to murderous acts in the computer game *Grand Theft Auto* (which many had played, despite its 18 certificate in the UK).

The pressure to conform to, and celebrate, masculine values of toughness and aggression was particularly obvious in a series of group interviews I conducted with children in Zak's and Faizel's class, when they were in year 5 (aged 9 and 10 years). One of the questions I asked in these group interviews was, 'If someone hit you, what would you do and why?' During group interviews with 13 girls in the class, six said they would not hit back, three that they would, and the remaining four girls did not express an opinion. However, during group interviews with boys in the class, all 12 participants said that they would hit back, and some subscribed to extreme physical violence. Consider for example the following extract, taken from one of these group interviews.

PAVANDEEP:	Miss I would tell the teacher, if the teacher doesn't listen, I'll start beating them up and swearing at them, and then throw 'em out the window.
RW:	Okay, so
ANIL:	Well you'll probably break your tooth cos you get beaten up by girls. [laughs]
PAVANDEEP:	Shut up, I don't get beaten up by girls, you do!
ANIL:	[still laughing] No, he gets beaten by Farah and that.
RW:	So you would try and tell the teacher, and if that didn't work then you would, like hit them back. Okay good.
ANIL:	Listen to this! Pavandeep gets beat!
RW:	Who did I say, Anil you go next.
ANIL:	Oh Miss, I wanna go last cos I'm thinking about what I'm gonna say.

RW:	Okay. Go on Sandeep.
SANDEEP:	I'll kill the fucking bastards! [laughter from Sandeep and others]
RW:	So would you hit them back?
SANDEEP:	Yeah Miss I would hit them back.
RW:	Seriously? [inaudible]
ANIL:	Miss I, I'd seriously hit them back.
SANDEEP:	Miss I'd do it, Miss people think I'm good but in the playground sometimes I do get annoyed really easily and I do start pushing people but Miss, um I'll ch– I'll chase 'em round the playground as far as I can go.
ANIL:	Okay come on, I'm annoying you. [starts slapping Sandeep]
RW:	Come on, not now! [inaudible]
MOHAMED:	He said outside not in school you idiot!
RW:	I know. If you do it in school all that will happen is that you'll have to go back to the classroom and I'll tell Mrs Samson [the boys' teacher].
ANIL:	Okay let's go outside Miss.
SANDEEP:	Miss, Amandeep came
ANIL:	Okay.
RW:	[laughs]
MOHAMED:	And now my turn Miss. If someone hits you what would you do and why. Um–
RW:	Okay try and think really, maybe think of a time when it has happened to you what you did.
ANIL:	Okay Miss.
MOHAMED:	I would chase him all around the playground and I'd fucking kill him, like I was blooming killing a bird, um, Miss, um, I get his face, put it [inaudible], scrape it on the floor, get the little dickhead, and, and
ANIL:	Suck his blood.
MOHAMED:	Shut up!

Mohamed, Pavandeep, Sandeep and Anil all subscribed to violent responses to being hit. These responses do not seem to be based solely on the concept of reciprocal justice because they are generally far in excess of the original provocation. In addition, in most cases the boys' accounts do not resonate with other sources of information about their levels of physical aggression. Mohamed did have a reputation among peers and teachers for being physically aggressive (his year 5 teacher saw him as sometimes physically and verbally aggressive and named him as one of the six children in her class she told off most often, and in questionnaires, 13 of his year 5 classmates named him as someone who got into arguments and fights a lot, the highest score among boys in the class). Anil's year 5 teacher saw him as sometimes physically aggressive and occasionally verbally aggressive, and in questionnaires, seven of his classmates named him as someone who got into arguments and fights a lot.

However, Pavandeep and Sandeep were not normally physically aggressive. Pavandeep's teacher saw him as occasionally physically and verbally aggressive, and he was named by five classmates for getting into fights and arguments. He told me in individual interviews that Faizel kept trying to pick a fight with him but that he would not fight back, because he was afraid of getting told off (see Chapter 4). Finally, Sandeep's teacher viewed him as never physically or verbally aggressive, and no classmates nominated him as someone who fights. Note that Anil mocked Pavandeep and Sandeep for their claims to violence, again suggesting that their words did not match their playground actions.

All 12 of the boys in this class who participated in group interviews claimed that if someone hit them, they would hit them back. Yet in individual interviews about the playground football scenario described earlier in this chapter, most told me that Ben or Priya should not hit back. Moreover, like Sandeep and Pavandeep, several made claims that were not supported by my playground observations or teacher and peer ratings. It is clear that in the group interviews, boys were motivated by impression management in front of their peers. This is only to be expected, but it is significant here for what it tells us about what sort of impression the boys sought to construct in front of one another.[6] Here it is clearly a celebration of violence and toughness, which were explicitly associated with masculinity by Anil, who teasingly claimed that Pavandeep got beaten up by girls.

The following quotes from boys in individual interviews give a sense of why such impression management was important. Both are taken from interviews about the physical aggression scenario described earlier in this chapter, involving Jenny and Priya. The first is with year 5 boy Idris, the second with year 6 boy Mansukh.

Interview with Idris

RW: How do you think Priya is feeling?

IDRIS: Miss Priya, Miss she might be feeling very sad that she just broke up and she wants to be back together but Miss if she makes up again Jenny'll think she's a pussy like if she has a fight with her again she'll always know I can beat her up, that's how she'll feel.

RW: Will they make friends do you think?

IDRIS: Yeah. Miss girls are always like that. They always make up with each other.

RW: Are boys different?

IDRIS: Boys have a fight and they don't come back together. Miss a long time ago I had a fight with Faizel and I never came back to him. We sometimes play on the same team [in playground football games] and everything. Miss that's how I am, if I have a fight with someone I never come back with them because if I just come back to them they'll just think I'll always come back to them, like whenever he hits me it's all right, he's just gonna do it again and again. That's why Miss I don't want people to think that about me.

Interview with Mansukh

RW: What do you think will happen next?

MANSUKH: Start a fight, and then they would both get in trouble.

RW: Would someone get the teacher or would the teacher come over?

MANSUKH: The teacher would come over cos they see everyone crowded round. In our playground, if someone starts a fight everyone goes to watch it and the teacher sees all the people and goes over to see what's happening.

RW: Why do they like to watch?

MANSUKH: Because they think it's really fun watching a fight.

RW: Like wrestling on TV I suppose.

MANSUKH: And quite exciting. And like sometimes children see if the other child's strong or not, like if he's bleeding.

RW: How do you mean?

MANSUKH: To see whether the kid who is getting beaten up can stand up for himself and if he's strong.

Both Idris and Mansukh note that children observe how a boy responds to a physical attack, making judgements about how tough he is and how able to stand up for himself. Similarly, when in a group interview with four other boys I asked why they all claimed that they would hit someone back, Farhan replied, 'It give you a better reputation at school'.

So it seems that in addition to (or indeed because of) associating masculinity with violence, boys gained status among peers by standing up for themselves in a fight. In this they were not unusual; sociologists have shown that boys in many settings use physical aggression to gain status and construct themselves as masculine (Boulton 1993a; Connell 1989;

Davies 1982; Ferguson 2000; Savin-Williams 1976; Swain 2003, 2004). The routine use by many boys at Woodwell Green of physical aggression to assert status created a dilemma for any boy who supported the school's position on harm avoidance, yet also wanted to command respect and authority in this peer group. This was exactly the problem faced by Zak and Faizel's classmate Paul.

3.3.2 'Mr Gardner said don't hit, tell a teacher, but it never worked': Paul negotiating hierarchy at Woodwell Green

According to school records, Paul's ethnicity was English and his religion Christian. He started at Woodwell Green at the beginning of year 4, when he was 8 years old. He became fairly unpopular, named in individual interviews by five classmates as someone they disliked and by only one as someone they liked. Children's reasons for disliking him implied a person who sought dominance unsuccessfully. For instance, children commented, 'Paul goes, I can run faster than you yeah, but he was the last person', 'He's bossy' and 'He always has to get his own way'.

Paul's teachers saw him as somewhat verbally and physically aggressive, a view that is supported to some extent by my interviews and fieldnotes. In an interview, Paul's classmate Joshua, who was not at all aggressive and usually played with girls, complained that Paul swore at him and called him 'gay'.[7] My fieldnotes document occasions when Paul was a victim of aggression, and others when he was perpetrator. For instance, he hurt his arm after several boys in another class pushed him over in the playground, and during a wet play Faizel screwed up his paper aeroplane; while he threw a beanbag in his cousin's face, justifying this with the claim that she was annoying him, and called Faizel 'a skinny little runt' during a dispute in a PE (physical exercise) class.

Paul certainly saw himself as unpopular. One playtime in October, when he had been at the school a month, I came across him sitting on a bench alone, looking fed up. I asked what was wrong and he said that the boys would not let him play football, going on to single out Faizel (see Chapter 4 for more on why it was Faizel specifically who excluded Paul). 'I've been here a month and I still haven't made a single friend,' he lamented. The following month, he and several other children were talking to me about my research. Paul suggested that I write about him because he did not have any friends. Paul's mother subsequently spoke to his teacher, Miss Chahal, who tried to tackle the problem by carrying out exercises with the class designed to help the children understand how it felt to be left out (these are described in more detail in Chapter 4). She and Paul also asked his classmates why they would not let him play football. On the two occasions I observed, the answer was the same: 'It's not me, it's Faizel!'

A few months later, during an individual interview, Paul told me that he disliked fellow year 4 boys and football players Faizel, Zak, Idris and Sam, but added that recently all four had become nicer to him. Wondering if Miss Chahal's interventions had been effective, I asked why he thought the change had come about. Paul replied immediately and with conviction, 'Because I hit Sam'. He went on to explain how it happened that he punched this notoriously aggressive boy:

PAUL: Well the thing was after maths he started saying stuff like, really horrible, and I asked Sandeep where is he and he said I'm not telling you.

RW: Did he? Why did he say that?

PAUL: Cos he knew I was gonna fight him. I went up to him

RW: [interrupting] How did you find him?

PAUL: I just looked around and I saw him. I went up to him and I said all right Sam and I just went *whack*!

Later in the interview, Paul commented on the fact that his teacher's interventions had not helped his situation. I had just asked Paul how he felt after he hit Sam.

PAUL: I wasn't really happy about it, but I had to do it. When I ask Miss something it never works really.

RW: Do you think it could've worked if Miss Chahal had done something different, or do you think it was just impossible to sort it out that way?

PAUL: It's impossible to do it the way Miss Chahal said. I won't punch anybody else. If Sam does it again really bad for another couple of months I'll do it again.

Later in the interview, Paul confided, 'My mum was saying one thing, why don't you hit him'. During my fieldwork, several children told me that despite school rules, their parents had told them to hit back if they were hit – an approach taken by many parents in the UK (Blatchford 1989, 1998). Like Paul's mum, these parents wanted their children to stand up for themselves and show that they cannot be pushed around by others. In other words, parents may encourage retaliatory hitting as a way of ensuring that their child is not positioned at the bottom of the social hierarchy and bullied.

Paul continued, 'Mr Gardner [head teacher] says don't hit, tell a teacher, but it never worked'. He clearly felt that one fight did more for his relations with the other boys than all the teacher interventions put together. He explained that since this event, which earned him a detention, Sam no longer swore at him and treated him with more respect, 'saying do you want this Paul, passing me my ball instead of kicking it down the end of the playground'. 'He's scared a little bit – not that much, just a little bit,' he said, describing how other boys including Faizel were also treating him more respectfully. In an interview early in year 5, Paul reported that this shift had persisted and that Faizel, who had formerly excluded him from football games, was now his friend. This claim is supported by fieldnotes, which document several occasions in year 5 when Paul was to be found playing football with Faizel and others in the playground. Soon after he changed schools, and Faizel and Zak told me that they were sorry he had left.

It is not that Paul was completely unaggressive until the day he hit Sam. As noted above, I had observed encounters between Paul and other boys, including Faizel, in which both parties swore at and insulted the other, and several of Paul's peers saw him as domineering. However, Paul's aggression prior to this turning point was primarily verbal, and when physical, it was directed towards unaggressive peers. Therefore the day he hit Sam, who was perhaps the most aggressive boy in his year, marked a decisive and transforming change.

Paul's struggles to become accepted and respected at Woodwell Green made little progress until he resorted to physical aggression, which was highly efficacious in improving his status with other aggressive boys like Sam, Faizel and Zak. In British and American working-class neighbourhoods, where many adults as well as children associate masculinity, status and violence, and where adults and children fear intimidation on the street, physical aggression is an important medium through which dominance and status are produced among boys (Connolly 1998; Evans 2006; Ferguson 2000; Swain 2003). It is difficult for a boy growing up in such a neighbourhood to achieve dominance, prestige and decision-making power without behaving aggressively, whatever they think of it morally. So it is not surprising that Paul, unpopular and longing for acceptance and respect, eventually followed his mother's advice and hit an aggressive peer.[8]

3.4 Implications for Schools

We have seen in this chapter that schools' requirement for children not to hit in response to a provocation is actually very difficult for some children to meet. The reason for this is that the value of harm avoidance promoted by the school conflicts with two other values or concerns: reciprocal justice and the construction and maintenance of dominance hierarchies among boys. For both of these competing demands, there are implications for how adults in school relate to physically aggressive children.

Taking first the competing value of reciprocity, fairness or justice, interventions designed to reduce physical aggression have often seen aggressive children as engaging in impaired moral reasoning, or as ignoring the moral dimension altogether (as noted by Astor 1994, 1998; Smetana et al. 2003). The psychological research demonstrates that in fact, the moral reasoning of aggressive and unaggressive children is remarkably similar. Both tend to condemn unprovoked hits, and both tend to judge provoked hits more leniently. Moreover, Zak's insightful analysis of his situation revealed that at least some physically aggressive children are well aware of the competing values and are engaged in an ongoing struggle to reconcile them. In addition, Zak, Faizel and their friends demonstrate that aggressive boys are strongly committed to the principle of reciprocity. In other words, it is not that they are amoral, but that they prioritise values differently from the school's official position.[9]

These insights into the perspectives of physically aggressive children suggest that interventions that assume such children's moral reasoning is simply flawed are misguided. It would seem more sensible to recognise the legitimacy of the concerns felt by aggressive children, and to use them as a starting point of anti-aggression interventions. For instance, Zak understood that one limitation of reciprocal justice is that it can lead to perpetual violence. Discussing this problem with aggressive children may help them to recognise the limitations of reciprocal justice. It would also be useful to discuss with aggressive children what kinds of provocation warrant a physically aggressive response. This is a question of the extent of harm perceived to result from different transgressions (e.g. racist insult; insulting a child's mother; kicking a child's football down the corridor), and a question of equivalence and fairness of response. Again, helping aggressive children to critically evaluate the fairness of reciprocal justice may help to avoid physically aggressive responses in some situations. This is especially important given the celebration of aggression that children may associate with masculinity, which seems to involve an excessive violence that is not proportionate to the original provocation.

The other value in competition with the school's non-aggression stance is the role that physical aggression plays in the construction of prestige and dominance in the peer group and the local community, especially for boys in working-class areas. The implication is that interventions that see individual aggressive children as the problem, and try to change them as individuals, are limited.[10] Such interventions neglect the social meaning that physical aggression has for these boys, in terms of masculinity and status. If a high-status, physically aggressive child like Zak stops being physically aggressive, he is very likely to lose status in his peer group because the individual intervention will not have changed the meaning that aggression has for other children in the group (and others in the wider community). Thus, it is crucial that individual interventions are accompanied by larger-scale shifts in how status and prestige are constructed in the peer group. This means finding plausible alternative ways for boys to achieve status that do not involve physical aggression. This is certainly not an easy task for schools situated in deprived urban neighbourhoods where physical aggression is widely associated with masculinity and status.

Finally, we have seen how Zak's and Faizel's distrust of teachers adds to their commitment to physical aggression, because it makes the main alternative offered by the school (to tell a teacher) undesirable. A typical element of a state society, the school demands that children do not take justice into their own hands but pass complaints onto an official (in this case, a teacher) to resolve. This is a big demand for children who do not trust their teachers to deal with complaints fairly. Zak, Faizel and their friends told me they believed their teachers to be sexist, racist and biased against them on the basis of their reputations. Their distrust was such that they refused point blank when I asked if I could express their concerns to their teacher – but they were enthusiastic about me writing about their predicament using pseudonyms. If Zak and Faizel are typical, schools will have to find ways to deal with aggressive boys' perceptions of unfairness in order to persuade them to tell teachers instead of hitting back. The first step will be for schools to be willing to examine their own practices and to be open to the possibility that teachers might show systematic subconscious biases against certain children.

Notes

1. Zak suggests here that a teacher would see an initial hit as more serious than a retaliatory hit. If this is the case, then despite the official school rule condemning all acts of harm, teachers' judgements of hitting may be influenced by the principle of reciprocity. Teachers' views on reciprocal harm are discussed further in Chapter 7.
2. See Chapter 7 on problems with applying the principle of reciprocity in practice.

3. The 5B girls were claiming that Simran's goal was not legitimate, and so the 5B goalie should be allowed to kick the ball into play (a goal kick), rather than 5S being awarded a goal.

4. A corner kick is awarded to the attacking team when the ball leaves the field of play by crossing the goal line (without a goal having been scored), having been last touched by a defending player. Zak is asserting that because, in saving the goal, he knocked the ball out of play across the goal line, the other team should be given a corner, which is a shot taken from the corner of the pitch nearest the place where the ball went out of play. In contrast, according to Zak, his team mate Yusuf wanted a goal kick, which is when the goalkeeper (i.e. Zak) kicks the ball onto the pitch. A goal kick should be awarded if someone in the opposite team kicked the ball out of play across the goal line, which was not the case here, according to Zak. Hence Zak is accusing Yusuf of cheating.

5. See Chapter 6 for more on the high priority assigned by children and adults to racism at Woodwell Green.

6. In the group interviews, I was concerned about boys exaggerating and repeatedly exhorted them to 'tell me what you really think' and 'tell me about a time when someone really hit you in the playground'. I wanted them to tell me the truth, and saw their exaggerations as obstacles to that aim. It was only later that I realised how unreasonable my request was. Impression management was far more important to these boys than my requests for 'the truth' were. Moreover, it is likely that the boys were also engaging in a degree of impression management in individual interviews with me. While I tried hard to distance myself from teachers and the school discipline system, I could not avoid being an adult in school and did occasionally intervene in fights. Thus children may have been more oriented to school values in individual discussions with me. I would expect this to be particularly true of children whose trust I had not been able to obtain. Children (and adults) will always be motivated to create a particular impression in encounters with others, so impression management is an unavoidable issue in social science research. We need not see this as a problem, though, for two reasons. Firstly, we can learn a lot about children's perspectives by observing the impressions they seek to create in front of particular others. Secondly, we can gather different kinds of data (such as playground observations, peer ratings, teacher ratings) in order to make judgements about how a claim made by a particular child in an interview relates to their claims and behaviours in other settings.

7. See Chapter 6 for more on children's use of 'gay' as an insult.

8. I am not suggesting that all boys at Woodwell Green were physically aggressive (we have seen that they were not). However, boys who refused to hit and punch did not usually command lofty positions in boys' hierarchies.

9. Children at Woodwell Green other than aggressive boys were also concerned about fairness and reciprocity in various situations other than physical aggression, as we shall see later in the book. My point here is that if we want to understand the subset of children at Woodwell Green who were physically aggressive (and mostly male), we need to recognise their concerns with reciprocity in situations of physical aggression.

10. Smetana et al. (2003) note that individualistic interventions for aggressive behaviours abound. This is partly the result of individualistic theories such as Dodge's social information processing model, which claims that children are physically aggressive because of flawed processing of information in their environment (e.g. Crick and Dodge 1994; Dodge and Coie 1987; see Woods 2009, 2010 for a critique of this theory).

4

'Whose Game Is It?'
Understanding Exclusion

4.1 School Rules: All Play Together

As we saw in the preceding chapters, Woodwell Green emphasised the principle of harm avoidance, summed up as 'We do not hurt others on the inside or the outside'. In this and the following chapter, I explore some aspects of 'hurting on the inside'. I focus in this chapter on cases where specific children were excluded from the peer group. Adults at Woodwell Green generally condemned acts of exclusion, stating instead that children should all play together, allowing anyone to join in their games, without selectivity. Here is an example, taken from a year 1 classroom (5- and 6-year-olds). Following a week off school, the class teacher, Miss Hart, reminded the children of their class rules:

> The children are sitting on the carpet. 'What are the rules?' Miss Hart asks them. Some hands go up. 'Akash?' 'No hitting and no punching,' he says. 'That's right,' confirms Miss Hart, 'No fighting.' She chooses Nayna, who also has her hand up. 'No kicking,' she says. Miss Hart says that that's also no fighting. Zain is chosen next. 'Don't put the chairs back cos someone will come and fall over,' he says. Miss Hart asks if he means that people shouldn't tip on their chairs, and he agrees. Miss Hart says that that's true, but that it's not the same kind of rule as no fighting, which she now homes in on. 'How does it feel if someone kicks you?' she asks the children. 'Is it a nice feeling?' 'Noo,' they chorus. 'How do you feel if someone kicks you, Mahdi?' After a slight pause, Mahdi says, 'Sad,' with a rising intonation. Miss Hart says that they never have any reason to hit or kick each

Children's Moral Lives: An Ethnographic and Psychological Approach, First Edition. Ruth Woods.
© 2013 John Wiley & Sons, Ltd. Published 2013 by John Wiley & Sons, Ltd.

other, continuing: 'Do you ever need to touch anybody?' 'Noo,' they chorus. 'If you have a problem in the playground, what should you do?' Lots of hands go up. Miss Hart chooses Bobby from amongst them. 'Go to Mrs Thomas or go to Jackie' [playground supervisors]. Miss Hart agrees, then asks, 'Is it nice – how do you feel if someone on your table or in the playground, if they say, I'm not gonna be your friend. How does it make you feel?' Hands go up again, and she chooses Bikram, who says, 'Sad.' Miss Hart says that this is hurting on the inside rather than the outside, and it still makes you feel sad. She urges them to 'be kind to each other'.

At first, the children focused on the rule concerning physical aggression, and Miss Hart reiterated the school's position that all physical aggression is wrong, and that telling a teacher is preferable to retaliation (see Chapter 3). But then the teacher drew the children's attention to excluding one another, calling this an example of hurting on the inside, which is also against school rules.

Teachers of older children also reprimanded them for excluding one another. For example, when year 4 boy Daniel complained to his teacher Mrs Samson that classmate Zohraiz would not let him play with him, Mrs Samson chided Zohraiz in front of the class:

> 'Zohraiz, I'm only going to ask you this once,' says Mrs Samson. 'You know the routine if you lie. Were you horrible to Daniel?' 'Yes,' Zohraiz answers quietly. 'Do you think it's a nice thing to say someone can't play?' 'No.' Mrs Samson asks how Zohraiz would feel if someone excluded him, finishing with, 'Do you have something to say to Daniel?' Zohraiz turns to Daniel and quietly says, 'Sorry.' 'Shake hands,' she commands, and they do. She tells them to sit down.

Fellow year 4 teacher Miss Chahal was also concerned about children in her class excluding one another. On one occasion, I saw her brush off a complaint about exclusion. Mohamed had complained to her that Amandeep would not let him play. Miss Chahal was not the slightest bit interested. 'Save it for the playground,' she replied in a bored voice. She saw Mohamed as quite popular (a perception borne out by children's comments to me in individual interviews), and so was not concerned about this complaint (which she probably saw as an instance of gratuitous tale-telling; see Chapter 7). However, on several other occasions she expressed concerns about Paul (who we met in Chapter 3) and Sarah (who we will meet later in this chapter), who both started at Woodwell Green in her class at the start of year 4, and struggled to settle in and make friends. Here are fieldnotes describing two separate instances when Miss Chahal tried to help Sarah and Paul by increasing their peers' awareness of exclusion.

Event 1: Miss Chahal puts children into groups and distributes a picture of a group of children standing together, with one child standing separate. She tells the class to discuss the picture, and then to act out a role play based on it. All the children I speak to interpret the picture as the group excluding the single child. Three groups act out their role plays. In one, Idris plays the excluded boy. 'Hey new boy, we don't like playing with new boys. Find your other friends,' exclaims Sarah. Miss Chahal stops them and asks the class how they think the excluded boy would feel. Suggestions include, 'Unhappy', 'Wouldn't want to go to school' and 'Cry every night', and Miss Chahal agrees that this is how she would feel. The group continues their role play. 'Jealous jellyface!' Farhan calls to Idris. 'See we're a gang,' adds Sarah. Miss Chahal gets them to freeze again, and asks the class who is in a gang. Quite a few children put their hands up. Then she asks what a gang is. 'A gang of bullies,' suggests Mohamed. Miss Chahal tells them that if you have friends like that you never know when they're going to turn on you. After some more discussion, the role play continues. The group approaches Idris saying, 'We're sorry, you can play. It's no way to treat a new person.' Miss Chahal asks them why they had a change of heart. 'Nobody will like us,' replies Sarah. Miss Chahal agrees. Sarah adds that they were jealous of him because he was clever and kind. In the ensuing discussion, Miss Chahal exhorts the children to welcome new people.

Event 2: Miss Chahal sends Mohamed, Zak, Amandeep, Anjali and Joanne out of the class with me. When we return a few minutes later, all the children are smiling. We have barely sat down when they suddenly all clap four times. This happens periodically, and is each time followed by some giggling amongst the children in the know. Mohamed and Zak ask why the others are clapping, and the children around them say, 'What clapping?' 'They've all gone mad!' Amandeep says to me. After a few minutes, Miss Chahal asks the children who were sent out how they felt. 'Interesting,' says Zak. Miss Chahal pushes him for more, and he adds, 'Interested to know what's going on'. 'It's weird,' comments Mohamed. 'They're disturbing me.' Some children laugh. 'Mohamed, you *are* disturbed,' Miss Chahal replies, smiling. She asks Anjali. 'Weird, because you don't know what's happening.'

'Imagine that (a), you're new in the school, and (b), you've got no one to play with in the playground,' says Miss Chahal to the class. She continues in this vein, then asks, 'Why do you think I've done this?' 'To make you realise how people feel?' Simran suggests. Miss Chahal agrees, and asks Mohamed again how he felt. 'Lonely,' he replies. Miss Chahal says that some children in the class don't have anyone to play with. She tells the children that they should look after each other in the playground; the class should stick together. 'If you see a child in your class on their own, what should you do?' Several children raise their hands, and one says, 'Ask them to play with you'. Mohamed raises his hand. 'When Paul was new I asked him to play with us.' Miss Chahal says that that's good, and asks whether he still asks him. Mohamed nods. Joshua raises his hand. 'Miss Chahal, we include Sarah when we play.' Miss Chahal says that if she hears about all the children taking care of each other she'll give them a house point.

These extracts demonstrate that like Miss Hart and Mrs Samson, Miss Chahal took the problem of children excluding one another seriously. The solution she recommended was that the children actively include one another, by approaching a classmate who is alone and asking them to play. Other adults at school expressed similar views. The leader of Woodwell Green's after-school club lectured the children there more than once about leaving out certain children and not letting them play, and at a meeting with the supervisory assistants who worked on the school playground at lunchtime, the head and deputy head teachers sought to identify children who did not have anyone to play with. Teachers saw exclusion as falling within the remit of their obligation to monitor and intervene in children's affairs, and the solution they usually proposed was indiscriminate inclusion; the children should all play together, and should invite lone peers to join them.

4.1.1   Children's views of exclusion

The extracts presented earlier show that children were well aware of teachers' view that exclusion, as a form of 'hurting on the inside', was wrong and that they should include others in their play. All three role plays performed by children in Miss Chahal's class began with a group excluding a lone peer and ended with the group apologising and inviting the peer to join them. Similarly, when Miss Chahal asked her class, 'If you see a child in your class on their own, what should you do?' a child responded, 'Ask them to play with you', and two others gave examples of how they had included new children in their play. Further evidence that children viewed exclusion as wrong came from interviews I conducted with children in years 1 to 6, about a series of hypothetical playground scenarios, two of which involved exclusion. They read as follows:

1.   Katie, Sani and Jasmine are in the same class. Katie and Sani are playing together in the playground. Jasmine comes up to them. Jasmine likes Sani but she doesn't like Katie. Jasmine keeps asking to

play with Sani on her own. Then Katie turns to Sani and says, 'If you play with Jasmine, I won't be your friend anymore'.

2. Five children are playing a game together. Then John, who is in their class, comes up and asks to play. The children don't really like playing with John because they think he's a bit pushy, bossy and rude. John asks to play.[1]

One question I asked children for each scenario was, 'Has anyone in this story done something bad do you think, or have they been okay?' In the first scenario, most children (72 of 122; 59 per cent) thought that Jasmine had done wrong. When explaining their answer, children criticised Jasmine's attempt to exclude Katie, and often commented that Jasmine should have asked both children to play. In the second scenario, 71 of 137 children[2] (52 per cent) said that the group (or part of the group) had done something wrong. Most children who gave this answer justified it by saying something like, 'They won't let him play'. As one year 4 girl explained when I asked why she thought it was wrong not to let the lone child play, 'Because everybody's supposed to just get on and play together, and they're being like really rude and saying she's not very nice to play with'. Children giving these answers echoed teachers' exhortations to play together.[3]

So many, if not most, children at Woodwell Green seemed to agree with teachers that excluding a peer was wrong. Nevertheless, there was evidence that children did still often exclude one another. For each hypothetical playground scenario, I asked children whether they had ever had a similar experience. Related experiences were reported by 48 of 122 children (39 per cent) for scenario 1, and 58 of 143 (41 per cent) for scenario 2. I also asked three playground supervisors how often they came across these scenarios. Their estimates for the first scenario ranged from once or twice a week to every day, and for the second, from 'not very often' to once a week.

4.1.2 Understanding exclusion on the playground

The prevalence of exclusion despite the official school line encouraging inclusion suggests that as with boys' physical aggression, children are orienting to other concerns that conflict with the obligation to prevent exclusion by including peers indiscriminately. There are many reasons why children exclude one another, and this chapter does not attempt to cover them all. Instead, I focus on cases of exclusion that do not resemble the way that teachers talked about exclusion in the classroom. Note how, in event 1 in Miss Chahal's class, described above, exclusion is depicted in a very specific form. A group of children is seen as uniting to exclude one lone peer, who is seen as blameless, excluded because of being clever and kind. In other role plays performed by class members, children were excluded because of being new, a geek (defined by the teacher as someone who likes, and is good at, studying) and wearing glasses. Consistently, the reason for excluding the isolated child is presented as trivial and silly. The group, in contrast, is described as 'a gang of bullies', cruel people who could turn on each other at any moment. Culpability is laid firmly at the door of the group as a whole. Similar views were expressed by many children at Woodwell Green in interviews about the hypothetical scenarios.

My data suggest that many exclusion events look rather different from this archetypal image, such that class exercises like those of Miss Chahal may have a limited impact. This chapter explores several ways in which exclusion can differ from the standard scenario portrayed in class. The first of these is the role of power in exclusion processes. Children's peer relations are often portrayed as 'horizontal', lacking the power asymmetries that characterise children's relations with family members (Pellegrini and Blatchford 2000, p. 33). In the section below, we will see that this is not so.

4.2 Exclusion and Power

4.2.1 *'Whose ball is it?' Exclusion from boys' football games*

In a survey I asked 70 boys and 80 girls in years 1 to 6 to name their three favourite playground activities; 83 per cent of the boys (and 16 per cent of the girls) named football (soccer), making it easily the most popular playground occupation for boys at Woodwell Green. However, space on the playground for football matches was scarce. The junior playground was marked out with two pitches, woefully inadequate given that 12 classes used this playground, and one pitch was usually used by two classes playing each other. Children also commandeered smaller spaces in other parts of the playground, creating makeshift goals from lunchboxes and coats. But this still left a lot of children wanting to play football but lacking the necessary space, creating competition to enter groups that did have space to play.

So how did groups decide who could join in and who could not? Boys at Woodwell Green adhered to a simple rule: whoever owned the ball decided who could play. The school did not provide footballs to the children, but a few children regularly brought in their own balls, marked with their initials. In the year 4 class I spent most time with, Faizel (Pakistani Muslim) and Pavandeep (Afghanistani Sikh) were the two boys who most often brought in a ball. The boys' rule meant that all the others abdicated responsibility for exclusion to them. Hence when their teacher asked Mohamed and Farhan why they would not let their classmate Paul play football (see Chapter 3), the two boys replied in unison, 'It's Faizel!' This abdication of responsibility to the ball owner has also been noted at other schools (Evans 1989; Sluckin 1981).

The importance of hierarchy
Actually, things were not quite as simple as this. The boys did adhere to the rule that the owner of the ball decided who could play, but this rule said nothing about whether an excluded boy would accept the ball owner's decision. When told that they could not play, some boys continued to play anyway. For example, when interviewing Idris, a classmate of Faizel and Pavandeep, about the hypothetical scenario in which a group is approached by a disliked child who wants to play with them, I asked him whether he had ever had a similar experience.

RW: Has anything like this ever happened to you?
IDRIS: That was, that was in the game, girls and boys were playing. I always usually play with those boys, Miss you know, Ali, Faizel. But there was a girl captain and the boys wouldn't let me be in their team cos sometimes they don't, and the girls wouldn't let me play cos they think I'm too rough, but I'm not too rough.
RW: Why wouldn't the boys let you play, do you know?
IDRIS: Cos they're copying the girls!
RW: So what did you do then?
IDRIS: I just joined in anyway. I always do that but because they wanna be bossy with the ball they say oh you can play anyway. I can't explain it.

So when boys like Idris were excluded from football games, they proceeded to play anyway, an act which amounted to a challenge to the ball owner's authority. How did ball owners respond to this challenge? One possible response is submission, allowing the invading boy to have his way, as Idris noted above. This was the path taken by Pavandeep. During an interview in year 4, I asked Pavandeep who he had the most arguments or fights with at school. Here is the discussion that followed:

PAVANDEEP: Miss I used to have a fight with Sam and Ali and Idris and Faizel [all fellow year 4 boys]. But Miss Sam and Ali don't beat me now, they used to, but Idris and Faizel still do, they still beat me up. Miss Sandeep says when someone beats you up don't let them play but I still let Idris play.
RW: Why do you still let him?

81

PAVANDEEP: Cos he just does innit. He just comes.
RW: Um, hang on, do you mean Idris just plays even if you tell him not to?
PAVANDEEP: Yeah Miss.

[Later in the interview]

RW: So what about, with Idris and Faizel, after you've had a fight with them do you make friends?
PAVANDEEP: Miss I never be friends with them. Miss but we still play with each other. Miss he just plays with me without asking me.
RW: Who does?
PAVANDEEP: Idris and Faizel.
RW: How does that make you feel?
PAVANDEEP: [pauses] Miss nothing. I said they can play.

In this extract, Pavandeep claimed that even though Faizel and Idris were aggressive towards him, he let them play with his ball, because they ignored any attempt on his part to stop them. So even though he is officially in control of who can play, he found his decisions overruled. In contrast, when the boys played with Faizel's ball, the evidence suggests that Faizel was much more likely to ensure that his decisions were respected. In interviews, two children during year 4 and three during year 5 commented that Faizel excluded them from football. Faizel himself also told me that he challenged children who tried to join in football games without his permission. I interviewed Faizel when he was in year 5 about the hypothetical situation in which one child (John) approached a group and asked to play. 'Have you ever been in this situation?' I asked Faizel. 'Which situation?' he asked, gesturing separately to John and the group in the simple picture I drew to accompany the scenario. 'Either, it doesn't matter,' I replied. 'Probably that,' he said, pointing to the group, 'Not that,' he added, pointing to John. 'Probably once, someone asks – actually it happens nearly all the time, someone joins in the football and I say you can't play who said you can play and they say a name but they're lying.'

Faizel gave a similar answer later in year 5 during a group interview I conducted with him and three classmates (including Zak and Idris). I presented them with the following scenario: 'You are playing a game with your friends, and someone you don't really like comes and asks to play. You say no, but they join in the game anyway. What do you do?' Faizel opened the discussion:

FAIZEL: You – go – and, well Miss that happened today, twice.
RW: Okay so this is
FAIZEL: Miss that happened today, honestly.
RW: All right then, so what happened?
FAIZEL: [interrupting] Miss, Mandeer I think his name was, he came and
           played with us, and then I said go away you're not playing
RW: This is playing football yeah?
FAIZEL: Yeah Miss and then he came again yeah, Miss, and then even
           though I, then I told Mrs Thomas [playground supervisor] yeah,
           Miss, and then Mrs Thomas said go yeah, and then, he never
           listened, he still carried on yeah. Then Miss afterwards I just said
           get lost, I moved, I threw his, I never really threw it I just moved
           his pack lunch, I said [inaudible] your pack lunch and go, Miss
           and then he just went.

These extracts suggest that Faizel's decisions to exclude were accepted
while Pavandeep's were sometimes overruled. The key seems to be the
relative dominance of the ball owner and the intruder – and as we saw in
Chapter 3, a central component of boys' dominance at Woodwell Green
was physical aggression. In Chapter 3, I described evidence that Faizel
was physically aggressive on the playground. During his interview about
the hypothetical scenario describing a lone child seeking to join a group,
his classmate Amandeep (Indian Sikh) told me how Faizel was prepared
to use physical aggression to enforce his decisions:

RW: Have you ever been in a situation like this?
AMANDEEP: Yeah. Once, Faizel didn't let us, me and Farhan, play foot-
              ball, and once I brought my football in and Faizel said let us
              play and I said no why should I? You didn't let me play!
              [laughs]
RW: [laughs] And do you know why Faizel wouldn't let you play?
AMANDEEP: No. But he won't ever let us play, he says no you're crap, you
              can't play. And Sam. We just play anyway.
RW: What happens when you do that, does Faizel try to stop you
              playing?
AMANDEEP: Yeah, but I just go I'm playing I don't care. Farhan just says
              come on man let's go, and I say no man don't do nothing.
              Farhan gets scared, he always says come on let's play some-
              thing else. Cos Faizel and Sam try and beat him up and he
              gets really angry.

So Faizel was willing to resort to physical aggression to ensure that as
ball owner, his decisions about inclusion and exclusion are adhered to.

In contrast, Pavandeep was reluctant to use physical aggression. He complained to me about this when I was interviewing him in year 5: 'I was playing football, thingy, and it was Faizel's ball, and he said no you can't play, because I scored for the other team. Miss *I'm* gonna let him play with my ball.'[4] A little later in the interview I asked Pavandeep why he thought Faizel behaved in this way towards him. 'Miss I don't know, he hates me,' he replied. 'Cos he starts fighting with me sometimes. When I like tackle him, he say you foul me, and he start pushing me and that.' He continued: 'Miss sometimes I think I might have to start a fight with him. Cos he tries to fight with me every day. But I'm afraid I'll get told off that's why.' Pavandeep's reluctance to resort to physical aggression, which seemed to be based on his respect for his teacher's authority, meant that he was lower in status than more aggressive boys who overturned his decisions.

'What if it isn't your ball?' Dominant boys playing by the rules
So the relative dominance (expressed mainly as physical aggression) of boys was an important factor in who was allowed to play football. What is surprising is that other members of the group respected the rule that the ball owner made the decision, even when those decisions were routinely overturned. This created a frustrating situation for dominant boys in the group who would be willing to enforce the decision themselves but were not in a position to do so because they did not own the ball.

During the interview about the hypothetical scenario in which John asks a group to play, I asked Zak, 'Have you ever been in a situation like this?' He replied, 'Sam's John, Sam's too rough, Sam's always rough, we don't want him to play football with us. But the person, the person, Pavandeep always brings the ball, it's Pavandeep's ball yeah. Miss at playtime, Sam kicked Pavandeep's ball away. At lunchtime, Pavandeep let him play again!' Zak was exasperated because Pavandeep would not stand up to Sam, a boy in another year 5 class who was notorious for his aggressive and confrontational behaviour (recall Paul's experiences in Chapter 3). Yet because Zak respected the rule that the ball owner made decisions, he felt he could not do anything about it. On another occasion, Faizel raised the same problem during a discussion group with Idris, Zak and another boy. We were talking about a question I posed: What would they do if someone they disliked joined in their game despite them excluding him? After some discussion, Faizel asked:

FAIZEL: What, what if it isn't your ball?
IDRIS: Exactly!
FAIZEL: And then Pav, if it is Pavandeep's ball, what if he says yeah
IDRIS: [interrupting] A-All the time, I play –
FAIZEL: [interrupting] And you don't wanna, you don't wanna?
RW: So does that happen sometimes?
FAIZEL: Yeah Miss it does, Pavandeep says yes and I say no. And what
            would you do then?
IDRIS: I'd stay playing like I usually do.
FAIZEL: No, if someone else came and you didn't want them to play but
            Pavandeep was saying yes, let 'em play.

Like Zak, Faizel felt frustration when Pavandeep failed to enforce exclusion, knowing that he himself would be willing and able to do so. Zak and Faizel both seemed to want the responsibility that Pavandeep struggled with. Yet despite their desire and frustration, they did not simply take charge themselves. Rather, and despite the problems it sometimes created for them, they showed great respect for ownership of the most crucial resource of all, the football. In so doing, they reluctantly abdicated responsibility for exclusion to just one child in the group. Thus, the archetypal image of a group uniting to exclude a specific peer did not accurately describe the process by which exclusion took place in playground football matches.

4.2.2   Dominance struggles: 'Holly tries to take over from me as leader of the gang'

What about when groups of children play together without a key object owned by a particular child? Do children in such situations still hand over responsibility for inclusion and exclusion to a single peer? And if so, how is that child selected? I attempt to answer this question via a case study of a group of girls who attended the after-school club at Woodwell Green. This group was an interesting case study for dominance and exclusion because two girls in the group both sought to be dominant. These two girls were Manpreet (year 5) and Holly (year 4). The group they both sought dominance over comprised Rachel (year 4), Leanne (year 3, Rachel's sister), Jasmeen (year 3, Manpreet's cousin) and Nita (year 1, Jasmeen's sister and Manpreet's cousin), plus a few others who joined the group sporadically. Manpreet, Jasmeen and Nita were all Indian Sikhs. Rachel and Leanne were labelled on school records as mixed ethnicity and not religious. Holly was English and Christian.

The girls at the after-school club often enjoyed making up dances together. However, Manpreet frequently excluded Holly from this activity. Here is a typical example:

> Manpreet, Rachel, Leanne and Jasmeen practise a dance on the stage with two girls in year 6. Holly and Roshni lean on the table nearby watching. Jasminder [who runs the after-school club] and I get out the pens and paper, and Holly, Roshni and Nita sit down to draw. I ask Holly and Roshni why they aren't in the dance. Holly says that she is in 'the band', but Manpreet says she can only be a background dancer, and if she wants to be in it properly she has to make up a dance for them all and can't join in the current one. She seems sulky about this. Nita disagrees and claims that Holly can join in this one. Holly insists she's right, so Nita approaches Manpreet and asks if Holly can join the dance. Manpreet says no. When Nita returns, I suggest that Nita, Holly and Roshni do a dance together, but none of them pursue this. Later on, after Manpreet has gone home, Rachel, Jasmeen and Nita are drawing and colouring. 'So why doesn't Holly wanna do the dance?' I ask them. 'She does wanna do it but she can't,' says Jasmeen. 'Why not?' I ask. Rachel and Jasmeen seem reluctant to comment but Nita says, 'Cos Manpreet doesn't like her.' 'Oh, they don't get on?' I say, and the others murmur agreement.

While Manpreet often excluded Holly from dance groups, she allowed her to join in some other activities, such as talent contests. Why was this? The answer became clear when I witnessed Manpreet arguing with the girls she usually played with at the after-school club.

Manpreet, Rachel, Leanne and Jasmeen had been putting a dance together. However, one day the other girls did not want to practise the dance, and ended up arguing with Manpreet. When I arrived at the after-school club, Rachel, Leanne and Jasmeen were chatting and laughing with Holly. At snack time, there were not enough chairs so these four girls shared three chairs between them. Manpreet's resentment was obvious; as the girls tried to work out who should sit where, she snapped, 'Leanne can sit where she wants, Holly'. After their snack, Holly and the other three girls played a game together at the other end of the hall. Manpreet approached first Jasmeen, and then both Jasmeen and Rachel, at one point kneeling down and begging them to rejoin her group.

Despite her efforts, Jasmeen and Rachel returned to Holly and Leanne, and the four began to practise a dance together. Manpreet sat at the other end of the hall looking glum. When I asked if she was all right, she replied, 'Yeah', in a half-hearted way. Then she explained how she had fallen out with Rachel, Leanne and Jasmeen, and 'Now they've gone off with Holly'. When I suggested that all five did a dance together, Manpreet pulled a face and looked unimpressed. 'Holly tries to take over from me as leader of the gang,' she said.

Shortly after this conversation, Manpreet spoke with Jasmeen again, and this time her efforts paid off as all the girls began to play games together, and harmony appeared to be restored. I attended after-school club again two days later, and saw Manpreet dancing with Rachel, Jasmeen and another girl (Leanne was not dancing). I asked Holly, 'Are you not doing the dance with the girls anymore?' She told me that they left Manpreet's group to come into hers, but then left hers and returned to Manpreet's.

Manpreet was explicit in this sequence of events about why she excluded Holly: because she threatened her position as 'leader of the gang'. Being leader was important to Manpreet, so in activities where there was room for only one leader (like making up and practising a dance), she did what she could to exclude her rival, Holly, and hence maintain her own leadership position. She did not attempt to exclude Holly from some other activities in which more than one child could take on a leadership role. For example, I observed the girls playing a talent competition in which Manpreet and Holly each led a different team, and when they played houses, the two girls each had a separate 'house'. Dominance struggles could still arise though. For example, when Manpreet suggested that they all play 'had',[5] Holly was not keen and suggested a couple of other games, which Manpreet turned down. 'Why do we have to play had, had's boring,' complained Holly. But Manpreet insisted. 'I won't play then,' countered Holly. 'Fine then,' replied Manpreet. Thus, Manpreet had to work hard in various situations to maintain her dominance, but it seemed a particularly pervasive issue when the girls practised dances.

How submission produces dominance

As with the boys in their football games, the more submissive girls at the after-school club assigned almost complete responsibility for decisions about exclusion to the leader, Manpreet. In an interview with Rachel, Holly and Leanne a year on from the above events, I asked them about the dance they were currently doing. They told me that Manpreet, Rachel, Jasmeen and Nita were in it.

RW: [to Holly and Leanne] Why aren't you two in the dance?
HOLLY: That's just the way it's always been, we're not allowed.
RACHEL: Leanne was in it.
HOLLY: Yeah but I didn't have anyone to play with.

LEANNE:	Yeah she was the manager.
RACHEL:	And she quit.
LEANNE:	Yeah she was so bored.
HOLLY:	I was fed up.
LEANNE:	She was bored.
HOLLY:	And I was fed up.
RW:	How do you decide who is in the dance?
HOLLY:	We don't, that's the end of it. We're not allowed that's the end of it.
RACHEL:	No it's basically, whoever the group leader likes can be in the dance.
LEANNE:	Yeah so if Manpreet likes us we can be in it.
RW:	Why is it Manpreet who gets to decide?
HOLLY:	Um, because she's the leader. Anyone she hates, we're never allowed in the band it's as simple as that.
RACHEL:	No, you don't know if she hates you.
HOLLY:	She does.
RW:	Why is Manpreet the leader?
RACHEL:	She's the best singer.
HOLLY:	Yeah and it's not fair because me and Leanne can't join in.
RACHEL:	Why don't you just ask her?
HOLLY:	No because she'll say no.
RACHEL:	You could ask Jasmeen.
LEANNE:	I asked Jasmeen and she let me in.
HOLLY:	She only lets her friends in and her relatives, it's as simple as that.
RW:	So let me just check, Rachel, you think Manpreet is the leader because she's the best singer?
RACHEL:	And dancer. She's the best singer and dancer, and she's the oldest.
HOLLY:	And the only people she lets in are her best friends and her relatives.
RW:	Why don't you guys
HOLLY:	[interrupting] She'll never let us.
RACHEL:	[to Holly] And Nita hates you.
HOLLY:	Yeah Nita hates me.
LEANNE:	And me. She just pretends to like me.

What I find most intriguing about this interview is the girls' almost complete surrender to Manpreet's (and, to a lesser extent, Jasmeen's) will. Even Rachel, who was a good friend of Holly's, did not seem to take any responsibility for her exclusion. Of course, it was this very submission that allowed Manpreet to dominate, and prevented Holly from being included and becoming leader. This was particularly apparent on another occasion, when some of the children played an imaginative game they called 'Queens and Princesses'. At the start of the game, Holly was in charge, but by the end, Manpreet had managed to take over. Here are my fieldnotes of the game:

Holly, Leanne, Roshni and Larry start to play 'Queens and Princesses'. Leanne is queen, Holly is her daughter and a princess, Roshni is a guest and Larry a servant. Manpreet, Rachel and Jasmeen wander up. 'Are you guys playing?' asks Roshni. Manpreet hesitates, and then says, 'Yeah, can I be the queen?' 'No cos Leanne never gets to be the queen,' Holly replies. 'No, let Manpreet be the queen,' Leanne says, electing to become a servant. Jasmeen joins Holly as a princess.

The children dress up and prepare for the queen to make a grand entrance for the ball. Rachel, who is not playing, announces the queen's arrival, and everyone stands. Manpreet walks grandly to her throne and sits down. Then she announces, 'Let the ball begin! Now, will you please get into partners of two. Who's gonna do the music?' Holly offers to, and everyone gets ready to dance. Manpreet gets up from her throne and then exclaims, 'Wait wait wait I forgot to do something. Before I dance I have to take off my crown. Can somebody get a special mat for me to put it on?' A couple of the children scurry around so that she can lower her imaginary crown onto a bench.

During the ball, Manpreet collapses dramatically. She lies on the floor, and says she's going to die. Holly leans over her and asks if she can be queen when she's died, but Manpreet says no, Jasmeen will be. Holly notes that she [Holly] is older, but Manpreet retorts that in the *game*, Jasmeen is older. Holly leans back exclaiming, 'It's not fair!' 'Don't play then,' says Manpreet. 'You can't do that, it's not your game, it's my game!' Holly protests. Manpreet reverts to her queen role, and orders imperiously, 'Go away.' Holly gets up and goes to the stage, where she takes up her 'throne' and talks with Jasmeen in hushed tones. 'It's not fair,' I hear her say. There follows a general discussion about what will happen next, and in the end Manpreet does not die, and they have a ball to celebrate, at which Holly sings. Manpreet comments on how beautiful Holly's voice is, and instructs Jasmeen to be jealous of this. 'Lovely voice isn't it?' she says to her.

Leanne starts to take her outfit off, calling, 'Manpreet I don't wanna play.' She goes to do crochet at the other end of the hall. Holly tries to persuade her to play again, but to no avail. Then she recruits Manpreet's younger brother, Jagpal. He agrees and she calls out triumphantly, 'Manpreet, Manpreet, Jagpal's gonna play!' He gets dressed up. 'Jagpal, you're gonna be my son,' Holly says. The children continue the game.

This extract demonstrates both Manpreet's skill and determination to dominate, and how the other girls enabled this through acts of submission. The shift began very early on, when Roshni invited Manpreet to play, rather than leaving her to ask the game owner, Holly. Then, despite Holly's resistance, Leanne gave up her role so that Manpreet could be the queen. Once in the most dominant role in the game, Manpreet made decisions about the other players, for example that Jasmeen would become queen after she died. When Holly protested that it was her game, Manpreet cleverly overruled her by switching back into imperious queen role, in which she was undeniably dominant over Holly who was her daughter and only a princess. By the end of the game, both Leanne and Holly had deferred to Manpreet. Leanne told Manpreet, not Holly, that she was quitting the game, and Holly jubilantly reported to Manpreet that she had persuaded Jagpal to join in. Similar examples of children deferring to a dominant peer during pretend play have been documented by several ethnographers of childhood (see Goodwin and Kyratzis 2011 for a review).

Power, exclusion and responsibility
By bowing to her wishes, Rachel, Jasmeen, Leanne and Nita often allowed Manpreet to exclude Holly. Although they may not have seen themselves as responsible for this exclusion, Holly did. I discovered this one evening at the after-school club, when Holly had an argument with Rachel and another child, and the three exchanged 18 notes before eventually making friends. In response to Rachel's note asking, 'Are you my friend?' Holly wrote: 'When Manpreet shut me out of the band you did not care so I don't know from Holly.'

Holly's resentment towards Rachel for failing to act when Manpreet excluded her is evident. This example shows that although they may not see themselves as responsible for what their 'leaders' do, submissive children like Rachel may still be held responsible for their leaders' actions by those on the receiving end of exclusionary processes. It also suggests that the negative effects of exclusion loom larger for the excluded child than for a peer who is an accepted part of the group. Killen et al. (2006) found that American children who had been recipients of discrimination were more likely to consider exclusion as a moral issue (using domain theory criteria; see Chapter 1 for more detail on these), while those who had not were more likely to see it as a personal issue. Similarly, Horn (2003) found that American adolescents in low-status peer groups saw exclusion as more wrong than did those in high-status peer groups, perhaps because the former had had more experience of exclusion than the latter.

There was tentative evidence that Woodwell Green children's judgements of exclusion were related to their experiences of it, from the interviews about

Table 4.1 Judgements of wrongdoing in exclusion scenario broken down by experience of children

Role of child in own experience	Who child blamed in hypothetical scenario				
	Lone individual	*Group or part of group*	*Individual and group*	*No one*	*Don't know/other*
Lone individual (*n = 34*)	2	22	4	6	0
Member of group (*n = 18*)	4	9	1	4	0
Individual and group (*n = 3*)	1	2	0	0	0
No experience (*n = 82*)	12	31	2	34	3

the hypothetical scenario in which a child asks a reluctant group of peers if s/he can play. We saw earlier in this chapter that 41 per cent of children reported having had a similar experience to this scenario. As noted earlier, one of the questions I asked children about this scenario was, 'Has anyone in this story done something bad do you think, or have they been okay?' Table 4.1 breaks children's answers to this question down according to the type of experience (if any) they reported.[6]

Table 4.1 shows that of the 55 children who reported an experience, 34 (62 per cent) described themselves as the lone child who was excluded from a group. The majority of these children (26 of 34; 76 per cent) said that the group had done wrong. Only six (18 per cent) said that the individual child was in the wrong. Eighteen children (33 per cent of those reporting an experience) described themselves as a member of the group. Ten (56 per cent) blamed the group and five (28 per cent) blamed the individual child. Of the 82 children who claimed not to have had a similar experience, 33 (40 per cent) attributed blame to the group, and 14 (17 per cent) blamed the individual. Many (41 per cent) thought that no one had done wrong.

Based on previous research finding that children's judgements of harmful acts are related to their previous experience of those acts (Horn 2003; Killen et al. 2006), I hypothesised that children who had experience of being excluded would be more likely to blame the excluders than would children who did not have such experience. Similarly, I hypothesised that children who had experience of excluding would be more likely to blame the excluded child than would children without such experience. Statistical tests found that there was indeed a relationship between children's experience and their tendency to blame the group (but not their tendency to blame the excluded child).[7]

There are some limitations to these results. Firstly, the group does not actually exclude the individual in the scenario, although many children assumed that they had or would do so. So children who did not blame the group might have reached this verdict either because they thought that exclusion was acceptable, or because no act of exclusion actually occurred. However, this does not explain why children's blame differed according to their experience. Secondly, researchers of moral development have debated how to word questions to ensure that they tap children's *moral* view of a specific situation (Shweder et al. 1987; Turiel et al. 1987). In this case, the word 'bad' might be used by children to refer not only to moral wrongdoing but also to transgressions that they might not consider morally wrong, just wrong in the sense that there is a rule against them (such as talking in assembly). Thirdly, the method relies on children's ability and willingness to recall and reveal what may be quite sensitive incidents, which may lead to under-reporting.

In spite of these limitations, the data provide tentative evidence that, as researchers have found elsewhere, children at Woodwell Green who had themselves been excluded saw acts of exclusion as more wrong than other children did. My observations may provide a concrete example of these processes in practice, as Holly condemned her friend Rachel for allowing Manpreet to exclude her, while Rachel showed few signs of taking responsibility for this. What my interview scenario did not take into account, however, is the role of power in these processes. Rachel's lack of concern seemed to stem not (or not only) from her lack of experience of exclusion, but from her relatively submissive role in relation to Manpreet, whom she held responsible for excluding her friend Holly. Thus, power relations may influence the way that children experience potentially harmful acts such as exclusion, and consequently affect what they learn from them.

4.3   Exclusion for Game Maintenance and Success

We have seen that power dynamics were an important factor complicating the simple exclusion scenario discussed in class. Another complicating factor was children's concerns with game maintenance and success. Some games have criteria that can lead to exclusion, such that a group leader might exclude but not necessarily out of cruelty or dislike. For example, children playing football required a (roughly) equal number of players on each team, the right number of players overall for the size of the pitch, players who were motivated and able to play the game according to the rules, and some stability of membership. Gatekeepers, in this case children who owned the ball, needed to place some limits on inclusion to enable the game to take place. For example, once when Idris (year 4 boy) told me that he was not allowed to play football, I called Mohamed (who was playing) over. He shook his head and insisted that Idris could not play, because it would not be a 'fair game' (since they already had the same number of players on each team).

Another reason for exclusion was competence. Again, football is a good example. Children wanted to win; their reactions to scoring were jubilant, and they argued over events largely because it mattered to them who won. So they wanted the best players possible on their own team. This of course means that those who were seen to be bad at football tended to be excluded. For example, recall Amandeep's comment that Faizel justified his exclusion of Amandeep and Farhan from football with, 'You're crap'. During the interview about the hypothetical scenario in which a group excludes a lone peer, a year 6 boy commented that he had seen this happen to a boy who wanted to play football. I asked why they did not want him to play, and he explained, 'It's because he never passes. When he gets the ball he doesn't pass it and he gets tackled by the other team and loses the ball and they get a goal and we lose the match'.

When combined, concerns with game maintenance and competence resulted in particular children being repeatedly excluded from football matches. This is what happened to Erickah, a Black African Christian girl who started at Woodwell Green in Miss Chahal's class halfway through year 4. Erickah had some problems making friends, and when she was in year 5, was identified when the head teacher asked playground supervisors which children seemed lonely on the playground. Soon after Erickah joined Woodwell Green, most of the girls in her class began to play football, first against their male classmates, and later in all-girl matches against another class. Erickah enjoyed football but often found herself excluded from these games. Here is a typical example from my fieldnotes:

Erickah and I stand watching the football match and chatting. I ask her if she'd like to play, and she says yes. Zena runs over to us, says she's having a quick break to go and get a drink. I ask if Erickah can play while she's away. She says Erickah can play all the time and runs off for some water. 'Come on Erickah!' she calls on her return. Erickah looks at me and I nod and smile, and Zena pulls her by the sleeve onto the pitch. The game continues all the while. Erickah stands a bit separate and doesn't join in properly, and after a couple of minutes she returns to me saying 'I'm too shy'. Zena sees and comes over, and I encourage Erickah to have another go. She and Zena go off again, but soon after they are talking with Simran [captain of girls' team], and Erickah comes away again. She says that Simran said that there are eight players on each side so Erickah can't play. Harpreet is nearby and I ask if Erickah can be a substitute. She agrees readily and makes to run off, so I ask who she is going to substitute. 'Not me, because me and Simran are the boss,' she replies, and runs off. Navneet and Zena refuse too. Zena tries to persuade Maria to swap, but she won't, and Erickah retreats to my side again.

The following week, I saw Erickah sitting watching the football on two separate occasions. On the first, Simran told me that she had told Erickah she could join in but she failed to do so. On the second, Harpreet told me that Erickah, Navneet and Maria were all excluded because the teams for the day had already been chosen. Three weeks later, Erickah, Maria, Navneet, Zena and I were sitting together in the canteen, when the following exchange occurred:

The girls are talking about football. Farah comes over to our table and tells Erickah she can only be 'in it' if she joins 5B's side [the opposing team]. Erickah refuses point blank and insists she wants to play for her own class, 5S. Zena and Navneet start to defend Erickah, asking Farah why she can't be on their team, but Farah replies that 5B have one less player than 5S, so it's either join 5B or not be in it. Zena and Navneet accept this and draw back, and Erickah says she won't be in it. 'Fine then,' says Farah and reports back to her table. I try to persuade Erickah to play for 5B but she refuses. She complains about Simran to me in a cross voice, pounding her fist on the table as she speaks. 'Why does Simran always have to be the boss of everything and she never lets me play. When Simran's the boss of the game I'm never gonna play.' Zena laughs at Erickah's words and actions and asks her to do it again, pounding her own fist on the table, but Erickah refuses. After Maria and Erickah have left the table, I ask Navneet why it is Erickah who can't play. She says that she was playing before, but they had to get rid of one player and Erickah is allegedly the worst.

Game maintenance requirements contributed to Erickah's exclusion on several occasions. And competence was also important; according to Navneet, the reason that it was Erickah specifically who was excluded was that she was the worst player – perhaps because of the reticence I witnessed on earlier occasions. Of course, there may be other factors involved as well. Erickah was the newest girl in the class, rather shy, and I witnessed Navneet (though not Simran) attempting to exclude her on other occasions. Nevertheless, the extracts presented above suggest that game maintenance and success were important. It is possible for repeated exclusion of one child to result from the combination of game maintenance and success pressures without any malice. Exclusion of this form does not fit representations of exclusion that teachers and children tended to assume in their discussions of the topic. Indeed, adults were in favour of children engaging in structured activities like football, and so tended to be sympathetic with the need to exclude for the sake of the game. For example, according to Faizel (quoted earlier in this chapter), a playground supervisor reprimanded a boy who joined their game without consent. Of course, the difficulty for adults is in identifying whether exclusion is purely the result of concerns with game maintenance and success, or whether other reasons are also important. Working this out is particularly difficult because children understood that it was more acceptable to exclude a peer for the sake of a game than for more personal reasons (see Chapter 7 for further discussion of strategies that children used to construct blame when narrating events to teachers).

4.4   Exclusion Without an Excluder

Not only could exclusion occur without malicious intent on the part of the excluder, it could also emerge without an active excluder at all. This was the predicament faced by Sarah, an English Christian girl who started Woodwell Green in Miss Chahal's class in September at the start of year 4. In class, Sarah was happy. She was enthusiastic, often putting her hand up to answer questions, and was an excellent actress, performing star roles in class assemblies. Out of the classroom was another matter, however. She played with different children in the playground but did not settle into friendships with specific peers, and sometimes spent playtime or lunchtime alone. For example, one lunchtime in October, I came across her sitting alone on a bench. I asked her how she was and she said that she did not have many friends. In November, during a religious education class, each child wrote an updated version of the ten commandments. Certain commandments appeared in many children's lists, such as not to pollute the earth, to respect one's parents and not to be racist. However, only Sarah included two pertaining specifically to exclusion: 'To let people play if they have not got anyone to play with' and 'Don't make secret and make people feel left out'.[8]

Sarah's teacher, Miss Chahal, tried several times to help Sarah make friends. In January, a new girl, Louise, joined the class. Miss Chahal sat her next to Sarah in the hope that the two might become friends. This did not work and in February, Sarah's mother told Miss Chahal that Sarah did not have any friends, and in addition, that two boys in the class were calling her names. Miss Chahal told me that she wanted to help but was not sure how. She observed that she could stop the boys being horrible to Sarah, but could not make others be friends with her. Later the same day, she carried out the clapping exercise with her class, described at the start of this chapter, which she hoped would make the children more aware of Sarah's predicament. In February, another new girl, Maria, joined the class, and Miss Chahal asked some of the other girls who were friendly to her to 'back off' so that Sarah could 'have a go'.

Despite her teacher's endeavours, Sarah continued to feel isolated. In fact, Miss Chahal's efforts to link her up with new girls may have back-fired, because Sarah's classmate and occasional friend Joshua (see below) told me that Sarah did not want to 'look after' the new girls and tried to evade this perceived responsibility. While she did play with classmates sometimes, I continued to see her alone in the playground quite often. In February, I interviewed her about her friendships (I interviewed every child in the class during the year). When I asked which children in her class she liked the most, she told me that she did not have any friends and dreaded coming to school for this reason. Three months later, in May, Sarah told me that she still did not have any friends. The following week, her mother contacted Miss Chahal again, who spoke to the class:

> Once the class is settled and quiet, Miss Chahal says, 'I've received a letter from a parent whose daughter still hasn't settled into the school.' She asks, 'Out of the girls, who plays Indian games out in the playground? Who tells children they can't play because it's an Indian game?' Many of the girls look round at each other curiously. 'Who calls children names?' she adds. Miss Chahal continues that she wants such behaviour reported, and she wants the new girls, 'Maria, Erickah, Sarah, Louise,' to be made welcome. Anjali raises her hand. 'Miss, Louise and Maria play with us sometimes, Louise most of the time.' 'Good. You need to make sure that Louise and Maria and Erickah and Zena and Sarah [all girls who had arrived at the school since the start of the academic year] all play with you.' 'They do,' Anjali replies quietly.

In July, Sarah still claimed not to have any friends, and she was given permission to stay in and read during lunchtime instead of being on the playground. July heralded the end of the school year and the end of Sarah's time at Woodwell Green; the following autumn, she did not return to the school. This rather depressing story of isolation raises the question: Why? How was it that for a whole year, Sarah did not make friends and remained excluded? My data suggest that this was a case of what we might call 'accidental' exclusion.

4.4.1   Three's a crowd

When I saw Sarah sitting on a bench alone in October, I asked her who she would like to be friends with. She named Joanne, the only other girl in her class of English ethnicity. Joanne was particularly friendly with Joshua, an English boy in their class. They spent some time as a twosome, and some time integrated into a large, loose, mainly female group that included Simran, Harpreet, Navneet, Sarina, Ayesha, new girls Maria, Zena and Erickah, and one boy, Sohaib. Joanne was quite often absent from school, and then Joshua would usually play with this large group.

Sarah did gradually become closer to Joanne and Joshua. I often saw her with one of the pair when the other was absent from school. When the absent child returned, sometimes they continued as a threesome, and other times Joanne and Joshua formed a pair, with Sarah alone again.

Joanne was positive about her friendship with Sarah. When I interviewed her about her friendships in April, she named Sarah as one of the children she liked most in the class. When I asked her if she thought Sarah had settled in by this time, she asserted firmly that she had. She also told me that she and Sarah lived on the same street and sometimes knocked for each other (i.e. went to each other's houses to see if the other wanted to play). Sarah even stayed over at Joanne's house one weekend.

But while Joanne seemed happy with the status quo, Sarah and Joshua were unhappy. Even when the three were together, Sarah felt excluded. For example, one day in April, the three approached me together in the playground. While Joanne and Joshua were out of earshot, I asked Sarah, 'How are you doing now? Are you feeling more settled in yeah?' 'Sort of,' Sarah replied, pulling a face. Later the same day, she confided, 'I don't really like Joanne all that much', complaining that when the three were together, one of them would say that they wanted to speak to the other one on their own, and she suspected that they were talking about her. In May, the three children fell out with each other. During this dispute, Sarah approached me in the playground saying, 'I don't think Joshua and Joanne wanna be my friend'. I asked why she thought that, and she complained that Joanne was her friend when Joshua was not around, but Joshua 'takes her away from me'.

Sarah's view was mirrored by Joshua's. During this same dispute, I interviewed him about his friendships and he did not name Joanne or

Sarah as among those he liked. 'What about Joanne – and Sarah?' I asked. Before I added Sarah's name, Joshua had already started to reply. 'Yeah but we've fallen out now. We've known each other for ages but Sarah's been turning her against me.' When I asked how she did this, he recalled an occasion when he asked Joanne and Sarah if he could join a dance they had made up, and Sarah replied that he could not because he was a boy. 'But now she got nobody to play with because Joanne's away and I don't wanna play with her,' he added. I asked why he thought he and Sarah did not get along, and he suggested that it was because he and Sarah's cousin, who was also in their class, 'hate each other'.

Months later, when he was in year 5, I interviewed Joshua about the hypothetical situation in which Jasmine approached Katie and Sani, who were playing together, and tried to make Katie go away (see earlier in this chapter). My first question asked how Katie was feeling. Joshua replied, 'Angry because she's, Jasmine's trying to take Sani away from her. And I felt like that before because Sarah always used to take Joanne away from me. When I used to go up to Joanne and Sarah and ask to play, Sarah would say no Joshua it's only a girls' game!' When I asked if anyone in the scenario had done anything wrong, Joshua singled out Jasmine, who he equated with Sarah. Joshua's involved recall shows that the situation with Sarah (who had by then left the school) had an enduring impact on him.

The three continued to sometimes play together until Sarah left at the end of the school year, but at other times Sarah was alone. In July, I saw her sitting with her cousin on a bench in the playground, while all the other year 4 children went to the canteen for lunch. They both complained of having no friends, and Sarah added with feeling, 'I especially hate Joshua and Joanne. They're acting like they don't even know me, even though we were best friends', going on to criticise Joshua in particular.

The problem seemed to be mutual dislike and rivalry between Sarah and Joshua over Joanne's friendship.[9] It seems that Sarah's isolation resulted partly because Joanne, the peer she most wanted as a friend and with whom she played happily out of school, was already in a stable pair with Joshua. This dyad incorporated Sarah to some extent, to become a chronically unstable triad, in which Sarah and Joshua grew to dislike each other, each perceiving the other as a threat to their own friendship with Joanne. Although this predicament was never completely resolved, by the end of the school year it seemed as though Joshua and Joanne had returned to their twosome, and Sarah remained isolated. Yet aside from Joshua and Joanne, there were 27 other children in the class. Why did none of them become friends with Sarah?

4.4.2   Ethnic identity and friendship

With notable exceptions (like Joanne and Joshua), cross-gender friendships are rare among children in this age group (Maccoby 1990). So let us rule out the 15 boys in the class as potential friends for Sarah. That still left 13 girls. Sarah did play with these girls sometimes, yet did not succeed in creating meaningful friendships with any of them. One possible reason[10] for this is the role of ethnic identity in the girls' friendships. None of the remaining 13 girls was of English ethnicity. Seven were Indian, three Pakistani, one Black African, one Black Caribbean and one 'other ethnic group'. At Woodwell Green, children named more friends of their own than of other ethnic groups (Woods 2005). Children's preference for peers of their own racial or ethnic group is very common and has been observed in the USA (Hallinan and Teixeira 1987; Shaw 1973), Canada (Aboud et al. 2003), the Netherlands (Baerveldt et al. 2004) and the UK (Boulton and Smith 1996; Davey and Mullin 1982). In some cases, children of a dominant ethnic group actively marginalise members of other ethnic groups (García-Sánchez 2011), but ethnicity can impact on integration in more subtle ways also, as I show below.

I realised that ethnicity might have something to do with Sarah's difficulties when Miss Chahal received a letter from Sarah's mother and spoke to the class about exclusion as a result. Recall Miss Chahal's rhetorical questions to her class: 'Out of the girls, who plays Indian games out in the playground? Who tells children they can't play because it's an Indian game?' Presumably Miss Chahal, who was herself of Indian ethnicity, asked these questions because of accusations made in the letter she had received. I spent a lot of time with the girls in this class out in the playground and never saw them playing an 'Indian game'. However, I did often hear them speaking in what they called 'Indian' (usually Punjabi, sometimes Urdu). In particular, children often swore at each other in 'Indian' during the types of playfully aggressive verbal exchanges described in Chapter 2, as well as during genuine disputes. In addition, the girls sometimes made up dances to songs from Bollywood films, as well as discussing recent Bollywood releases and the actors and actresses who appeared in them.

The largest single ethnic group at Woodwell Green and in the local community was Indian. It is not surprising, then, that Indian cultural expertise, such as knowledge of 'Indian swear words' and Bollywood films, was a valuable commodity. Those who did not have this knowledge were not able to understand or participate in some interactions. For example, in a game of Red Rover between year 5 boys and girls,[10] the girls chanted for Amandeep (Punjabi speaker) to come over. Amandeep hesitated, so Farah (Urdu speaker) shouted, 'Come on you budha, are you a wimp?' The Indian and Pakistani girls shrieked with laughter, and one translated the term for my benefit as 'old man'. Without the linguistic knowledge, a child would be excluded from this joke.

To aid my integration among the children of Woodwell Green, I learned a couple of 'Indian' words, watched the latest Bollywood film and bought the soundtrack. Some children who, like me, were not Indian or Pakistani pursued the same tactic. For example, Anjali ('other ethnic group') did not speak Punjabi but acquired an impressive vocabulary of 'Indian'. She used this knowledge to banter with her friends and to exclude classmate Sohaib (who was Pakistani but did not speak Urdu), by recruiting 'Indian' words as secret passwords. Zena, a Black Caribbean girl who joined Woodwell Green during year 4, also made efforts to learn about Indian language and music. Here is an example:

> Zena and Farah [Urdu speaker] begin a playful aggressive exchange with each other. Zena says 'Koota!' and Farah replies with something that I don't catch. Zena retorts with 'Koota!' again. I ask them what this word means. At first, Farah claims not to know. Zena says it is swearing at your mother. Then she changes her mind, claiming that it means a female dog, and Farah corrects her, stating that it is any dog. Farah starts to walk away, and I ask Zena, 'How do you know Indian words?' She replies in a lilting Indian accent, 'Cos I can speak Indian! I can dance Indian, look!' She puts her hands and arms to her sides, and moves them forward and backwards. Farah sees and comes back over, saying that Zena's efforts are not Indian. 'She's trying to do Bhangra,' she comments in amusement. I ask Farah if she can do Bhangra and she says yes, and I ask her to show me. At first she refuses, but then agrees to show me in a secluded part of the playground, without Zena present. After demonstrating Bhangra to me, she tells me that her two-year-old sister is learning to dance, and can already sing a song from the latest Bollywood film.

Zena used her rather partial knowledge of Bhangra and 'Indian' to good effect in this playfully aggressive exchange with Farah. We saw in Chapter 2 that these playfully aggressive exchanges were an important component of friendship among children at Woodwell Green. So Zena's willingness to learn how to participate in these may have contributed to her popularity; two girls (one Pakistani, one Indian) wanted to be her best friend (see Chapter 5), and at the end of year 4, she was named by six of her classmates (including Farah) as one of their four closest friends.

Zena and Anjali demonstrate that even children who are not Indian or Pakistani can acquire sufficient knowledge of language and culture to interact competently with peers. Yet I never witnessed Sarah, Joanne or Joshua 'speaking in Indian' or referring to Bollywood films. My field-notes suggest that it was quite rare for English children to demonstrate knowledge of Indian language or culture (but it occasionally occurred; see, for example, the extract in Chapter 2 in which English boy Paul used an 'Indian swear word' during a playfully aggressive exchange with Amandeep). This may be because children at Woodwell Green (and their parents) subscribed to a view of 'Indian' and 'English' as opposites. English and Indian children alike used these terms in a polarised way to label particular foods (roti as Indian, chips, pizza, pasta as English), clothes (jeans or tight clothes as English, saris as Indian), hairstyles for girls (short hair as English, long hair in plaits as Indian), religions (Christian or non-religious as English, usually Sikh as Indian) and languages (English versus 'Indian', which usually meant Punjabi). This opposition may result from the fact that in the space of only one generation, the local area had transformed, the largest ethnic group changing from English to Indian. Thus, English ethnicity had become a local minority whilst remaining, of course, a national majority. English and Indian ethnic identities were the dominant ones on the scene, but in tension with one another.

Apparently in response to this opposition, children policed peers who engaged in activities associated with the opposite ethnic group. For example, I heard one Indian girl teasing another over the fact that her family ate spaghetti bolognese and pasta rather than roti, calling her 'an English girl'. When an English boy told his peers that he had made roti at home, an Indian boy laughed and said, 'He can't make roti, he's English!' A Welsh girl told me that she had watched Bollywood films at the house of an Indian Sikh friend and wanted to go to the Sikh festival Vaisakhi with her, but that she did not want her big brother to know, 'Cos he will make fun of me cos he will say like *you're* an India, that's what he says when I sing Indian song. He tells me to go back to India cos that's my country'. I myself was not immune to this policing; Anjali told me that some of her Indian friends disapproved of me, an English person, going to watch Bollywood films.

I have argued elsewhere that the reason for this policing is that the children of Woodwell Green saw eating, appearance, leisure interests and religion as partly constitutive of ethnicity (Woods 2007). In other words, by participating in the activities of another ethnic group, children believed that one to some extent took on the identity of that ethnic group. This was particularly problematic in the case of Indian and English because these terms were seen as mutually exclusive and opposite, so to become more Indian was by definition to become less English. Therefore it is possible that learning about Bollywood films and 'Indian swear words' was more difficult for an English girl like Sarah than for a Black Caribbean girl like Zena, because for Sarah this knowledge challenged her own sense of identity and, moreover, the identity ascribed to her by others, including her own family.[11]

Friendships between Indian and English children did exist at Woodwell Green. For example, we will see in Chapter 7 that English boy Robbie was good friends with his Indian classmate, Soraj. And Joanne and Joshua were friendly with the large, loose group of mostly Indian and Pakistani girls in their class. They sometimes played with them in the playground, and in the individual friendship interviews I conducted during their time in year 4, Joanne and Joshua both named three Indian children, and were named by four and three Indian children respectively, as someone they liked in their class.

Nevertheless, ethnic identity may still have been an issue for Joanne and Joshua. When Kosovan girl Kanina joined their class, Joanne approached me in the playground to excitedly tell me that the new girl was white. Joshua's mother complained to his teacher that he had to wear an 'Indian' costume for their class assembly (see Chapter 6). This does not necessarily mean that Joshua himself objected, but he was probably aware of his mother's concerns.

To conclude, many studies have found that children find it a bit harder to develop friendships with peers of other ethnic groups. I have argued that this is partly because of the shared knowledge (such as language and cultural references) that same-ethnicity children are more likely to have. This in itself may explain why Sarah did not achieve a stable friendship with any of the other (non-English) girls in her class. In addition, because children saw 'English' and 'Indian' as mutually exclusive opposites, it may have been particularly difficult for English children, like Sarah, to participate in 'Indian' activities. Such a barrier need not be insurmountable, but could be enough to deter Sarah from creating a close friendship with any of the ten Indian and Pakistani girls in her class.

4.4.3 Distorted perceptions

In addition to ethnic differences, ethnic identity processes and a problematic dynamic with two English children in her class, another possible contributor to Sarah's exclusion was her own perception of her situation. We have already seen that Sarah saw herself as friendless; she told me several times that she had no friends. Yet my sociometric data actually suggest that she was well liked by her classmates. In individual interviews conducted during year 4, seven classmates (three Indian, two English, one Pakistani, one Black African) named Sarah as someone they liked. Here are the reasons they gave:

- 'I want to be with Sarah because she hasn't got any friends and I want to play with her.'
- 'She's kind and, um, she helps me with my homework, and when she's alone I play with her. She looks after me all that.'
- 'She's kind as well.' [like previously named child]
- 'When I play with Joshua, she comes to play with us.'
- 'She was friendly, she was nice to people.'
- 'She plays with me and she doesn't say anything bad and stuff, the same as the other people, and she sticks up for me sometimes, and I stick up for her. Cos we get called names a lot that's why we go to Mr Gardner's [head teacher] room to read sometimes.'
- 'Same' [as previously named child, about which this child said, 'She is good from her heart and she's a good girl, and she always hug me.']. RW: 'Exactly the same?' 'Yeah. But Miss, one thing of Sarah I don't like yeah, she does help me but she doesn't help me, she does help me but she doesn't play with me; when I go to her she just makes faces … In the playground, when I go to her she moves.'

The first two children in the list above alluded to Sarah's friendlessness in their reasons for liking her. Both were interviewed soon after Miss Chahal carried out the clapping exercise with their class (described near the start of the chapter) to increase the children's awareness of exclusion. So it is possible that although the friendship interviews were confidential, they were influenced by this exercise to assert friendship with Sarah. Nevertheless, the children's reasons overall convey the impression of a girl who was seen as friendly and kind by her peers. This impression was sustained at the end of year 4 when children completed questionnaires listing their four best friends at school. Five children nominated Sarah, three of whom had also named her in friendship exercises during the year, suggesting that the liking she received was enduring.

Yet Sarah did not seem to be aware of this liking. Indeed, there is some evidence that she may have pushed others away. Firstly, the last peer in the list above who named Sarah as someone she liked in her friendship interview gave a caveat: 'She doesn't play with me; when I go to her she just makes faces.' Obviously this is the claim of just one child, but it might indicate that Sarah did not want to be friends with some of the children who liked her. Secondly, once when I saw Sarah alone in the playground, I asked her why she did not join the big group of mainly girls in her class, who were playing 'had' nearby, and she replied that she did not like running around.

It is of course perfectly legitimate for Sarah not to want to participate in particular activities or to play with specific children, but this reluctance may have contributed to her exclusion. It is possible that over time, Sarah's perception of herself as friendless became self-reinforcing, leading her to underestimate her status among her peers and to make less effort to integrate. This process arguably culminated in her regularly spending lunchtimes in the head teacher's office (as noted earlier) rather than in the playground, further reducing opportunities to make friends.

4.5   Exclusion as Reciprocity

This book is full of examples indicating that reciprocity or justice was important to the children of Woodwell Green. The principle is discussed further in Chapters 3 and 7. Here I describe a case study in which children excluded a peer in retaliation for harmful acts that peer carried out. It concerns Michael, a boy who came to the UK from eastern Europe and joined Woodwell Green in September, at the start of year 6. I began fieldwork in his class of 10- and 11-year-olds in January. On my second day with the class, the children had a science lesson in which they worked in groups allocated by the teacher, Miss Lock, who asked me to work with one group of seven children (one of whom was Michael). Here are my fieldnotes describing what followed:

> The table around which the group is working has only six places, all of which have already been taken when Michael attempts to draw his chair up to one of the corners. Paula resists this move, commenting, 'You ain't gonna have enough room to put your book.' Another girl adds quietly, 'And you can't sit here either, because [inaudible name]'s book goes there.' So Michael sits well back from the table, unable to participate in conversation about the experiment. Eventually, after another attempt to join the group is rebuffed, he moves to an empty desk nearby and sits on his own there. I ask him why he's not sitting with the group. 'They say there ain't any room,' he says. 'But I think there is,' he adds in a softer voice.
>
> I go over to help the main group. Once they have gathered the results (which are written on one piece of paper), they all need to transfer the data to their individual books. I tell a girl in the group that she will need to make space so that Michael can do this. 'There ain't room,' Paula replies. 'Well how's he supposed to get the results?' I ask, annoyed now. But Michael seems distressed by my intervention and says that he'll borrow the

sheet after everyone else has finished writing up. I am dissatisfied with this solution since he cannot start to do any work until he has the results, so I tear a piece of paper from my notebook and write them out for him. 'It's only cos there ain't room,' Paula says, but I don't reply.

Several members of the group continued to exclude Michael for the rest of the lesson. Bemused, at lunchtime I asked Miss Lock why the children were excluding him. She explained that Michael had made racist comments to at least two children in the class, one of whom was very popular (and a friend of Paula's). Since then, the whole class closed ranks against him. Miss Lock worked hard to challenge her class's behaviour, lecturing them on more than one occasion about including and accepting each other. Yet her efforts were at best partially successful; in the playground more than a month later, Paula told me that Michael still did not have any friends, which she attributed to his making fun of people all the time.

In some respects, this example of exclusion fits archetypal school representations more closely than the other examples I have described in this chapter: it was deliberate, and while some children seem to have been more active than others, nevertheless many group members united in excluding Michael. However, it does not fit the archetypal image insofar as the children were (at least partly) motivated by widely accepted values (harm avoidance and reciprocity) to exclude. We will see in Chapter 6 that children and adults alike at Woodwell Green took racism extremely seriously. In a sense, then, it is not surprising that the children in this year 6 class wanted to retaliate and punish Michael for what they saw as very offensive and hurtful behaviour. Children might also exclude on the basis of other values, not only reciprocity. For instance, Evaldsson (2007) describes how 11- and 12-year-old working-class girls of various ethnicities at a Swedish elementary school excluded a peer on the basis of her alleged moral inadequacies, including disloyalty and dishonesty. The possibility that children might be motivated to exclude for principled reasons is not acknowledged in standard school discussions of exclusion.

4.6   Implications for Schools

4.6.1   *Mismatches between classroom representations and playground reality*

Woodwell Green provided a clear stance on exclusion. It was seen as wrong, a type of 'hurting on the inside'. Teachers sought to minimise exclusion by urging children to play together and to invite lone peers to join them. They also sometimes carried out exercises to help increase children's awareness of exclusion. These exercises and incitements to play together tended to assume that exclusion took a particular form: a group uniting to exclude an innocent lone peer. Almost everyone agreed in this simple scenario that the children in the group were in the wrong and the single child was the innocent victim – recall children's role plays in Miss Chahal's class, all three of which depicted a mean group excluding a peer for trivial reasons like being new, wearing glasses and being clever.

If such discussions and exercises are to be genuinely beneficial in increasing children's awareness of exclusion and empathy with excluded children, they need to be realistic. They need to be sufficiently similar to children's own experiences of exclusion on the playground for children to recognise the latter as exclusion. While exclusion sometimes resembles this archetypal scenario (Adler and Adler 1998; Goodwin 2006), this chapter has demonstrated that at other times, it looks quite different.

For one thing, at Woodwell Green it was not usually the group as a whole who carried out acts of exclusion (although there are exceptions, such as the year 6 class uniting to exclude Michael). Rather, children generally abdicated responsibility for inclusion and exclusion to one group member. Children who were not allocated this responsibility seemed willing to leave those decisions entirely to the group leader, and as such may not have seen *themselves* as excluding at all (although the excluded child may have seen things differently – I return to this issue shortly). In the examples I have described, one child in the group generally took responsibility for exclusion, but researchers have described other configurations also, such as two dominant girls, colluding with a third, to exclude a fourth (Svahn and Evaldsson 2011). There is a need for more research to understand when and how particular distributions of power develop within children's peer groups.

For another thing, exclusion was not always carried out with malicious intent. Even adults at the school seemed sympathetic to the need to exclude children for the sake of game maintenance (a game of football cannot operate if there are too many children and is not seen as fair if one team has more players than another). Children also excluded those they perceived to be incompetent at specific games, because of a desire to win. While this was undoubtedly unpleasant for the excluded child, and could be used as a ruse to cover a more malicious reason for exclusion, it was not in itself malicious.

Extending this idea of non-malicious exclusion, sometimes children ended up isolated apparently through an unfortunate combination of events. In the case of Sarah, her English identity may have acted as an obstacle to her integration into a predominantly Indian peer group, and her isolation was exacerbated by the fact that the English girl she most desired as a friend was already in a stable dyadic friendship with another child who felt threatened by Sarah. The exact reasons for such cases of incidental exclusion are likely to vary; for example, the resistance among English children to Indian activities likely arises from the specific situation in Woodwell Green, where there were many more people of Indian ethnicity than English, despite English being the majority group nationally. Nevertheless, ethnic identity is likely to be an issue in any multicultural school (Aboud et al. 2003; Baerveldt et al. 2004; Boulton and Smith 1996; Davey and Mullin 1982; Hallinan and Teixeira 1987; Shaw 1973), children lacking locally valued knowledge and skills are likely to be marginalised, and any new child entering a pre-existing group has to grapple with the fact that desirable peers may already be in exclusive friendships. Schools might consider how they could support children coping with these issues.

Even when children's exclusion was malicious, it could be motivated by other values. We saw in the case of Michael that children were willing to exclude a peer as a form of retaliation to what they saw as a serious act of harm (racism). This is a rather different situation from one in which children exclude a peer for trivial reasons relating to appearance or academic competence.

Like the standard depiction of exclusion, the standard solution provided by teachers – to all play together – is also limited in several ways. First, it is arguably unfair to expect children to spend all their free time at school affiliating with someone they may not even like. Teachers were, of course, somewhat selective about who they spent time with in the staffroom. Why should children be any different in this regard? Second, this chapter suggests that having someone to play with and having a *friend* are not quite the same thing. Having a reliable friend may be a guarantee of having someone to play with (provided they are not absent from school, of course), but the converse does not necessarily apply. In Sarah's case, she sometimes played with children in her class, but this association did not lead to enduring friendships, and ultimately, it was her lack of friends, rather than her aloneness in the playground, that she lamented. It might be useful for schools to consider what they are aiming for with their interventions; to enable children to build up meaningful friendships, or to avoid being alone on the playground. If the former, then simply encouraging children to play together may not be enough. We may need more active interventions, based on an understanding of what friendship means to these children. Third, as we saw with Sarah, Joanne and Joshua, asking children to play altogether is likely to challenge concepts of loyalty held by many children (see Chapter 5).

The most important practical implication is that schools need to broaden their representations of exclusion, to make them more relevant to children's playground lives. Many children clearly had experience of various types of exclusion and the complex issues they raised, yet they never mentioned them during classroom role plays, exercises or discussions about exclusion. There seemed to be an unspoken agreement about the intrinsically negative nature of exclusion, and hence no space for children to acknowledge its complex and varied form. The result was that classroom discussions ignored key motivations for exclusion, and hence were not genuinely enlightening to either teacher or children. To acknowledge these motivations would make such discussions more complicated, with various possible perspectives rather than a simple black and white judgement upon which everyone could agree. But at least they would become real discussions, allowing genuine learning and innovation to arise.

4.6.2   Power, status and accountability

We have seen in this chapter that one member of the group usually took responsibility for decisions about who can join the group. In football matches, this was the ball owner, while among the girls of the after-school club it was usually Manpreet, who was assertive, the eldest, and also perceived by some as the best dancer and singer. These responsible children weighed inclusion against other concerns, including status and dominance maintenance. Thus, Faizel (but not Pavandeep) asserted his dominance over defiant excluded peers, while Manpreet sought to exclude Holly in an effort to maintain her own dominance at the after-school club.

We have also seen that the other members of the group usually allowed the group leader to include and exclude on their behalf. Relatively dominant children contested or struggled with the group leader's decision (whether as the excluded child, e.g. Idris and Holly, or as a group member without decision-making powers, e.g. Zak). But more submissive children in the group allowed the group leader to exclude without challenging them. These children may not have wanted the responsibility associated with leadership and decision-making, or may have been afraid that standing up to the group leader would result in their own exclusion.

Previous research has demonstrated that perpetrators and victims experience exclusion and other harmful acts differently, with victims tending to see the acts as more serious and harmful than perpetrators do (Horn 2003; Killen et al. 2006; Wainryb et al. 2005). My own analyses of children's responses to a hypothetical scenario about exclusion also pointed to the same conclusion, with those who had experienced exclusion blaming the group significantly more often than those who had not experienced it.

The case studies of boys playing football and the girls at the after-school club show that perspectives on acts of exclusion differ not only between victim and perpetrators, but also between perpetrators, in the sense that not all members of an excluding group take responsibility for the act. Rather, group members' experiences vary as a function of their dominance within the group. For instance, group decision-makers may tend to blame the excluded child for their exclusion (e.g. Manpreet might blame Holly for trying to 'take over' her dominant position), while other more submissive group members may tend to blame their group leader, whom they assign responsibility for exclusion. However, excluded children may not always differentiate between group members in this way and may hold them all responsible for their exclusion, as seemed to be the case with Holly, who criticised her friend Rachel for not intervening when Manpreet excluded her. These varying experiences and perspectives on responsibility may have contrasting implications for moral development, a possibility I consider further in Chapter 8.

These insights into power dynamics suggest a new direction for schools concerned about exclusion: encourage submissive group members to take more responsibility for decisions made by their leader. It is probably unrealistic to aim to remove this abdication of responsibility to a leader altogether (it would make management of large stable games like football very difficult). But we could perhaps aim for a more weakly stratified peer group, in which everyone's voice counts, and in which all children accept a sense of responsibility for decisions that affect the whole group. Perhaps classes could try out semi-formal mechanisms for exchanging opinions and reaching decisions in groups that do not rely on complete abdication of responsibility to one person. Children could then be encouraged to transfer these skills in group decision-making to the school playground. By the same token, children who often lead groups could be encouraged to think about how they could share that responsibility and also to critically assess the competing values, such as dominance and status, that lead them to exclude in some instances.

Notes

1. There were two versions of each scenario. For the first scenario, half the children heard a version involving three girls, Katie, Sani and Jasmine, and the other half, three boys, Adam, Matthew and Hinesh. For the second scenario, the composition of the group (as depicted in an accompanying picture) remained the same, but for half the children, the lone child was a boy, John, and for the other half, a girl, Joanne.

2. The reason that more children answered questions about scenario 2 than 1 was because year 1 children found scenario 1 too confusing so I omitted it from their interviews. A total of 143 children were interviewed about scenario 3, but due to experimental error, the question about blame was omitted from six interviews.

3. Note that in the second scenario, the group does not actually carry out the act of exclusion, although most children assumed that that was what would happen. This omission may explain why 44 children (32 per cent) said that no one had done anything wrong in scenario 2.

4. Note that according to Pavandeep, Faizel is unfair insofar as he plays with Pavandeep's ball but does not allow Pavandeep to play with his ball. We saw in Chapter 3 that fairness was important to Faizel in many situations, but Pavandeep's comment is a reminder that there may have been situations in which Faizel prioritised other concerns over fairness.

5. 'Had' is a game in which one child (who is 'on') chases the others. When he or she touches another child, that child becomes 'on' and the former chaser becomes one of the chased. The game continues indefinitely in this way.

6. Although I interviewed 143 children about this scenario, I accidentally omitted the question about blame from six interviews. Therefore I focus here only on the 137 children who answered all questions for this scenario.

7. I used two χ^2 tests of association to assess whether there was a relationship between the role of the child in their own experience (either as excluded individual, member of group, or no experience reported) and whether they blamed, firstly, the individual excluded child, and secondly, the group. I found a significant association between child's experience and blame of group, $\chi^2(2) = 12.766$, $p = .001$ (one-tailed). Children who had experience of being excluded blamed the group much more often than did children who had experience of being in the group. Children without relevant experience blamed the group least often. There was no significant association between experience and blaming of the excluded child.

8. Spelling mistakes have been corrected for the sake of clarity.

9. The experiences of Sarah, Joshua and Joanne as an unstable triad were very common at Woodwell Green. Children's expectations of loyalty and exclusivity of specific peers often created tensions. See Chapter 5.

10. In Red Rover, two teams stand in lines opposite each other, holding hands. Teams take turns to calls for one person on the other team to run over and attempt to break through the line of children holding hands.
11. See also Chapter 6, where I describe how English parents felt threatened by their children's participation in 'Indian' practises, like dancing to Bollywood songs, at school.

5

Loyalty in Girls' Friendships

5.1 Possessiveness, Loyalty and Independence

In addition to exclusion, the focus of Chapter 4, adults at Woodwell Green were also concerned about possessive behaviours, in which children tried to force particular peers to play with them. These were seen as problematic because they limited children's freedom to choose their own affiliations. For example, in an assembly for years 3 to 6 (ages 7 to 11 years), Mr Gardner, the head teacher, commented that friendships were important, but that the previous term he found that some children were being too possessive of their friends, 'acting like they owned them'. He continued that if a child wanted to sometimes play with someone else, it did not mean that they were no longer friends with their usual companions, since it was possible to have many friends.

On this occasion, Mr Gardner argued in favour of children's independence in the playground, in an effort to counter what he saw as problems with possessiveness. Year 5 class teacher Mrs Samson seemed to share his view. Concerned about her class's playground relations, she devised several 'problem cards', which she gave to groups of children to use as a basis for role plays. One card, which she gave to a group of five girls, read: 'Stephanie usually plays with Marie, Elaine and Shannon. Stephanie wants to have a change of friends today. She decides to play with Beth. Marie, Elaine and Shannon are very upset. They approach Stephanie in the playground to ask her why she isn't playing with them.' The wording

Children's Moral Lives: An Ethnographic and Psychological Approach, First Edition. Ruth Woods.
© 2013 John Wiley & Sons, Ltd. Published 2013 by John Wiley & Sons, Ltd.

Table 5.1 Children's judgements of wrongdoing in exclusivity scenario

Protagonist who was blamed	Number of children (N = 122)	Percentage of children
Katie	32	26
Sani	4	3
Jasmine	72	59
No one	31	25

Numbers add up to more than 122 because some children blamed more than one protagonist.

used to describe this situation expresses sympathy for Stephanie, who is described as wanting the freedom to play with someone different.

There was some evidence that children were sympathetic to teachers' valuing of independence and concerns about possessiveness and ownership. As noted in Chapter 4, one of the hypothetical scenarios I discussed with children in individual interviews concerned possessive behaviours:

Katie, Sani and Jasmine are in the same class. Katie and Sani are playing together in the playground. Jasmine comes up to them. Jasmine likes Sani but she doesn't like Katie. Jasmine keeps asking to play with Sani on her own. Then Katie turns to Sani and says, 'If you play with Jasmine, I won't be your friend anymore.'[1]

Table 5.1 summarises children's answers to the question, 'Has anyone in this story done something bad do you think, or have they been okay?' While 25 per cent of children thought that all protagonists had been 'okay', most thought that Jasmine's and/or Katie's possessiveness of Sani was wrong. These data suggest that, like Mr Gardner, children were ready to condemn possessive behaviour.

Nevertheless, acts of possessiveness were common at Woodwell Green; 39 per cent of the children interviewed reported having had an experience like this scenario, and I witnessed many examples during my research. As I analysed these examples, I began to realise that the value the head teacher and many children placed on choice and independence in the playground was in tension with two other values. One was the value teachers placed on inclusion, i.e. all children playing together (described in Chapter 4). The other was a value which I rarely heard teachers refer to directly: children's expectations of loyalty from their friends. We might define one child's loyalty to another as their obligation to privilege their friendship over their other relationships and concerns. The form of privilege took various forms, such as lying to a teacher to protect each other or a willingness to help each other in class. In this chapter, I explore two types of loyalty that were important for children at Woodwell Green, and which could lead to claims of possession: the obligation to be available to one's friend, and the obligation to share a friend's enemies.[2] The case studies that follow focus on girls, among whom I witnessed most examples of loyalty and possessiveness, for reasons I discuss later in the chapter.

5.2 Loyalty in Best Friendship

One form of loyalty that was widespread at Woodwell Green was associated with best friendship. A few children claimed to have more than one best friend but, more usually, best friends were pairs who made a mutual commitment above all others. One element of loyalty between best friends was availability; to be loyal to one's best friend was to be always available to him or her. Insofar as best friendship was ideally a two-way obligation between a pair of children, this form of loyalty bore some resemblance to the value of reciprocity.

This conception of best friendship is not unusual. Australian working-class children saw availability as part of what makes a good friend (Davies 1982), while best friends among an ethnically diverse group of teenage girls in London were expected to spend more time with each other than with anyone else (Wulff 1995). Similarly, teenage girls in Quebec saw being together as an obligation of friendship (Amit-Talai 1995).

The obligation to be available to one's best friend is most obvious when it is not met, as I discovered from year 4 girls, Navneet (Indian Sikh), Maria (Pakistani Christian), Zena (Black Caribbean Christian) and Erickah (Black African Christian). I met Navneet at the start of year 4, when she was 8 years old. At that time, she was usually to be found with a large loose-knit group of children (mostly girls) on the playground, but not with any one child in particular. Zena, Maria and Erickah all joined Navneet's class (and the school) over a period of two months during year 4. Maria was the first to arrive, in mid-February.

5.2.1 Maria: 'I let her play with other people but why can't I play too?'

During her first month at Woodwell Green, Maria spent time on the playground with different children in the class, usually in large groups. When Zena arrived in mid-March, she and Maria paired up almost immediately and became 'best friends'. In mid-April, Erickah started at the school. She quickly joined up with Zena and Maria. About a week later, Zena began to spend more time with other girls in her class, particularly Navneet. She remained friends with Maria, but they no longer spent much time as a twosome.

At this point, I conducted an individual interview with Maria in which I asked her who she liked most in her class. Maria named Zena and Erickah, amongst others, but when explaining why she liked them, she spoke of her distress about how Zena was behaving towards her:

MARIA: [explaining why she likes Erickah] Miss she's quiet and she, she always help her.

RW: What do you mean?

MARIA: I help her and she helps me. She says that I'm your best friend, I won't leave you, like Zena does, Miss she leaves me, one day she be's my friend and one day she doesn't. I like Zena but I don't like her when she goes like that. I tell Erickah all my secrets, not like my brother and sister.

MARIA: [explaining why she likes Zena] Just like her – so – so – I liked her more before.

RW: Is that because she goes off with other girls now?

MARIA: Yes.

RW: Why do you think she does that?

MARIA: Because – when she gets a new friend yeah, like she gets Anjali now, she becomes rude, and she only comes to me to pull faces, and I say don't be my friend, because I don't like it. Sometimes be my friend and sometimes don't, I don't like it.

Having developed a best friendship with Zena, Maria continued to expect her to be available to her. Zena, meanwhile, seemed keen to pursue other friendships in addition to Maria's. From Maria's perspective, this amounted to disloyalty, and she expressed her distress about Zena 'leaving her'.

In July, very near the end of their time in year 4, this dynamic was still causing Maria distress. It was lunchtime, and most girls in the class had

115

been playing their male classmates in a heated football game. Maria and Zena argued fiercely with several boys, kicking and swearing at them, and Mohamed threw a football at Zena's head. Zena started to cry and Mohamed was taken inside by the head teacher.

> The whistle goes, indicating the end of lunch break, and the children make their way across the field to line up. Maria and Zena walk together near me. Anjali, Amrita and Louise approach them. Anjali puts her arm round Zena and talks with her closely. Maria is hanging back on the edge of the group, looking dejected. She comes over to me and asks 'Why does Mohamed hate Zena so much?' I say I don't know.
>
> I hear Anjali say to Zena, 'You come with us now,' and then Zena, Anjali, Amrita and Louise walk off among the trees nearby, Anjali's arm still round Zena's shoulders. Maria runs after them, but soon comes back to me. She takes my arm and we walk along together. 'Why doesn't Anjali like me?' she ponders sadly. 'She always tries to take Zena away from me.' I say that Anjali probably does like her. She replies that when the five of them were standing together just now, Anjali had leaned into Maria's face and said loudly, 'BYE!' (Maria demonstrates this on me.) Maria didn't move, so then Anjali said to Zena, 'Tell Maria to go away.' Zena turned to Maria then and said 'Go away'.
>
> I tell Maria that Anjali is like this with other children as well, not just her, but she seems convinced that she's the only one. 'What shall I do? Why doesn't Anjali like me?' she wails. I say not to worry about that, she and Zena are still friends and she just needs to let Zena have other friends too. 'I do,' she says in the same frustrated, aggrieved tone. 'I do everything for Zena. I play with her, I give her things. I let her play with other people but why can't I play too?' I find this hard to answer.

In this incident, Anjali, a strong, dominant girl (see Chapter 2), excluded Maria with Zena's help, and Maria was left struggling with Zena's failure to meet her expectations of loyalty. From Maria's perspective, Anjali was trying to 'take Zena away' from her and no matter what she did, Zena was slipping through her fingers. She gained no solace from my 'independence' solution, which did nothing to address her key concern: As Zena expanded her friendship network, why would she not take Maria with her?

A few months later, having moved into year 5, Maria expressed similar concerns, this time about Zena and Navneet. I was interviewing Maria about the hypothetical scenario about possessiveness (described earlier in this chapter). As I read out the scenario, Maria started to pace the room and all her answers were rapid and animated. Here is her answer to the first question, and our resulting discussion.

RW: How do you think Katie is feeling?

MARIA: Bad cos, sad cos, cos she, if she's playing with Sani, like somebody, Miss I'll tell you one thing. When I play, when I used to play with Zena, Navneet always comes and take her away from me.

RW: How did she do that?

MARIA: Cos she hasn't got friends so she thought, I'm gonna take Sani away from Katie, I'm gonna feel very proud cos Katie won't play with me. Miss, you know today, you know Sarina, she's a bit rude to me. As I walked past the bookcase, Navneet was tidying it and she dropped a load of books on the floor. Sarina turned round and said, uuhhh, oohhh, Maria, pick them up, pick them up. I said I didn't drop them why should I pick them up, and she said pick them up, pick them up! I said Navneet did it and Sarina still said pick them up.

RW: Did Navneet say anything?

MARIA: Navneet always be rude to me. I said to Navneet, Navneet I know you're not my friend, and she said I *am* your friend. Then another time, again I ask her, Navneet are you my friend, and she said yeah, but I think Zena and Navneet, they don't like me. But Zena, does like me, and Navneet, a bit they do like me, but I don't know *why* they don't want me to play with them.

Maria still seemed to expect loyalty from Zena. She struggled to understand Zena's failure to meet that expectation, interpreting her behaviour as meaning that she and her new friends did not like Maria (although in questionnaires in years 4 and 5, both Zena and Navneet named Maria as a friend). In our discussion above, Maria seemed to see Navneet as the cause of the problem. For example, she claimed that 'Navneet always comes and take her [Zena] away from me'. The phrase 'taking away' refers to a triad: the one who takes away, the one who is taken away, and the one who is taken away from. For Maria, these are Navneet, Zena and Maria respectively. In this formulation, Zena and Maria are passive; it is Navneet who is actively removing Zena from Maria's company.

I was surprised, therefore, that when I asked if anyone had done anything wrong in the scenario, Maria said that Katie had, her reason being, 'She must say, come on Sani, let's play together'. I asked her if she had tried saying this to Navneet and Zena. She replied, 'Yeah I did, they said come and play with me yeah, but when I did, they don't talk to me'. It is unclear why Maria thought that Katie was to blame, given that her account of her own experience suggested blame of 'the one who takes away' – Jasmine in the hypothetical scenario – and given that she found her own suggestion to play together ineffective. Possibly she meant to blame Jasmine, rather than Katie. Meanwhile, although Maria seemed to see Navneet as responsible for 'taking Zena away', Navneet herself had surprisingly similar concerns to Maria.

5.2.2   Navneet: 'She's running off with Sarina'

As noted above, in late April, soon after Erickah arrived, Zena began to spend increasing amounts of time with Navneet. By the end of the month, Zena was often to be seen in a pair with Navneet, and Maria with Erickah. In June, I heard Zena tell Navneet, 'You're my best friend', and the following week, Zena told me, 'Maria used to be my best friend but now Navneet is'. Yet just a week after that, tensions erupted between the newly formed best friends. As Zena, Navneet and I walked together during a school trip, Zena told me, 'I'm not Navneet's friend anymore'. 'Why not?' I asked. 'Because I want to be Simran's friend and Navneet won't be Simran's friend so I'm not Navneet's friend,' Zena replied. Once I had grasped this (I had to get Zena to repeat it), I suggested, 'But you can still be Navneet's friend'. 'No, because I want to be Simran's friend more,' Zena replied.

According to Zena, Navneet issued her with an ultimatum: her friendship or Simran's. Navneet and Simran usually got along reasonably well with each other (Navneet named Simran as someone she liked during interviews in year 4, but Simran did not name Navneet), and I never witnessed them arguing (although Simran did tell me in year 5 that Navneet had once spread rumours about her). So it seems unlikely that Navneet's ultimatum was the result of a dispute between her and Simran. Rather, I suggest that it was triggered by Zena's desire to be friends with Simran, who was very popular (named by eight classmates as someone they liked in interviews during year 4, and by 11 classmates as a friend in questionnaires at the end of year 4 and again during year 5). Navneet seems to have felt her own friendship with Zena to be threatened by Zena's blossoming friendship with this high-status, popular girl, and so she tried to force Zena into an exclusive relationship with her, a tactic that backfired on this occasion. I saw a similar sequence of events later (when the girls were in year 5), this time with Sarina instead of Simran:

> As Navneet and I walk over to the canteen together I ask, 'Why aren't you with Zena?' Until then we'd been chatting pleasantly, but now she switches instantly into a complaining, aggrieved tone, starting high pitched and sinking a little. 'She's running off with Sarina. I'm on my own and she

didn't even come and ask me to play with them, or ask me if I was okay.'
I ask Navneet if she asked to play with them. 'Yeah, and they just run off,'
she replies.

We join the queue for lunch inside the canteen, next to Maria. Zena is
further forward in the line, next to Sarina. Zena leaves Sarina's side and
stands behind Navneet who is talking to me. I smile and greet her, but
Navneet doesn't. Zena gently fiddles with Navneet's hair, but Navneet still
does not respond, so Zena returns to Sarina. Navneet starts talking with
Maria, who is next to her in the queue, and I talk to someone else. When
I turn back, Navneet is saying to Maria, in a plaintive tone, 'She's my best
friend.' Maria doesn't say much. The line moves forward. Zena drops back
again to talk to me and so is near Navneet again, but Sarina waits for her.
'Zena!' she calls in a warm, friendly voice, and Zena and Sarina go through
lunch together. Navneet clings to me fervently.

I sit with Navneet, Maria and Erickah, and Sarina and Zena sit at
another table. During the meal, Navneet says to me in a resentful tone,
'See, she's sitting with Sarina.' 'She did come to stand with you in the line,'
I point out and she says nothing. I suggest that this is a chance for her to
play with someone different, and ask who, apart from Zena, she likes to
play with. She says Maria and Erickah, so I suggest she plays with them
today. She doesn't look inspired, and says she likes to play with Simran and
Harpreet too. I suggest she plays with them. She adds that she plays with
Maria quite often. 'Sometimes I play with Maria, sometimes with Zena
and Maria.'

Like Maria, Navneet sought loyalty from Zena, which she did not get
when Zena played with Sarina without her. The extract above shows that
Navneet was distressed by Zena's actions, this time withdrawing from
Zena rather than issuing an ultimatum. When I interviewed her about the
hypothetical possessiveness scenario, she, like most children, blamed
Jasmine (the protagonist who sought to play with one member of a dyad
and exclude the other). When I asked if she had ever had a similar
experience, she replied, 'I have with Zena'. However, contrary to my
observations, she said her position was that of Sani (the child desired by
both Jasmine and Katie). I asked what happened, and she explained:

NAVNEET: I don't remember, cos sometimes what it is I break up by, one
            friend says that, if one friend says that, say if I said shall we
            play Ring a Ring o' Roses, just pretend yeah, Zena says let's
            play [pause] had. Okay let's pretend that's [points to picture
            of Katie] Maria, and Maria says let's play Red Letter or Stuck
            in the Mud, and Maria says okay you have to vote for Red
            Letter or Stuck in the Mud, and we don't want to, so we go off

119

> together, and Maria goes with someone else, Erickah. And
> Zena says that's a good idea actually, let's play Stuck in the
> Mud or Red Letter on our own and I say that's boring let's
> play Ring a Ring o' Roses or Cat's got the Measles[3] and Zena
> says that's boring, and she goes away from me. And Maria
> goes with Erickah.

This account did not fit my observations of Navneet and Zena in the playground, and it also did not fit the scenario which we had been discussing, and which Navneet seemed in her other answers to have understood very well. There is no claim to exclusive friendship, no attempt to exclude one member of a threesome, and no ultimatum in her tale, despite the fact that I knew from my fieldnotes that Navneet had experienced these issues. Her account did emphasise her friendship with Zena, and she mentioned how she and Zena, and Maria and Erickah, formed pairs. Perhaps Navneet found it unpalatable to recall her own friendship troubles here, and/or to explicitly acknowledge the vulnerability evident in my fieldnotes.

So although they might not have acknowledged it, there were parallels between Maria's and Navneet's experiences. Both became best friends with Zena. Both were distressed and jealous when Zena spread her wings and played with other girls, and attempted to secure their own inclusion through what we might call possessive behaviour. They responded differently, Maria trying harder to win Zena over, Navneet punishing her by withdrawing and threatening to terminate the friendship. But the overall aim of both seemed to be the same: to induce in Zena the loyalty they expected from a best friend.

Despite Zena's resistance to Maria's and Navneet's demands both girls continued to expect loyalty from her, and to be distressed when they did not get it. This raises the question of why they did not withdraw from Zena and invest in friendship with someone else – perhaps even each other. The girls may have got caught in a vicious cycle. By being unavailable, Zena increased her desirability to Zena and Navneet, so they worked harder to maintain their friendship with her, making themselves more available and hence less desirable to Zena. In contrast, because she is not available to them, Maria's and Navneet's feelings of insecurity are likely to increase, leading them, again, to try harder and be more available to Zena.

Zena's desirability to Maria and Navneet was probably also a consequence of her increasing popularity. Sociometric data suggest that

Zena was quite popular, Maria less so, and Navneet seemed to become less popular over time.[4] One way in which girls demonstrate status is through their relationships (Eder 1985; Goodwin 2002; Hey 1997). Girls who have many friendships, particularly with other high-status, popular girls, accrue more status than do peers who have fewer friendships, or whose friends are mostly low status. So Maria's and Navneet's enduring loyalty to their relatively high-status friend Zena may reflect their desire to improve their own status.

5.2.3   Zena: Prioritising independence and popularity

Zena's experience and perspective were very different from Maria's and Navneet's. She stated explicitly that first Maria and then Navneet were her best friends, but she seemed to have a different idea of what best friendship meant. As we have seen, she repeatedly resisted Maria's and Navneet's expectations of constant availability. Instead, she eagerly expanded her friendships with other girls, including, as we have seen, Anjali, Simran and Sarina.

In the process of friendship expansion, Zena sometimes seemed unconcerned about the impact of her behaviours on Maria and Navneet. For example, in November of year 5, Zena, Navneet and their popular classmate Harpreet started to make up a dance together on the playground. A couple of days later, Zena and Navneet quit together, and were replaced by Simran and Joanne. However, later the same day, Harpreet agreed that Zena could rejoin the dance. Upon learning this, Navneet began to cry, and she and Zena walked off to talk. At this point the whistle was blown indicating the end of lunch break. When I next saw them several days later, Zena was doing the dance with Harpreet, Simran and Joanne. I asked her what Navneet thought about that. 'She's with Sarina,' Zena replied, continuing cheerfully, 'I told her, I don't care if you're not in the dance! So she's gone off with Sarina.' The following day Navneet finally entered the dance group again, but it was with the help of her popular, prosocial classmate Harpreet, not Zena.

It would seem that loyalty was less important to Zena than it was to Maria and Navneet because of the high value she placed on independence. She wanted to be free to develop new friendships with peers of ever higher status. In doing so, she was acting to increase her own popularity and thus status.

121

Choice and contingency friendships

Freedom in one's peer relations is only appealing to children who have a choice about who to play with. Zena could take risks in extending her friendship network because she could always fall back on Maria and Navneet, who were what Davies (1982, p. 70) calls 'contingency friends'. Contingency friends have been observed in various school settings (Davies 1982; Griffiths 1995) and I knew of several children at Woodwell Green who had them. Harpreet had a friend in the year above her to whom she would go when she argued with girls in her class. And when I interviewed him about the hypothetical scenario in which a group excluded a lone peer (see Chapter 4), the girls' classmate Anil commented, 'I've got two sets of friends. Ones like Mohamed and that and one, when I have a fight with one and he has the ball then he probably won't let me play so then I play with my other friends'.

Contingency friends provide children with choice on the playground. This was clear in an interview with Zena in year 5, about the possessiveness scenario. She told me that she did not think any of the protagonists had done anything wrong, and went on to recount an experience of her own in which her position resembled that of Jasmine in the scenario:

ZENA: When um I play with, no when Erickah plays with Maria, and Navneet's playing something else that I don't like. So I go to Maria and I don't want to play with Erickah cos I don't like her.

RW: Why don't you like Erickah?

ZENA: I don't know! Cos she swears all the time and I don't like it.

RW: But loads of people swear in the playground.

ZENA: Yeah but it's different, she swears in a rude way and the other people swear in a jokey way.[5]

RW: How does it happen when you come up that Erickah goes away? Does Maria ask her to go?

ZENA: No. She doesn't stand up, she just goes away.

In this extract, Zena explained that when she did not want to play with Navneet, she went to Maria and insisted that Erickah, the child already with Maria, had to go. Her actions in this account are almost identical to Jasmine's in the scenario. Zena expressed no remorse about excluding Erickah so she could play with Maria on her own. Unlike most of her peers, she did not see this behaviour as wrong. From Zena's point of view, the playground was full of choices and she was free to make whichever choices she wishes.

The connection between contingency friends and choice was also made during a group interview I held with Maria, Navneet, Zena and their classmates Ayesha, Kiran and Joanne when they were in year 5.

Here is part of their discussion about the following hypothetical scenario: 'Abigail and Debbie both want to play with Priyanka, but Abigail and Debbie don't want to play with each other.'

MARIA: Miss, if you've got more friends then why do you wanna play with er them [the protagonists in the scenario], they, they being rude to you, go play with other people.

NAVNEET: But Priyanka might be the most popular.[6] [Navneet and Zena laugh]

RW: So you think it would be best to go off and play with someone else?

MARIA: [interrupting] Yeah. If somebody be rude, be rude to them just don't, ignore them and that.

AYESHA: Yeah, go play with your other friends.

KIRAN: [interrupting] Yeah, I know! [inaudible]

JOANNE: [interrupting] I got an idea.

[Several girls talk at once, all inaudible except Joanne]

JOANNE: What if you ain't got any friends, what if you ain't got any more friends?

NAVNEET: Miss, while you're playing you can make up.

AYESHA: You, you don't know [inaudible]

ZENA: [interrupting] Let Priyanka choose who she wants to play with.

In this extract, Zena again prioritised freedom over other considerations by suggesting that Priyanka, the desired protagonist, should choose who she wants to play with. Maria and Ayesha also prioritised Priyanka's freedom by suggesting that she should choose neither girl but should play with her 'other friends' instead. Then Joanne highlighted a problem with this solution: 'What if you ain't got any more friends?' To consider this question, let us turn to Erickah's experiences.

5.2.4 Erickah: Loyalty and loneliness

Children with contingency friends have a safety net, protecting them from aloneness on the playground if their usual friends are unavailable. Corsaro (1985) argues that the avoidance of being alone is a powerful force motivating American nursery school children to develop stable relations with several playmates.

Being alone on the playground is a perennial fear among school children, and understandably so. Playgrounds are open places full of people, a setting in which being alone has many negative connotations, including the knowledge that one has no friends and the very public nature of the aloneness, reminiscent of the vulnerability many adults feel when going to the cinema, restaurant or pub alone. American children as young as 5 and 6 years old define the term 'lonely' in a similar way to adults, referring to sadness, boredom, 'feeling left out' and feeling 'like no one likes you' (Asher et al. 1990, p. 255). Children feel vulnerable when alone at school (Davies 1982; Griffiths 1995), and there is evidence that friendless and isolated children are particularly liable to be bullied (Blatchford 1993). At Woodwell Green too, children were concerned about aloneness. When I interviewed children about the exclusivity scenario, 46 per cent of them spoke about one or more of the protagonists being alone, lonely or having no one to play with, often suggesting these as motivations for Katie's and Jasmine's attempts to secure exclusivity with Sani.

Erickah was among those children at Woodwell Green who did not have the luxury of a contingency friend. She was unpopular, named in questionnaires at the end of year 4 by only one classmate as a friend (Maria). She was very quiet, shy and serious looking when she joined the school, which some children interpreted as superiority or unfriendliness, and we saw above that, according to Zena at least, she was not competent at the playful aggression so valued by children at Woodwell Green. Zena and Navneet both told me that they disliked her. When I interviewed her about her friendships in year 4, Erickah told me that Navneet shouted insults at her and Zena told others not to be her friend.

Erickah did have a strong friendship with Maria. The two named each other as a friend in both the interviews during year 4 and the questionnaire at the end of year 4. By the time I distributed the questionnaires in year 5, Erickah had left the school (her family moved to a different part of the UK), but in an expression of loyalty, Maria still wrote her name down and told me that they were emailing and phoning each other.

For unpopular Erickah, loyalty from Maria was the one thing that stood between her and isolation on the playground. This placed a lot of pressure on their friendship and may have led Erickah to value loyalty more than any of the other three. Yet that same loyalty threatened to stifle them, limiting their opportunities to interact with other classmates and to develop a broader range of friendships. In addition, Erickah's lack of contingency friends may have rendered her overly eager to please Maria, allowing Maria to take her friendship for granted. When I asked Erickah why she liked Maria, she explained, 'She's um, nice friend, and she, when she says she not your friend, she come back and say sorry and be your friend again. She's friendly'. Her reply hints at a situation in which Erickah had no option but to allow Maria to come and go, since she had no contingency friend to fall back on. Like any child at the periphery of a friendship group, she was vulnerable (Svahn and Evaldsson 2011).

Consequently, Erickah was sometimes alone. This seemed to result from two different sets of circumstances. For one thing, she was often excluded from girls' playground football games, in which Maria was normally included (see Chapter 4). For another, Maria continued to make herself available to her former best friend, Zena. As we have seen, when Zena wanted to play with Maria, Erickah was shunted out and left to walk around the playground alone. Without contingency friends, Erickah was vulnerable to Maria's ongoing loyalty to Zena. No wonder that when I interviewed her about the possessiveness scenario, she blamed Jasmine, the protagonist whose position was most similar to Zena's, explaining, 'Katie is sad because she took away um, the friend, so this one [Jasmine] has done wrong'. However, Erickah claimed not to have had a similar experience herself, either for this scenario or the following one, which involved exclusion from a group, so she may have understood her situation differently from how I have presented it here.

5.2.5   Multiple values: Reconciling loyalty with freedom and status

This case study has shown that girls encounter the value of loyalty not in isolation but in the context of at least two other values, freedom and status. We have seen that freedom, or independence, which was the value promoted by some school staff, was in tension with loyalty. So girls like Zena, who placed a high value on freedom, were likely to prioritise this over loyalty. In contrast, girls who did not value freedom as highly (typically because, like Erickah, they did not have a choice of friends to which to apply their freedom) were more likely to prioritise loyalty. Indeed, a girl without contingency friends is liable to find freedom threatening in that if her friend chooses freedom over loyalty, she will be left alone. So a girl's popularity had a bearing on her commitment to loyalty via its implications for her orientation towards freedom.[7]

The extent to which girls valued loyalty was also related to their status, and that of their best friend. I noted earlier that girls often demonstrate status through their relationships with one another, such that a girl can move up the hierarchy by developing friendships with higher-status peers. This seemed to be what Zena was doing, as she expanded her friendship network and cultivated friendships with high-status peers like Simran and Anjali. Friendships with lower-status girls like Maria did not aid her status; if anything, they decreased it. Therefore for Zena, loyalty (to Maria) and status were in tension with one another. This tension has been noted among the white working- and middle-class British secondary school girls studied by Hey (1997).

However, it is also possible for concerns with status and loyalty to support one another, when the loyalty is directed towards a higher-status peer. Thus, if Maria were concerned to improve her standing in the peer group, this would add to her commitment to Zena rather than detract from it. In other words, concerns with hierarchy can either promote or undermine loyalty concerns, depending on the relative positions in the hierarchy of the girls involved.

Girls will not necessarily consistently value loyalty or independence. A girl might forsake loyalty to a current best friend in order to solicit a best friendship with another, higher-status peer (see Hey 1997 for an example). Alternatively, girls may 'over-commit' themselves, seeking loyal relationships with more than one girl at a time. This seems to be the case with Maria, who was loyal towards her current best friend, Erickah, and her former best friend, Zena. Zena's account suggests that when these came into conflict, Maria prioritised her loyalty towards the more popular Zena, by allowing her to interrupt her play with, and exclude, Erickah (perhaps because Maria was motivated to improve her own status through her friendship with Zena).

Girls may also be inconsistent in the loyalty they demand from their friend, and the loyalty they are willing to show their friend in return. In other words, children may prioritise loyalty when it comes to their friend's obligations to them, but prioritise independence when it comes to their obligations to their friend. Children are likely to exert pressure on each other to equalise these (Davies 1982), but if these pressures fail, then the friendship is unbalanced, which is likely to lead to jealousy and possessiveness. My analysis suggests that such a situation is likely to occur if the members of a best friendship differ substantially in popularity and/or aspirations regarding status.

Loyalty obligations need not lead to the exact formation we have seen here, involving four core children. The form it takes will depend on the number of children connected by loyalty demands, and the willingness of each child to fulfil them. For example, another possible formation was the unstable threesome, where two children compete for the loyalty of the third, desired child. I saw this dynamic quite often (see, for example, Joshua's and Sarah's struggle over Joanne, described in Chapter 4), and it is also documented by other researchers (Davies 1982; Hey 1997).

In summary, the extent to which a girl values loyalty (as availability) in a specific friendship is (partly) dependent on her popularity (which affects how much she values freedom and independence), on her status relative to her friend, and on the extent to which she wants to improve or maintain her status. Tensions may arise when best friends differ in how much they value these various concerns and, thus, the extent to which each is willing to meet the obligations the other makes of them. Best friendships, then, will generally be more stable and less fraught when they are between children of similar popularity and with similar aspirations regarding status.

5.3 Loyalty through Sharing Enemies

Another form of loyalty that was important to children (especially girls) at Woodwell Green was the obligation to share the enemies of one's friend. For example, during an interview in year 4, Zena told me about an argument she had had the previous day with her classmate Anjali, 'And we still didn't make up, even today!' I asked her if she thought they would make friends soon. 'Never,' she replied. 'Anyway we never made up when I came to this school.' 'What, you weren't friends before this anyway?' I asked. She confirmed this, explaining that when she started at the school, 'I couldn't be friends with her. She wasn't friends with Maria and Maria was my best friend at the time'. Similar expectations of loyalty have been described among white working-class teenage girls in northern England and girls of varying ethnicities at a Swedish elementary school (Evaldsson 2007; Griffiths 1995).

The obligation to share enemies usually faded into the background during peaceful periods but appeared forcefully as soon as two girls fell out with each other, especially when those girls were popular and/or influential, like Harpreet and Anjali.

5.3.1 *'She'll say if you talk with Anjali I won't be your friend': Taking sides*

I met Harpreet (Indian Sikh) and Anjali ('other ethnic group', Christian) at the start of year 4, when both were 8 years old. Harpreet was a very popular girl, named by 13 of her classmates in interviews during year 4 as someone they liked, and named as a friend by nine and seven classmates at the end of year 4 and partway through year 5 respectively. The equivalent figures for Anjali were three, one and two respectively. Both girls were dominant and influential in the peer group, although in different ways. As we saw in Chapter 2, Anjali was an assertive, aggressive girl, receiving the most nominations in her class in year 5 for the question, 'Which girls in your class get into arguments or fights the most?' Harpreet was more sensitive (see Chapter 2), but nevertheless a leader among the girls in the class, often organising games and inviting peers to join in, offering to care for upset, lonely or sick children, and with a reputation among her friends for being bossy.

Harpreet was part of a large, loose-knit group of mostly girls. Anjali spent most of her time in the playground with Louise (Indian Christian), Amrita (Indian Sikh) and sometimes Farah (Pakistani Muslim). However, quite often these two groups joined and intermingled, and Anjali was particularly friendly with the two most popular girls in the large group, Harpreet and Simran. Occasionally, Harpreet and Anjali could be found as a twosome. For example, they made up a dance together for their class's Christmas show, and refused to let another classmate join in. Occasionally they argued, and when that happened, each girl expected her friends to demonstrate loyalty by 'breaking up' with the other, leading to the polarisation of this normally fluid group of girls into two gangs. Here is an example, which occurred one lunchtime when the girls were in year 5:

I walk into the playground and Zena and Navneet run up and hug me. They are breathless and excited. 'Guess what just happened!' Zena exclaims. 'What?' I ask. 'Anjali and Harpreet just had a cat fight!' They tell me that Anjali stabbed Harpreet's hand with a pencil in class, so Harpreet did the same back, got told off by their teacher and cried. Out in the playground the girls apparently fought and swore at each other's parents. Now the fight is over and Harpreet is standing in a corner of the playground with Simran. Zena, Navneet and I go over but she won't talk to us and wants to find Mr Gardner, the head teacher, to tell him about the incident. Zena says dramatically to Navneet, me and a couple of others, 'Yesterday was there any fights? Was there swearing or punch-ups? No, and Anjali wasn't here yesterday!' She makes a gesture of mock despair and smiles.

We go to the canteen and, while lining up outside, someone tells Kiran what's happened and she begins to tell me excitedly, until someone else tells her I already know. In the canteen, Anjali, Louise and Amrita sit together, and at the next table sit Simran, Zena, Navneet, Farah, Sarina, Joanne and Kiran. A place has been saved for Harpreet on this table, and she comes and sits down, but almost immediately gets up again and moves to another table further away from Anjali. All the others get up and follow, except Kiran, who asks me to sit with her. After I sit down with Kiran,

Navneet comes over from the other table and asks me if I would come and join them. I tell her I'm already sitting with Kiran, so Navneet asks Kiran if she would come over too. She agrees readily. As Kiran and I get up to move to the other table, Anjali beckons me over, and I tell Kiran and Navneet I will be over in a minute and go to talk to her.

Anjali tells me that poking Harpreet with the pencil was an accident and she didn't even think the pencil hit Harpreet. She says that she is worried that she will get in trouble and I try to reassure her. While Anjali and I are talking, Farah comes over from the other table, stands between Anjali and me so that her bag prevents us from being able to see each other, and asks me to come and sit with them. When I have finished talking to Anjali, I do so.

When they have finished eating, the girls leave in small groups until only Zena, Navneet and a couple of others remain. The canteen is almost empty and as I help canteen staff to stack chairs, Zena and Navneet hover around me. 'Don't blame me if I'm still a little bit Anjali's friend,' Zena says, and Navneet agrees. 'That's okay, I'm not blaming anyone,' I say. Then Zena says something about Harpreet not being her friend that I don't hear properly. 'Did Harpreet say she won't be your friend if you're friends with Anjali?' I ask. 'No but she will,' Zena replies. 'She'll say if you talk with Anjali I won't be your friend.'

Zena and Navneet leave the canteen slightly ahead of me, and I watch them approach Anjali, Amrita and Louise, who are hanging about nearby. I walk up to them, and Zena and Navneet leave together just as I arrive. Anjali looks pleased. 'At least I've got two of my friends back!' she says. We walk over to the playground. Harpreet is playing a game called Red Letter with Simran, Sarina and several other children. After a while Anjali, Amrita and Louise approach and sit on a bench very nearby. A few minutes later, the whistle goes for the end of lunchtime. As the children begin to make their way to their lines, Sarina comes up to the bench, leans towards Anjali and says, 'Oi Anjali, Simran said she's not your friend!' Simran is standing close by and on hearing this, whirls round to face Sarina and shouts, 'When did I say that? I didn't say that!' Sarina giggles and turns away without saying anything. 'Don't stir Sarina,' I say, then turn to Anjali, saying that it wasn't true. Anjali smiles wanly, saying of Sarina, 'She always does that.' I say that she can trust Simran, and Anjali replies, 'Yeah I know Simran's my friend. She's always on both sides.'

Harpreet's and Anjali's fight triggered a situation in which every girl was expected to demonstrate allegiance to one of the two. Thus, Zena commented of Harpreet, 'She'll say if you talk with Anjali I won't be your friend'. Consequently, girls who were normally friendly with both Harpreet and Anjali (such as Amrita, Louise, Zena and Farah) chose their side and terminated their friendship with the other. Sometimes this termination of friendship had a ripple effect, such that friends of Harpreet ended their friendships with friends of Anjali (this happened with Zena and Farah in another similar dispute, in which Zena took Harpreet's side, and Farah took Anjali's).

Allegiance was demonstrated primarily by the physical location of the girls, as we saw with Harpreet's desire to sit as far as possible away from Anjali, and with Zena's and Navneet's decision to discreetly make friends with Anjali out of Harpreet's sight. Location was probably important because physical proximity enables communication – for example, Anjali telling me that she did not stab Harpreet with a pencil, and Farah attempting to prevent our conversation with the physical obstacle of her bag.

The result was two gangs. In this particular incident, Harpreet's gang was much larger than Anjali's. On another occasion, they were more evenly distributed, with Harpreet, Zena, Navneet and Erickah in one group, and Anjali, Amrita, Louise, Simran and Farah in the other. The numerical size of the two geographically separated groups was a clear symbol of the relative popularity and strength of the warring girls.

No wonder, then, that in these situations dominant girls worked hard to manoeuvre more submissive peers into their gang and away from the opponent. In the extract above, Navneet and Farah even attempted to get me into Harpreet's gang, a move I resisted by talking with Anjali. As an adult, I was relatively protected from censure for doing this, but it was much more difficult for the girls to remain 'on both sides'. In the argument described above, only Simran succeeded in doing so, reacting to Sarina's allegation swiftly and angrily with 'When did I say that?' Simran, a popular, assertive girl (see Chapter 2 for examples of her assertiveness), was the only girl I witnessed directly resisting the pressure placed on her to commit to one side in situations like this. It was much more common for girls to allow themselves to be manipulated.

5.3.2 'Sarina wanted to talk to me but Anjali kept saying no': Submission and possession

Most examples of loyalty through shared enemies I witnessed involved a hierarchical relationship between dominant and submissive children. When dominant children like Anjali and Harpreet argued, their submissive peers were expected to take a side, whereas the converse was not necessarily the case (i.e. if two more submissive children argued, the rest of the peer group would not necessarily feel obliged to demonstrate their allegiances). The obligation from submissive to dominant children was so strong that even without doing anything at all, submissive children found themselves involved and assigned to one or other of the gangs. Of course, some children willingly took a side. For example, Sarina usually sided with Harpreet. This was not surprising because Sarina and Anjali had a longstanding dislike of each other. However, the quieter, more submissive girls did not actively choose a side but allowed themselves to be manoeuvred into one by more dominant peers.

In individual interviews, some of the quieter girls referred to this phenomenon. For example, when I asked Louise what she did when her friends argued with each other, she replied, 'I just stay out of it'. But when I asked if they tried to get her to 'take sides', she agreed, with a smile of recognition, recalling a recent example: 'Cos Sarina wanted to talk to me but Anjali kept saying no.' Similarly, Louise's classmate Ayesha said of a recent dispute between Anjali and Sarina, 'Miss you know what? Me and Amrita don't say anything, it's Anjali and Farah'. She said of herself, Amrita and Louise, 'We don't usually say anything, we just follow them'. I asked her why she didn't go away and leave them to it, but she said this was because she wouldn't have any other friends to play with.

The passive approach of girls like Ayesha and Louise allowed more dominant girls to possess and manipulate them. This was evident in Harpreet's account of another dispute between herself and Anjali. During an interview with Harpreet in year 4 about her friendships, I asked her 'What about Anjali, what do you think of her?' 'Well, she's very annoying,' Harpreet replied. When I asked her why, she proceeded to give me a lesson on possession and power:

'Well, because Miss you have to listen to me cos I'm the teacher.' As Harpreet says this she finds a board pen and positions herself in front of the whiteboard. I'm sitting at the desk nearby taking notes, in a bizarre reversal of roles. Harpreet complains that Anjali always has to be boss of everything. She begins, 'I was playing with Louise, Simran and Navneet, what happened was' and breaks off to draw two small circles next to each other [which, she explains, represent herself and Simran], and a short distance away, two more circles, also next to each other [representing Louise and Navneet].

Harpreet tells me that Anjali 'pushes away' her and Simran, and as for Louise and Navneet, she 'pulls them to her'. As she explains she adds two sweeping lines, one starting at Simran and herself, and the other starting at Louise and Navneet. 'Do they let themselves be pushed and pulled?' I ask, carefully copying her diagram. 'Well Miss there's a gang,' Harpreet explains. 'Used to be Ayesha, Amrita, Navneet and Louise, but now she's [Anjali] losing some people because Ayesha is out of the gang.' I ask why. 'Because she doesn't like Anjali because Anjali bosses her around. Louise is out of the gang. Amrita used to be out of the gang but she came back into the gang.

'Now about that pushing problem,' she continues, rubbing out her first diagram. She draws a second, with four equidistant circles in a horizontal line (representing herself, Simran, Louise and Navneet), and a scribble to the left of them, representing Anjali. She draws a curved line from Anjali to Louise and Navneet, another line leading from Navneet away from the circles, and an arrow above Louise and Navneet pointing to the right. This represents Anjali approaching and 'taking away' Louise and Navneet from Harpreet and Simran.

'Does Anjali actually *pull* them, or does she *act* like she's pulling them?' I ask. By way of explanation, Harpreet draws below this diagram, two dots, arranged vertically, which she labels as Navneet and Louise. Then she draws two huge arms, with their hands touching the two dots. 'Do you like my arms?' she grins. 'Navneet nearly fell over Louise but she doesn't care.'

'About the pushing stuff again,' she announces in an authoritative tone, cleaning the board. 'She does it in the playground.' Harpreet redraws her second diagram again (minus the arrow), and writes 'in the playground' alongside it.

The dispute Harpreet described here culminated in two gangs, one led by Anjali, the other by Harpreet, with Harpreet's 'Bubblegum Club' writing a letter to Anjali on a small whiteboard during wet play, which read: 'Anjali, We hate you. You are a stupid fool. We have copied your dance and we have already told Mr Gardner [head teacher] on you. Hatred from the Bubblegum Club.'[8] Anjali took the whiteboard to Mr Gardner and Harpreet and her gang got into trouble. The following day the girls wrote 'a sorry letter' to Anjali, and most of them made friends soon after.

This intriguing lesson reveals how dominant girls like Anjali and Harpreet sought to possess other girls during disputes, and also how this process of possessing was very physical, with girls pushing and pulling each other from one gang to another (hence Harpreet's drawing of arms). The result of these physical processes of possession was that submissive girls unwillingly found themselves in one gang and not the other. By handing over their agency and responsibility for who they affiliated with, they became pawns to be possessed by their more dominant peers.

Even though they did not take direct responsibility for their affiliations, they were sometimes still held accountable for these by others. When telling me about a dispute that Anjali and Farah were having with Sarina, Ayesha commented, 'You know Farah and Anjali, they keep telling Sarina that they're her worst enemy. She thinks that it's us [Ayesha, Louise and Amrita] too'. So according to Ayesha, Sarina assumed that quieter girls shared the views of their more dominant, vocal friends.

At other times, they were seen as unwilling members (and might therefore also be seen as less culpable). For example, in another interview, Harpreet told me about a dispute between Anjali and Sarina, and how she and Sarina devised various strategies to gain the advantage. One of these strategies was, 'We were trying to get Louise out of their gang, trying to bring her here', so that Louise could tell them what Anjali and her gang had been saying. Here, Harpreet seemed to see Louise not as a committed member of Anjali's group but as a pawn who could be a useful resource on Sarina's side.

Why did girls like Louise and Ayesha allow themselves to be manipulated by their more dominant peers? There are several possible reasons. They may have enjoyed being fought over and desired. They may have felt, as Ayesha did, that they did not have any one else to play with. However, this does not explain why Ayesha and the other girls not involved (such as Louise) did not go away together. The quieter girls seemed to feel unable to leave their group leader, in this case, Anjali, even when this drew them into a dispute.

The submissive girls' behaviour makes more sense when we bear in mind that these girls demonstrated loyalty through shared enemies. Simran's experiences are instructive. I noted earlier that she was the most successful at remaining friends with both Harpreet and Anjali during their disputes. However, she worked hard to achieve this. She boldly countered Sarina's attempt to alienate her from Anjali, and she also experienced problems when she tried to leave the 'Bubblegum Club'. According to Simran, she was not involved in the letter to Anjali, and when she found out about it, she told Harpreet that she wanted to leave the gang. She told me that Harpreet was annoyed, saying, 'Fine then, go away'. 'Because she thinks you don't want to be her friend anymore?' I asked, and Simran agreed.

Simran's wish not to take sides was challenged, I suggest, because it defied girls' widely accepted understanding of loyalty, according to which friendship is demonstrated by sharing enemies. If we accept this definition of loyalty, then we must see Simran's refusal to take sides as jeopardising her very friendship with Harpreet. It may be that some submissive girls allow themselves to be possessed by one side because they accept this definition of loyalty and are afraid of losing their friendship with a dominant peer. This is the explanation suggested by Griffiths (1995) for why girls took the side of their group leader during a dispute that did not involve them. Alternatively, they may simply feel unable to carry out the bold, assertive behaviours that Simran required in order to maintain her independence.

The only alternative open to girls who wanted to remain on both sides but disliked direct confrontation was to pursue friendship with their friend's enemy in secret, a strategy pursued by several girls. For example, Sarina told me that she and Louise were 'secret friends', 'Cos she, she doesn't want Anjali and that to know'. According to Zena, even bold Simran employed this tactic sometimes. She wrote the following story, entitled 'Play ground fight', which she later told me was true at the time:

> When its play time at school me Simran and Harpreet always play football. like most of the kids but sometimes Simran goes off to Anjali. So Harpreet doesn't really like it you see Harpreet isn't really Anjali's friend so she gets quite angry. One day when Simran was playing with Anjali Harpreet got fed up because she thought Anjali was taking Simran away. So Harpreet said to Anjali 'Anjali I'm quite fed up with you trying to take Simran away! So why cant we be friends.' 'Yes Anjali why cant you be friends with Harpreet because you wont have any friends left.' I said. 'Oh shut up I will have friends and I'm never going to be Harpreets friend the only time I'm going to be Harpreets friend is over my dead body. Even ask Simran she doesn't want to be your friend isn't that right Simran!' said Anjali in a loud and annoying voice. 'Ya I'm not your friend Harpreet I think,' said Simran in a confused voice. Next morning Simran went to Harpreet and asked her. If she can be her friend. Harpreet said yes but secretly Simran some times plays with Anjali. But with out Harpreet knowing. Till today the secret playing with Anjali goes on. The End.

Maintaining secret friendships was a short-term measure for coping with friends who were enemies. This might work quite well for friends of Harpreet and Anjali, whose disputes tended to be short-lived. For most girls, loyalty as sharing an enemy arose sporadically, when dominant girls argued. But for some girls at Woodwell Green, this aspect of loyalty became a defining feature of particular relationships. In other words, some friendships seemed to be *predicated* on sharing an enemy.

5.3.3   Toxic loyalty: Friendship through sharing enemies

The assumption that being 'with' one person meant being 'against' another seemed to underlie some of the most unstable friendships I observed at Woodwell Green. I saw several instances where triads of girls were almost constantly divided, two against one, with the members of each side endlessly changing. It was very rare in such triads for all three girls to be friends at the same time, suggesting that their friendships relied on alienation of the third.

Anjali, Farah and Sarina were caught in this dynamic. I documented six changes in their affiliations during one week in year 4:

Tuesday morning, classroom: Anjali and Sarina approach me together, Anjali complaining that Farah is 'stirring up trouble' between herself and Sarina.

Tuesday lunchtime, playground: Farah tells me that previously, she and Anjali were friends and Sarina was not, but today, Sarina said to her, 'Anjali isn't your friend anymore and I'm not either.'

Wednesday lunchtime, playground: Sarina, upset, tells me, 'I fell out with Anjali and now she, Amrita, Louise, all that lot keep coming up to me.' When Harpreet, Sarina and I approach Anjali's group [which includes Farah] to challenge them, Farah retorts that Sarina kept approaching them, shouting insults, and running off.

Thursday morning, computer room: While lining up to leave the room, Sarina moves from near the front of the line to stand next to Anjali. Back in class, Farah and Sarina share a worksheet, and Farah turns to me and whispers, smiling, 'We're friends now!' pointing from herself to Sarina and back again. 'That's good!' I whisper back. Later in the lesson she whispers to me, 'We're all friends, even Anjali!' I ask her when it happened and she says in the computer room.

Thursday lunchtime, playground: Anjali and Farah play with a few other girls [but not Sarina]. When the whistle goes [for their year group to go to the canteen], Farah tells me in an injured tone that Anjali said she wasn't Farah's friend. We discuss what Farah should do, and Farah adds hopefully, 'Maybe she was only joking.'

Thursday hometime, corridor: Sarina shows me two bracelets that Anjali has just given her. Farah, lingering nearby and sounding hurt, says they are from a jewellery-making set she recently gave Anjali.

Monday playtime, playground: Sarina is off sick. I see Farah chatting with Anjali and Amrita.

Monday lunchtime, playground: Farah informs me, 'We're not friends with Anjali.' I ask why not and she says Anjali is telling everyone that Sohaib [a boy in their class] and Sarina 'had S-E-X'. 'I feel sorry for Sarina,' she adds.

In this short space of time, we see alliances between Anjali and Sarina, Anjali and Farah, and Farah and Sarina, plus a brief interlude when all three were (according to Farah) friends together. This dynamic extended both before and after the one-week window I have provided here and was summed up nicely by Farah in an interview, when I asked her whom she argued with most often. She named Sarina, explaining, 'If Anjali's not my friend and I'm not Anjali's friend, Sarina come up and says, I'm not your friend because you're not Anjali's friend'.

Are the friendly relationships that children forge in unstable triads like this really friendships? That, of course, depends on how the children concerned define friendship. When she was in year 6, I told Anjali about my analysis of the data above, which, at the time, I saw as evidence that she was sometimes friends with Sarina. She disagreed strongly with this claim, saying, 'I was never friends with Sarina. I don't know why you wrote that, I was never friends with Sarina'. Anjali's and Sarina's relationship with each other was notoriously fraught, and so it makes sense that Anjali did not see occasional periods of friendliness as signs of friendship *per se*. In interviews during year 4 and questionnaires at the end of year 4 and during year 5, Anjali never named Sarina as a friend. Similarly, Sarina never named Anjali, so it is likely that she did not interpret these moments of friendliness as signs of friendship either. However, Farah's experience was a little different. In her year 4 interview, she named both Anjali and Sarina as friends, although neither named her. In questionnaires at the end of year 4, she named neither girl (and neither named her), but during year 5, she and Sarina both named each other. These data suggest that for some girls in unstable triads, friendliness constitutes actual friendship. Note, though, that such friendships are fragile and fluctuating.

We might ask why children enter and engage in such an unstable dynamic, which was clearly upsetting for the alienated one (evident in Farah's distress when Anjali used a gift from her to make a gift for Sarina). But it was also a source of excitement and intrigue, and every time a girl reforged a friendship and pushed another into the 'enemy' position, she got affirmation. Similar dynamics have been observed elsewhere too. Goodwin (2002) describes how elementary school girls in California marked the boundaries of their friendship groups by forming alliances against others, and Hey (1997) argues that being 'with' one girl and 'against' another is a key aspect of girls' friendships. At Woodwell Green, however, this dynamic seemed to be more important to some girls than others. Some children (like Ayesha and Louise) only had an occasional need to demonstrate loyalty through shared enemies. For other children, this type of loyalty seemed so central to their idea of friendship (or at least, their relationships with some peers) that it was an almost constant preoccupation.

5.4 What About Boys' Loyalty?

The head teacher of Woodwell Green told me that possessive behaviours were more common among girls than boys. He confessed that he sometimes struggled to understand girls' disputes and occasionally asked the (female) deputy head to clarify and intervene. My fieldnotes include many more instances of possessiveness among girls than boys, and when asked if they had had an experience similar to the possessiveness scenario (in which two children competed over the possession of a third child), 65 per cent of the girls answered in the affirmative, compared with only 29 per cent of the boys. Other researchers have found that what they term 'relational aggression' (of which possessiveness is an example) is more common among girls than boys (Blatchford 1998; Crick and Rose 2000).

It is not that loyalty was unimportant to boys. Rather, it generally took different forms that seemed less prone to lead to possessiveness. Take loyalty as availability. Most boys at Woodwell Green played football regularly in fairly stable groups in the playground. Since friends were likely to be playing the same game of football together, expectations of availability were less of an issue, and because football is a group game, expectations of exclusivity inappropriate. Most girls, on the other hand, did not engage in such regular activities. Their groupings and locations were more varied, making the issue of exactly who plays with whom more significant, and making fear of loneliness a perennial concern.

Loyalty as sharing enemies was also important for boys. But because boys expressed hostility through physical aggression more often than girls, this form of loyalty often translated as willingness to enter a fight on the side of one's friend. For example, in an interview about his friendships, Farhan named his classmate Amar as a friend. One of his reasons was, 'On the field, if someone pushes me over, Amar goes up and kicks them'. He proceeded to recount several examples of Amar joining fights on his behalf. Similarly, Zak said of a couple of his friends, 'He sticks up for me, and I stick up for him'. This 'sticking up' involved a range of behaviours for Zak, including not telling a teacher if he broke school rules. But it could also involve supporting him in a fight.[9]

Sharing a friend's enemy during a physical fight made possessive behaviours unlikely, because it would be physically difficult for a boy involved in a fight to force friends to join in. In addition, in order to demonstrate toughness and status, a boy needs to show he can stand up for himself (see Chapter 3). Encouraging friends to join in a fight on one's behalf may undermine a boy's show of strength. In contrast, girls in a range of settings have been found to demonstrate status through their relationships (Eder 1985; Goodwin 2002; Hey 1997). It is not surprising, then, that during a dispute girls are eager to get as many peers as possible 'on their side'.

This does not mean that boys *never* experienced loyalty in the form typical of girls. For example, we saw in Chapter 4 how Joshua struggled to secure an exclusive friendship with Joanne. In addition, year 4 boy

137

Idris told me in an interview about a classic case of loyalty through shared enemies involving himself and two other boys, Sam and Ali. He was telling me about an argument he had had with Sam a few days before. 'But Ali, I don't know why he's had a fight with me, just because he wants to stick up with Sam. But if I make up with Sam, I dunno I might, he's [Ali] gonna be sad like I am now, cos he's with Sam now, and then I'll be with Sam,' he mused. I asked Idris if it was true to say that if he was Sam's friend, then Ali would not be Sam's friend anymore, and Idris agreed. A few months later, when he was in year 5, he brought up a similar issue in response to the hypothetical possessiveness scenario.

RW: Have you ever been in a situation like this?

IDRIS: I think, I don't know, I think I been in this situation before.

RW: What happened?

IDRIS: Like Miss me yeah, I was like Katie, I don't know why I said this but I said if you go with her, then I won't be your friend. But everyone does this Miss, they just say I'm not your friend for this day and then they make friends again.

RW: Was it a boy or a girl?

IDRIS: A boy.

RW: Why did you say I'm not your friend?

IDRIS: Because Miss that might make you feel to go back to me, and not go to the other boy.

RW: And what happened?

IDRIS: I think Miss we just left each other for some days or till lunchtime, and then we just came back together.

Idris's experiences suggest that there is overlap between the forms of loyalty that girls and boys expect of their friends. Nevertheless, the kinds of loyalty that led to possessive behaviours did seem to be more common among girls than among boys. So it is with a focus on girls that I turn to consider the implications of loyalty for schools.

5.5   Implications for Schools

Adults at Woodwell Green viewed girls' possessive behaviours as a problem and countered them with the principle of freedom, encouraging children to associate freely with whomever they wished on the playground, a principle promoted in other UK schools too (Hey 1997). From the school's point of view, independence and freedom are laudable values for the playground, and possessiveness is purely negative. Adults at school may well have valued loyalty, at least in some forms, but I rarely heard them talking about it with children, suggesting that it was a relatively silenced value.

Yet we have seen in this chapter that many girls (and some boys) strongly valued loyalty, a selective, enduring allegiance to particular peers, in the form of availability and/or sharing enemies. Loyalty has been shown to be important to working- and middle-class girls in various countries (Amit-Talai 1995; Davies 1982; Griffiths 1995; Hey 1997; Wulff 1995). While some valued it more highly than others, almost all the girls I studied acknowledged to some extent loyalty obligations they held towards their friends. These obligations often led to possessive behaviours. In the case of best friendship, a child whose best friend refused to fulfil the obligation of availability might issue ultimatums, threaten to withdraw friendship, become upset and/or withdraw from her. If one accepts the obligation of availability, then these 'possessive' behaviours can be seen as reasonable acts designed to encourage the best friend to fulfil her obligation. In the case of sharing a friend's enemy, possessive behaviours might be seen as reasonable measures to ensure that friends demonstrate loyalty appropriately, with the additional benefit of strengthening one's own side and weakening the other, and demonstrating status through popularity.

In other words, the meaning of possessive behaviour shifts dramatically depending on one's priorities. If one prioritises independence and freedom, then possessiveness and, to some extent, loyalty itself, look negative. If, however, one prioritises loyalty, then independence and freedom represent betrayal, irresponsibility and selfishness.

Not only do adults and children tend to differ in their priorities, but individual children do too, with some much more invested in loyalty than others, who are more preoccupied with independence and/or status. These differences made it much harder for some children than for others to conform to the school's 'freedom of association' position. By promoting freedom on the playground, teachers inadvertently support popular children who enjoy independence and high status, and undermine unpopular children who, lacking contingency friends and choice, are more likely to value loyalty.

Things were complicated still further for children by adults' concerns about exclusion, which led them to encourage children to play altogether, indiscriminately (see Chapter 4). This value, of inclusion, is in tension with both the values of independence and loyalty. Loyalty, as a selective association with *some* other children, sits between the two adult values of independence and inclusion, pleasing neither.

What can adults in schools take from this analysis? They must begin by acknowledging the importance of loyalty to children, and recognising that it is in tension with the value of freedom promoted by teachers. They might also consider different responses to loyalty demands and possessiveness depending on which type of loyalty these emerge from – loyalty as availability, or as shared enemies. I discuss these in turn below.

5.5.1   Loyalty as availability

The loyalty that best friends show each other is, in many circles, seen as a desirable thing (a key component of social competence in middle childhood according to education researchers Pellegrini and Blatchford 2000, p. 17). While it can clearly cause distress, especially in cases of imbalance between best friends, it may also have a positive side, with availability constituting a form of care and commitment. If so, then perhaps schools should accept this form of loyalty as a legitimate value for children. This means adjusting the ideals of playground association that adults at school promote to children, since neither 'freedom' nor 'inclusion' acknowledge loyalty.

If we accept children's expectations of loyalty as availability, then we probably also have to accept some possessive behaviours as unavoidable. Nevertheless, schools might take steps to reduce them. In other words, it seems possible to accept the inevitability and positive aspects of loyalty as availability whilst still working to curtail its more negative aspects. One focus could be on the place of loyalty to protect unpopular children from loneliness on the playground. Fears of loneliness may motivate some children to demand that their friend be available to them. The idea of providing resources for children who are alone in the playground (e.g. an adult-supervised structured play area, buddy bench) is not new, but my analysis suggests it could help unpopular children like Erickah to cope with failed loyalty demands. The difficulty with such schemes is to avoid them becoming stigmatised.

Children might also benefit from class exercises or discussions of relevant literature[10] that increase their awareness and understanding of their own expectations of loyalty, and how these are mediated by freedom, choice, popularity and status. This might help best friends to better understand their own and their friend's behaviour, and perhaps to find more creative solutions to tensions between best friends of differing popularity levels. Such exercises might also help them to cope with possessiveness, insecurity and jealousy when they arise. In addition, by helping children recognise how ubiquitous these issues are, such exercises might help to destigmatise ventures designed to support children having problems with loyalty, such as buddy benches.

Loyalty as availability was, on the whole, less of an issue among boys who played in large, stable groups (as in football). On average, on school playgrounds, girls form smaller groups (Benenson 1994; Hartup 1983) and spend more time 'hanging out' and talking (Boulton 1992) than boys. If girls spent more time in large, stable games, then provided both members of a best friendship participated in the same game, availability claims would be less relevant. For example, if most girls in their class played skipping together every day, then Maria and Navneet might not worry so much about whom Zena is playing with (although loyalty obligations and acts of possession could still occur in other settings, such as the canteen).

Finally, it is possible that Woodwell Green's relatively high turnover of children may have contributed to the prevalence of problems with possession. If group membership of a particular class did not change over the course of several years, children might be more likely to settle into stable friendships than if class membership is constantly changing. Of course, friendships still evolve and shift even among a stable group, but it may be that schools with lower turnovers will not need to focus on possessiveness as much as schools like Woodwell Green.

5.5.2   Loyalty as sharing enemies

Unlike loyalty as availability, this form of loyalty necessarily involves a harmful act of alienation. Therefore schools may want to act more decisively against this type of loyalty.[11] Most crucially, schools could challenge the very need to demonstrate friendship through sharing enemies, and challenge children's assumptions that being *with* one means being *against* another. Children could learn conflict resolution skills that support them in allowing arguments to unfold without any obligation for others to become involved. Additionally, as suggested above for loyalty as availability, girls might be encouraged to play large-group, stable games in which loyalty as shared enemies is harder to enact.

Another area that schools could address is the issue of power and responsibility. We have seen that submissive girls claimed not to be involved in their dominant friends' disputes, yet became so because they allowed themselves to be physically manoeuvred into one group. Once there, and without even saying anything, they could be interpreted as 'for' one girl and 'against' the other. Thus, their failure to take responsibility for what dominant girls did with them had serious repercussions for them, and also tended to allow the dispute to escalate, as more and more children became involved, and girls vied to possess these more submissive girls. This is another form of allowing dominant children to make decisions on their behalf (see Chapter 4). If submissive girls could be empowered to take responsibility for decisions about whom they affiliate with, then many possessive behaviours would no longer be possible.

Notes

1. Half the children heard this version, involving three girls, and the other half, three boys, Adam, Matthew and Hinesh.
2. It is possible that possession sometimes arose from other motivations, but this chapter focuses on cases where loyalty appeared to be a key cause of possessive behaviour.
3. 'Ring a Ring o' Roses' and 'Cat's got the Measles' are songs with actions. 'Had' and 'Stuck in the Mud' are chasing games. 'Red Letter' is a game in which one child calls out letter names and the other children move forward according to the frequency of that letter in their name, with a penalty for children who move when the 'red letter' is called.
4. In interviews during year 4, Navneet, Maria and Zena were named by eight, four and three classmates respectively as someone they liked. Seven classmates (five of whom were girls) were interviewed before or in the same week that Maria joined the school, and this was true of 12 classmates (ten of whom were girls) in the case of Zena. So while Navneet was certainly popular in these interviews, Maria and Zena were actually well liked considering the smaller number of possible nominations available to them. At the end of year 4, and again during year 5, children were asked to name up to four friends in questionnaires. Navneet, Maria and Zena were named by seven, three and six children respectively in year 4, and by two, two and five children respectively in year 5.
5. The distinction Zena makes here recalls the subtle and fine line that Woodwell Green children walked between playful and hurtful aggression, described in Chapter 2.
6. Navneet's comment here supports my argument that her loyalty to Zena may have been partially motivated by her desire for friendship with a relatively high-status, popular peer.
7. By 'freedom', I mean the freedom to affiliate with whomever one wishes. There are, of course, many other domains of life to which the concept of freedom also applies, where popularity is irrelevant. Girls who valued freedom in the domain of playground companions need not necessarily value it in other aspects of life, and vice versa.
8. Spelling mistakes have been corrected for clarity.

9. Interestingly, Zak's friends may not have felt the same compulsion to intervene if Zak's enemy was a friend of theirs. Zak had just told me that he and Mohamed stuck up for each other. I asked what he meant and he explained, 'Like, if I get in a fight, yeah, he helps me and hates the person. But if he likes him, like if it's Faizel, he tries to break it up'.

10. My thanks to the head teacher of Woodwell Green for the suggestion that children's literature could provide a way to address children's loyalty concerns.

11. This is a challenge in itself because loyalty as availability can lead to demands to share enemies if a particular peer is seen as a threat to the best friendship. For example, we saw earlier that, apparently feeling threatened by Zena's blossoming friendship with popular Simran, Navneet gave her an ultimatum: her friendship or Simran's.

6

Racism
A Special Type of Harm?

Woodwell Green was situated in a multicultural area of west London (see Chapter 1 for more information on pupils' ethnicities and religions). Given its diverse composition at a time when migration, multiculturalism and integration were frequently political hot potatoes in the UK, it is not surprising that staff at Woodwell Green were very motivated to encourage good relationships between children of differing ethnic, religious and language groups (and their families). The school employed various measures to encourage children to take pride in their diversity and to discourage expressions of prejudice. Racism was strongly condemned, and diversity celebrated in religious education (RE) lessons, assemblies and posters throughout the school. This chapter explores how this ethos impacted on children's moral experiences in school. I look first at the implications of the school's emphasis on racism as a particularly serious form of harm, and then at various struggles and disputes regarding what counted as racism.

6.1   Prioritising Prejudices: Racism versus Homophobia

6.1.1   'There is simply no room for racism at Woodwell Green'

Racism was treated very seriously by staff at Woodwell Green. There were several anti-racist posters around the school, one of which was

Children's Moral Lives: An Ethnographic and Psychological Approach, First Edition. Ruth Woods.
© 2013 John Wiley & Sons, Ltd. Published 2013 by John Wiley & Sons, Ltd.

often commented on by teachers and children: a poster of four brains, three the same size labelled 'European', 'Asian' and 'African' brains, and a fourth smaller brain labelled 'racist'. Others had pictures of young teenagers of various ethnicities, with text emphasising shared interests across children from different backgrounds. For example, a poster featuring a mixed-race boy read 'He's a lot like you. He's wicked on a skateboard. Doesn't love United. Plays Tomb Raider'.[1] At the top of each poster, produced by the Metropolitan Police, was written in capital letters, 'Make up your own mind about the people you meet. Remember, it's a crime to abuse or attack people because of their race, culture, or ethnic origin'. When these posters arrived at the school, the head teacher, Mr Gardner, devoted an assembly to discussing them with children. On a teacher training day, he distributed typed notes that included the following:

> Another core value of Woodwell Green is anti-racism. It is a value we must defend vigorously on a day-to-day basis. With this in mind, I was disappointed by the number of children who were reported to me for racist remarks last term. Therefore, I am going to make this subject a key theme in assemblies – the message will be strong and uncompromising – there is simply no room for racism at Woodwell Green. I would like all cases of it reported directly to me.

Racism was taken so seriously at Woodwell Green that it was seen to outrank other types of harmful behaviour. For example, at an assembly for children in years 3 to 6 (aged 7 to 11 years), having just finished talking about children being too possessive in their friendships (see Chapter 5), Mr Gardner continued, 'But much more serious even than that', and began to discuss racism, which he told the children was worse than insults like 'four eyes', because it attacked something that was a part of them, and that linked them to their families and communities. The seriousness attached to racism made it difficult for adults to see racist insults as anything other than harmful, creating problems for children who used such insults playfully between friends (see Chapter 2).

Woodwell Green's prioritisation of racism above other types of harm reflects UK government documentation. For example, government department Ofsted (Office for Standards in Education, Children's Services and Skills) wrote, 'Racial harassment is a particularly insidious form of bullying, affecting not only individuals but their families and communities' (Ofsted 1993, p. 16). This echoes the earlier Swann Report produced by the government's Department of Education and Skills in 1985 (cited in Blatchford 1998, p. 111):

> We believe the essential difference between racist name calling and ... other forms of name calling is that whereas the latter may be related only to the individual characteristics of the child, the former is a reference not only to the child but also by extension to their family and indeed more broadly their ethnic community as a whole.

There is some evidence that these attitudes towards racism were shared by children at Woodwell Green. When witnessing someone being accused of racism, they were often hushed, and sometimes one or two would gasp dramatically. In an interview with Zak (Somali Muslim) in year 5, I asked when he would tell a teacher about a problem in the playground. Zak said, 'If it's just a little thing like someone push me then I won't say anything but if it's like someone being racist then I will'. Troyna and Hatcher (1992) found the same attitude at other UK primary schools, quoting, for example, a girl saying, 'It doesn't really bother me about the other sorts of names, it's just the racist ones' (p. 57). Children may hold such views even if they cannot explain why. For example, when Troyna and Hatcher (1992, p. 168) asked a girl why children got into more trouble for saying a name about someone's colour than another sort of name, she replied, 'I don't know really, it's just horrible, like if I call someone "Dickhead" it doesn't really hurt them, but if I call someone a "black bastard", something like that, it would hurt them'.

6.1.2   Homophobia: The silent harm

The attention the school gave to racism contrasted starkly with its silence on homophobia, which was widespread in the playground. As researchers have found in other British schools (Griffiths 1995; Hey 1997; Renold 2002), children at Woodwell Green frequently used the words 'lezzie' (lesbian) and 'gay' as insults to girls and boys respectively. When I interviewed the 30 children of one year 4 class individually about their friendships, five boys told me that they did not like particular classmates because they had called them 'gay'.[2] For example, Faizel complained of his classmate Pavandeep, 'Yeah Miss, I wasn't saying anything to him and he started calling me, you know, the gay word'. Two boys also described how the use of 'gay' as an insult led to arguments or fights between friends.

Boys often used the word 'gay' as a way of undermining or mocking the toughness and masculinity of another boy (see Chapter 3 for more on boys' associations between toughness and masculinity). For example, when explaining why he preferred to play with boys than girls, Paul noted, 'I play with some girls sometimes but mostly boys. Like, Sohaib plays with girls quite a lot and people call him names and I think that's horrible'. I asked him what names Sohaib got called. 'They call him girly and that, they call him gay and that,' Paul replied. Here is another example, from my fieldnotes:

> I am walking from the canteen to the playground, when a year 6 boy stops me and points out two other boys, announcing, 'I'm gonna beat them up.' I ask why. 'Cos they called me *gay*.' He walks along beside me with a pronounced swagger, and continues, 'But soon they won't be calling *me* gay, they'll be calling *themselves* gay when I've finished with them.'

These boys linked heterosexuality with toughness in their perceptions of normal, desirable masculinity. They opposed this with homosexuality, which they associated with femininity, weakness and abnormality, as found in other British primary schools (Epstein and Johnson 1998; Renold 2002).

Children also used 'gay' and 'lezzie' as accusations towards peers who were physically affectionate. For example, year 4 girl Amrita commented to Anjali in my presence, 'Sarina is all lezzie, she keeps hugging us all the time'. She acted out an impression of Sarina hugging, and she and Anjali exclaimed, 'Urgh!' Amrita's accusation worked to distance herself and Anjali from Sarina's behaviour, thus protecting their own heterosexuality (similar moves among white working-class British girls are described by Hey 1997). I only once saw a child not rejecting the label in this context. Anil's friends were teasing him about being gay, in reference to his friendship with Mohamed. 'So, maybe I do love him,' he replied lightly.

Some children saw homosexuality as a reason to dislike someone. On two occasions, when chatting about a TV talent show that was running at the time featuring an openly gay male contestant, different girls told me that they did not like this contestant because he was gay. Finally, children also demonstrated aversion to the word gay in a light-hearted injunction, 'If you touch the door you're gay'. Here is an example from a year 4 class (8 and 9 year olds):

> On the way back to class, the teacher stops Idris and tells him to go back, 'and walk the last part again properly' because he let a door slam shut in the next child's face. Idris's classmates Farah and Mohamed hang back in the corridor to watch, looking amused and ignoring the teacher's instruction to go into the classroom. I watch with them as Idris hangs back at the other side of the closed door, and Farah explains to me, 'If you touch the door

handle it means you're gay.' Eventually Idris emerges through the door, and as we walk to the classroom, he protests to the laughing Mohamed, 'I didn't touch it!' As he says this, he holds up his fist; he has his jumper sleeve pulled over his hand.

The efforts Idris went to to avoid the label 'gay' reflect the negativity which he and others assigned to it. Yet despite the frequent use of the term, in a range of different, almost all pejorative, ways, I never heard a child reporting homophobia to an adult, an adult reprimanding a child for being homophobic, or an adult speaking to children about homophobia. In fact, one teacher mockingly described to me an effeminate boy at the school as gay. Adults' silence allowed homophobia to flourish in a way that would not be possible were there a clear school policy against it. Moreover, their silence may have added to the harm caused by homophobia by implicitly condoning it.

Adults' silence on homophobia is unsurprising when considered in relation to wider societal trends. Homophobia is widespread in most societies, although it has reduced in the West (Hooghe et al. 2010). It remained institutionalised in the UK at the time of the research in the form of Section 28 of the UK Local Government Act (which has since been repealed), which prohibited local authorities from promoting homosexuality (Renold 2002). This legislation made it difficult for teachers to address homophobia in primary schools. Furthermore, given this national context, it seems likely that some adults at the school, as well as children, were homophobic. From their point of view, it is homosexuality that is wrong, not the vilification of homosexuality.

An additional contributor to teachers' silence on homophobia may have been assumptions adults typically make about childhood innocence, making references to sexuality seem inappropriate (Epstein and Johnson 1998; Robinson 2005). This is changing in some countries; for example, the UK government's anti-bullying pack for schools addressed bullying relating to sexuality from the year 2000 (Renold 2002).

It is possible also that Woodwell Green's status as a multicultural school made homophobia particularly difficult to confront. The school worked hard to promote good relations between children (and parents) from different ethnic and religious backgrounds. It used the notion of respect, particularly for religious beliefs and practices, as a way of managing its diversity. Teachers often told children that they might not believe in a particular religion themselves, but they should still respect it. For example, when some year 6 children groaned at the prospect of an RE lesson on Christianity, their teacher reprimanded them, saying, 'You respect everyone's religion, everyone's belief. You may not believe what they believe but you still respect them'. Similarly, when a year 1 child said of a Hindu god, 'I don't believe in that god', Miss Hart told the children, 'You don't have to believe in it yourself, but other people do believe it and you should respect that'.

This injunction not to criticise other religions was enshrined in one of the seven aims in Woodwell Green's policy document concerning what children should learn from religious education lessons: 'To encourage the children to respect and value the rights of people to hold differing beliefs and to cultivate understanding and respect in a religiously diverse society.' This continues to be the approach promoted by the UK government's Department for Children, Schools and Families (DCSF; since renamed Department of Education), which in 2010 released updated non-statutory guidance for RE in English schools. The document advocates helping pupils to feel that their religion is respected and valued, and explicitly enlists the notion of respect as a way to manage diversity when it states, 'RE also contributes to pupils' personal development and well-being and to community cohesion by promoting mutual respect and tolerance in a diverse society' (DCSF 2010, p. 7).

The notion of respect enabled the school to manage widely contrasting beliefs about reality. But it also committed the school to a degree of moral relativism, by placing religious beliefs and practices beyond criticism. Many religious texts have been interpreted as anti-gay and religiosity is positively associated with homophobia (Adamczyk and Pitt 2009; Hooghe et al. 2010; Olson et al. 2006). So it is likely that if it were to explicitly address homophobia, the school would trigger concerns that religious beliefs condemning homosexuality were not being respected.

The implication was that any adult at Woodwell Green who was concerned about homophobia was in a dilemma. They could prioritise multicultural harmony and avoid tackling the issue for fear of offending school members' religious beliefs. Or they could prioritise tackling homophobia, challenging prominent religious views of homosexuality and, thus, potentially undermining harmony between different groups in the school's diverse community. The notion of respect as not questioning religious beliefs or practice meant that addressing racism and homophobia became mutually incompatible. It is ironic that promoting tolerance of one form of difference (racial, ethnic or religious) may have contributed to intolerance of another form (differences in sexuality).

Given the importance assigned at the time of the research to harmony between ethnic and religious groups, both in the local community and nationally, it is not surprising that the school focused on multicultural harmony at the cost of tackling homophobia. Researchers have noted the existence of similar hierarchies in Australia and Canada (Kobayashi and Ray 2000, p. 406; Robinson 2005). The implicit message to children was unequivocal: adults at Woodwell Green were teaching children to prioritise between different kinds of harm, with racism seen as extremely damaging and homophobia barely recognised as a problem.

6.2 Defining Racism

In designating racism a particularly serious form of harm, the school precipitated the question of what exactly counts as racism. We have already come across this issue in Chapter 2, where children and adults disagreed over whether racist insults could be used in a playful way between friends. It arose in various other forms too. The remainder of this chapter explores some of the ways in which members of the school community differed in their definitions of racism, and examines the resulting tensions and disputes regarding whether specific incidents were seen as racist (and hence, particularly serious harm) or not.

6.2.1   Race, religion or language?

The rising significance of religion
Traditionally, definitions of racism have focused upon skin colour and race. For example, Dennis (1996, p. 715) defines racism as 'the idea that there is a direct correspondence between a group's values, behaviour and attitudes, and its physical features' while the Concise Oxford English Dictionary (1995) describes it as 'a belief in the superiority of a particular race; prejudice based on this' and 'antagonism towards, or discrimination against, other races, esp. as a result of this'. Some researchers of childhood racism have accepted such definitions (Olweus 1991), but others have defined racism more broadly. For example, in their effort to establish the amount of racism children encounter, Eslea and Mukhtar (2000) asked children in the UK whether they had been bullied 'because of your name, your skin colour, the language(s) you speak, the God(s) you believe in, your place of worship, the festivals you celebrate, the food you do or do not eat, the clothes you wear' (p. 211).

Within Woodwell Green, there were similarly contrasting definitions of racism. The posters around the school described earlier mentioned race, culture and ethnic origin as potential bases of racism, but Mr Gardner, the head teacher of Woodwell Green, defined racism slightly differently.

In a junior assembly (for 7- to 11-year-olds), he told children that racism was when people were horrible to other people because of their religion, the language they speak, or the colour of their skin. However, this broader definition was not easily embraced by all adults at the school. The following extract is taken from a year 6 (10- and 11-year-olds) RE lesson:

> Jaskaran [Indian Sikh] comments that a lot of Sikhs live in Southall [an area of London quite near Woodwell Green]. Miss Lock agrees, 'As Jaskaran said, a lot of Sikhs live in Southall.' Another boy comments, 'If people come from India they feel more at home if they come to Southall, cos it's like India.' Miss Lock agrees. Then another boy says that he saw on a TV programme that Bradford [a city in northern England] used to be all white, but when Asian people arrived, the white people started moving out. There is some laughter from the class at this. 'It's not a funny issue,' Miss Lock says. 'People who live here might decide to move away.'
>
> Jaskaran says of what happened in Bradford, 'That was racist.' Miss Lock said that it could be racist. She says that moving away is one thing that can happen. 'What else can happen?' she asks, 'What happened last year?' One child says, 'The Bradford riots.'[3] There is a brief debate about whether the riots took place in Bradford or elsewhere. Then Miss Lock continues, 'All that stems from racism. It's hoped that you, coming from a multicultural school, growing up with children of different backgrounds, you develop an understanding, and a respect, for different backgrounds.' She says that racists are ignorant, and mentions the poster of four brains pinned up in one of the school corridors.[4] Many of the children make sounds of recognition and approval.
>
> Leon [other ethnic group, Christian] calls out, 'It could've happened with Ireland Miss.' Miss Lock at first denies that the situation in Ireland is racism, saying that it's to do with religion. 'Racism tends to be related to the colour of skin.' But then she adds, 'It is a type – you could say it's a type of racism.'

In this extract, Leon seemed to view the tensions between Catholics and Protestants in Northern Ireland as parallel to the hostilities between Asian and white youths in the north of England, in spite of the lack of racial difference in the former case. His teacher is more ambivalent about seeing the Northern Ireland situation as racism, although it clearly qualifies given the head teacher's definition.

There was some evidence, aside from this extract, that children at Woodwell Green held relatively broad definitions of racism. During interviews in pairs, I asked 26 year 4 children (8 and 9 years old) what they thought the word 'racism' meant. Twenty-one children provided a definition. Their responses are categorised by the attribute of the victim

Table 6.1   Year 4 children's definitions of racism categorised by basis

Bases of racism	No. of children	Examples
Race	12	'If you say to other people, you're brown. It looks like this, if you see a brown banana, you say "you're like a brown banana". If there was a white person, you could be racist to them as well.'
Religion	12	'When somebody doesn't believe in your religion and they say something rude about it.'
Country of origin	3	'When people are being mean saying, oh you're not born here, you're not allowed in this school, you are racist, you haven't got the same hair colours as us, you're black and horrible.' [also coded as race]
Other	2	'Some people have those turbans on, people make fun out of their turbans.'
Unclear	2	'If your mum's Muslim and my mum's Sikh, saying, "Your dad's a Paki".'
No reference to bases of racism	4	'It means rudeness.'

upon which the racism was based, in Table 6.1.[5] Most children mentioned more than one attribute in their definitions, which is why the total of the 'number of children' column exceeds 21.

The table reveals that race (usually referred to as skin colour) and religion were the most common attributes on which children's definitions of racism were based, both mentioned by 12 children (eight of whom included both race and religion in their definitions). Smaller numbers mentioned other bases: place of origin, religious clothing and culture. None mentioned language.

These definitions, broader than traditional ones, were also applied to some extent in practice. During my fieldwork, I witnessed or was told about 11 acts of racism carried out by a child towards another child, which were labelled as racism by a member of the school community.[6] Six of these were not specific about the basis of the racism; for example, I was told that one child called another 'racist names'. Of the remaining five, one concerned skin colour ('black shit'), two concerned country of origin ('Afghani', 'All the Indians should go back to India'), one concerned clothing ('Turbanator') and one concerned religion ('bloody Muslim').

So the evidence from fieldnotes and interviews indicates that some children at Woodwell Green defined racism more broadly than traditional definitions. Connolly (1998, p. 10) argues that definitions of racism have shifted, 'directed at people not only because of their skin colour but also because of their nationality, in the case of the Irish, or their religion, in the case of Muslims or Jewish people'. This expanded conception of racism may be part of a widespread historical change, as new generations, especially in multicultural areas like Woodwell, respond to the salience of religious difference in general, and Islamophobia in particular, in contemporary Britain.

What about language?

There is good evidence that, like the head teacher, many children at Woodwell Green saw harmful acts based on religious difference as racism. However, although the head teacher mentioned language in his definition of racism, none of the year 4 children did, and I did not witness a single instance of language-based harm being called racism.

Children often teased peers who joined the school from overseas about their accents and pronunciation. For example, Maria joined a year 4 class at Woodwell Green from Pakistan. She and I were working on a task together in class, in which she pronounced vet as 'wet'. Her classmate Zak laughed and repeated 'wet' in a humorous tone (see Chapter 2 for another example of Maria's classmates teasing her about her accent). I only once saw a child criticise a peer for this kind of teasing. Usually children did not comment on it; in fact, they were more likely to join in.

Some adults saw such behaviour as wrong. For example, Maria's teacher, Miss Chahal, told me that she 'came down hard' on Amrita when she heard her laugh at Maria's accent. However, some teachers may have seen language-based teasing as more benign. For instance, a girl who had recently joined the school from India complained to Jasminder, the leader of the after-school club, that a boy in her class teased her for her accent. Jasminder (who also spoke English with an Indian accent) asked her if she had told the teacher, and the girl responded that she had but that the teacher had done nothing to intervene.

Still other adults were unsure about the status of language-based teasing. For example, a teacher recounted to me a shared joke that emerged in a class she taught whereby they would add 'jeet' (a common ending for Sikh names) to the end of English words; for example, 'Pass me the scissorsjeet'. Having participated in this class joke for a while, she began to feel uncomfortable about it, wondering if it was racist, and brought an end to it.

Overall, and in contradiction with the definition provided by the head teacher, children and adults at the school seemed less perturbed by language-based than religion- or race-based teasing, and less likely to consider such teasing as racist. Why was this? The key difference indexed by accent was the length of time that children had been in the UK, and, more specifically, in west London (since the UK is characterised by strong, distinctive regional accents). Since most children attending the school (whatever their ethnicity) were born in the UK and spoke English with a west London accent, accent-based teasing did not map onto more traditional tensions, such as those between English and Indian ethnicities or black and white skin colours.

In fact, children of Indian and Pakistani ethnicities were often perpetrators as well as victims of language-based teasing. Language-based teasing at the school may, then, be more about differences *within* the local South Asian community rather than *between* different ethnic or religious groups. It may also be linked with the use of accented English in British Asian TV comedies that were popular at the time, such as *Goodness Gracious Me* and *The Kumars at No. 42*.

A second possible explanation for why language has not been incorporated into definitions of racism in the way that religion has is that the ability to speak more than one language can be very useful at Woodwell Green, creating opportunities that do not exist for monolinguists (who constituted a minority at the school). In particular, having some knowledge of 'Indian' enabled a child to understand and join in playful boisterous exchanges of 'Indian swear words' in the playground, to share 'secret words', to gossip without non-speakers being able to understand, and (provided that one's teacher did not understand 'Indian') to converse more easily with friends in the classroom.[7] The advantages and prevalence of second-language speaking at Woodwell Green may have contributed to its lack of meaningfulness as a source of racism for the children there.

6.2.2   Name-calling or discrimination?

Children's experience of racism as name-calling
Another dimension along which definitions of racism can differ is the type of act that is understood to be a vehicle for racism. Researchers have found that name-calling is the most prevalent type of racism among children, although other forms, such as racist graffiti and physical attack based on ethnicity or religion, do exist (Connolly and Keenan 2002; Troyna and Hatcher 1992; Verkuyten and Thijs 2002).

At Woodwell Green, too, name-calling seemed to be the most common form of racism between children. Table 6.2 categorises the definitions of racism provided by 21 year 4 children by type of behaviour described.

Table 6.2 Year 4 children's definitions of racism categorised by type

Type of racism	No. of children	Examples
Making fun of	7	'Taking the mick out of people's colour skin, religion, God, or of their features.'
Rudeness/ insults	6	'When they're not really nice people and they be rude about your religion and the colour of your skin.'
Swearing	4	'Like someone's swearing about your colour of your skin.'
Bullying/ fighting	2	'If someone was fighting and they say racist attack, if someone was fighting over religion, cos they don't like a different religion.'
Discrimination	1	'Whites were treated nicely and the blacks weren't and that's not fair.'
Unclear	1	[inaudible]
No reference to bases of racism	4	'It means rudeness.'

Numbers add up to more than 21 because some children mentioned more than one type in their definitions.

Almost all definitions involved verbal abuse, in the form of teasing or making fun, insults and swearing. Three children did mention other, potentially non-verbal forms of racism: bullying, fighting and discrimination. I also asked these children whether they thought that racism occurred at their school. Eight of the 17 children who defined racism appropriately said that it did, and all the specific examples they gave involved racist name-calling. Similarly, of the 11 instances of racism that I witnessed and heard labelled as such by school members, nine involved verbal abuse.

Children at Woodwell Green may have defined racism in terms of name-calling and direct verbal insults because these were indeed the commonest forms of racism they encountered, but they may also have been influenced by their head teacher's definition. For example, during a junior assembly Mr Gardner told the children that racism was worse than other kinds of insults. Implicit in the head teacher's comments is a definition of racism as name-calling. Similarly, he wrote to staff of 'racist remarks' (see earlier).

Racism plus fairness = discrimination
There is evidence that children are capable of understanding racism much more broadly than only name-calling (McKown 2004). American

6- to 10-year-old children were told stories about an imaginary land inhabited by 'the Greens' and 'the Blues', and then asked whether the real world was like this imaginary world in any way. They came up with many forms of racism, including stereotyping (e.g. 'The White people don't think the Black people are smart'), prejudice ('Whites don't like Blacks'), rights violations ('Whites say that Blacks don't have the right to do things') and exclusion ('If there's a new kid and he's Black, people might not pick him. They'll pick somebody else') (McKown 2004). While these definitions do not necessarily refer to the children's own experiences, they do demonstrate that young children are capable of quite sophisticated understandings of racism.

This raises the question of whether the children of Woodwell Green also understood racism beyond name-calling. We have seen that a few, at least, did; Table 6.2 includes references to bullying, fighting and discrimination in addition to verbal abuse. Further evidence that some children in this class were developing a broader understanding of racism, and applying it to their own experiences, emerged during group interviews they participated in when in year 5 (aged 9 and 10 years old). Several children (of varying ethnicities, but none of them English) interpreted events they had witnessed in terms of preferential treatment of English or white people over ethnic minorities. These observations were made during interviews which did not ask about racism at all. The children's spontaneous references to racism suggest that they were using the concept to make sense of their own experiences:

1. During a group interview with Harpreet, Simran and Sandeep [all Indian Sikh], I am in the middle of discussing fights with Sandeep, when Harpreet, who is currently wandering around the room, comments:

    HARPREET: Guess who won in Fame Academy? David. I wanted
                Lemar to win.[8] They're being racist.
    SANDEEP: They're not being racist!
    SIMRAN: They are being racist.
    SANDEEP: Why are they racist?
    SIMRAN: Cos Sinéad and David were the last two.
    SANDEEP: It was a bit racist.

2. I am interviewing Faizel [Pakistani Muslim], Zak [Somali Muslim], Amar [Pakistani Muslim] and one other boy about getting into trouble with teachers. In the middle of discussing their class teacher, Mrs Samson, Faizel comments:

156

FAIZEL: I think she's racist.
ZAK: Me too.
AMAR: Me too.
RW: Who do you mean?
FAIZEL: I think Mrs Sampson's racist and this other dinner lady, I
          don't know her name, Leon's mum. She always tells me
          off. Like, Dylan kicked me under the table yeah, I didn't
          touch him. He strangles me and pushes me to the wall and
          all I did was kick him and I got in trouble just because he
          started crying yeah.
RW: Why do you think she's racist?
FAIZEL: Cos she always takes the other side.

3. I am interviewing Zak and Faizel. The two boys are talking about
    football, when Zak comments:

ZAK: Miss I was playing for Woodwell football club and they're
          racist, and there's one way I know they're racist. You know
          Lee yeah
FAIZEL: [interrupting] No she doesn't know Lee!
RW: [interrupting] No I don't know Lee!
ZAK: Well Lee yeah, whenever I score he starts to cry. Then Lee's
          dad, he's the manager yeah, he takes me off.
RW: Why do you think that's racist though?
ZAK: Because he always takes me, Sandeep and Sufyan off yeah,
          and puts Lee, Alex and Sam on.
RW: I didn't get it, tell me again.
ZAK: You know the manager, he subs me for Lee, he subs Sandeep
          for Alex, and he subs Sufyan for Sam. Miss isn't that racist
          yeah, he takes us all off and we're the best players! Just cos
          his son always cries when I get a goal.

In extract 1, Harpreet, Simran and Sandeep agreed that racism
occurred in a TV talent show because the black finalist was voted out
before the two white finalists. In extract 2, Faizel complained that a dinner lady (who was Asian) was racist, telling off Faizel (Asian) but not
Dylan (white). In extract 3, Zak saw his football coach as racist because
he substituted two black (Zak and Sufyan) and one Asian (Sandeep)
boys for three white boys. These children spontaneously interpreted situations in which white people succeeded over non-white people as racism.
None of the children quoted above explicitly mentioned the basis for the
discrimination they claimed to have witnessed (e.g. skin colour), so one
might question whether they really understood what racism is. However,
all six of these children defined racism appropriately several months

previously when they were in year 4, referring to skin colour and/or religion. It is likely, then, that they did interpret these situations in terms of racist discrimination.

As noted in Chapter 3, Faizel and Zak's perceptions of racism were part of a more general view of adults at school as unfairly biased against them, on the basis not only of race or religion, but also of gender and reputation. I argued in Chapter 3 that such a viewpoint arises by applying ideas of fairness and justice to adults' behaviour. Here, I suggest that these children have combined their concepts of justice with definitions of racism to arrive at a sophisticated understanding of racism as discrimination.

The children's accusations of racism are troubling, particularly those relating to school staff, and I do not have the data to evaluate their accuracy. However, it is also possible to see these accusations in a positive light. McKown (2004) suggests that children's developing understanding of racism contributes to their evolving political consciousness, which can help them to negotiate racist incidents in their own lives and inform their participation in society in general. Considered in this light, the accusations made by these 9- and 10-year-olds reflect a maturing grasp of the forms that racism can take, hence preparing them to cope with it in their own lives and to engage with problems of racism in wider society.

However, these children did not get much support at school to develop and apply appropriately this understanding of racism as discrimination, because the school focused on racist name-calling instead. The result is an ambiguous situation in which children see some forms of racism (verbal abuse between children) treated very seriously, while other forms (discrimination by adults) are glossed over. If such young children are grappling with the sensitive issue of discriminatory racism from adults in their lives, then schools must similarly branch out from their focus on racist name-calling to seriously consider other kinds of racism that children may be concerned with.

6.2.3 'I'm not racist but': English parents and ethnic identity

This section explores clashes between (usually Indian) teachers and (usually English) parents regarding children's participation in activities typical of another ethnic group. These clashes were associated with disagreements about what constituted racism. It was common for (usually Indian) teachers to involve the children in their class in practices that were associated with Indian ethnic identity. Examples included wearing Indian clothes, making mehndi designs[9] and dancing to Bollywood songs. It was also common for parents of English children to complain about their child's participation in these practices. For example, one teacher told me that when an English girl in her class went home with a bindi,[10] her mother complained to the teacher angrily that this was 'taking it too far'.

Another teacher chose an Indian-themed 'Cinderella' for her class's assembly. Class assemblies were performed on a rota by each class in front of parents, several other classes and their teachers, who often discussed and judged them. So it is not surprising that teachers put a lot of effort into them. For this assembly, some of the children wore Indian costumes and danced to a Bollywood song, and the King and Queen were renamed Raja and Rani. There was some opposition to this among English parents. The teacher told me that the mother of an English boy in her class told her that her son was not doing the dance. The mother of another English boy in the class complained that some English parents kept their children off school as the assembly date approached, so that they would not have to wear Indian costumes.

Not all English parents were averse to their children's participation in Indian practices. The after-school club was run by Jasminder, an Indian woman who usually wore Western clothing. One day she wore Indian dress to mark Vaisakhi, a Sikh festival. An English girl who regularly attended the after-school club was reluctant to go on this date because, as she put it, Jasminder 'speaks Indian'. Both amused and concerned, Jasminder spoke to the girl's mother about her shyness and suggested that they get some Indian clothes as dressing up material for the after-school club to help familiarise her with them. Her mother, who managed a charity shop, noted that they had a surplus of Indian clothes that did not sell, and readily agreed to bring some in for the club.

While some parents seemed unconcerned about their children participating in cross-ethnic activities, we have seen that others were worried enough to complain to teachers. They often preceded their complaints with a disclaimer: 'I'm not racist but', or 'I know this is a multicultural school but'. Nevertheless, their complaints were generally interpreted as racist by teachers, who were very offended and upset by them. The head teacher (himself English) also considered that these complaints often arose from racism.

In contrast to these English parents, many of the English (and other non-Indian) teachers at the school enjoyed opportunities to engage in 'Indian' practices, finding them fascinating and cosmopolitan. For example, on one occasion many non-Indian teachers dressed in Indian costume for the day.

What is happening here? Why did English parents object so strongly to practices that English teachers happily embraced? I suggest that the answer lies in the different understandings that these groups had of ethnic identity, which themselves related to different experiences of the local area of Woodwell.

Religious practices, ethnic practices and identity
We have seen that teachers at Woodwell Green often asked children to participate in activities of other ethnic groups. In contrast, they never required children to practise any *religion* other than their own. Woodwell Green was a non-religious school. There was no praying or singing of hymns or other religious songs in assemblies, in which the head teacher discussed not only Christian but also Sikh, Hindu and Muslim festivals and beliefs. Assemblies did not involve an act of worship, and the school policy document was clear that assemblies should not tread on religious toes:

> Our school serves children from a number of different faith groups. It also has many other children with no experience of the habits or traditions of any faith group in their home lives. We have a commitment to all children and will seek to avoid offence to anyone at any time in the themes which are addressed and the manner in which we address them. Our aim is to include all children at all times.

A similar attitude was taken to RE. The school's policy documents stated very clearly that in RE lessons, children should learn *about* and *from* religion, but they should not learn to *do* religion. This careful avoidance of religious commitment was promoted nationally by the government's then Qualifications and Curriculum Authority (QCA), which stated, 'RE does not seek to urge religious beliefs on pupils nor compromise the integrity of their own beliefs by promoting one religion over another', and advocates that teachers 'Encourage the use of "owning" and "grounding" language such as "in my opinion" or "some Hindus would say". This allows belief statements to be made in the classroom without everyone feeling they have to agree' (QCA 2004, p. 29).

It is clear that teachers saw religious practice in school as inappropriate, compromising the integrity of children's own religious (or non-religious) beliefs, practices and identity. In this, they were probably in agreement with English parents at the school. However, where they differed is that as we have seen, some English parents extended the same reasoning to non-religious practices typical of particular ethnic groups.[11] In contrast, teachers drew a sharp distinction between religious and ethnic practices. They frequently required children to participate in activities associated with other ethnic groups (especially Indian), and embraced opportunities to do so themselves.

I do not have enough data to be sure of why this difference exists, but can speculate. Many of the English parents had grown up in Woodwell and seen dramatic changes during their lifetimes. For example, an English woman who worked at the school and whose children used to attend it told me that she had lived in Woodwell all her life, and had seen huge changes: when she was at school, there were just two non-white children in her class. She told me that she felt that the change was too great, and that people moving into the area should try to adapt. Tellingly, when I asked if I could interview her in more detail about her views (which were very much in tension with the official school rhetoric promoting multiculturalism), she looked panicked and refused.

In the context of rapid change in the place where they grew up, English parents may have felt that the distinction the school drew between inappropriate religious practice and appropriate ethnic practice was irrelevant, because both essentially required their children to adopt the behaviours of incomers who should, in their view, be adopting the behaviours of the pre-existing community. Hence, they were just as upset at the prospect of their child dancing to a Bollywood song as teachers would have been about non-Christian children reciting the Lord's Prayer.

I suggest that English parents' worries were exacerbated by the fact that children and adults at Woodwell Green tended to oppose Englishness and Indianness, especially when referring to food, clothes, religions and languages. Children teased Indian peers who engaged in what were seen as 'English' practices (such as eating pasta rather than roti at home), and they teased English children who engaged in 'Indian' practices (such as singing Bollywood songs). In both cases, children were accused of being the other ethnicity; 'You're an English girl', 'You're a India' (see Chapter 4 for examples). This understanding of English and Indian as opposites probably results from the fact that the largest ethnic minority at the time in Woodwell was Indian, in an area that was previously mainly English. The opposition may have made English parents more anxious about their children's participation in specifically *Indian* activities, because it was as if by carrying out practices associated with the 'opposite' ethnicity, children took on a little of the other ethnic identity and lost a little of their own.

In contrast, teachers' experiences of ethnic identity and place were very different. Most teachers at Woodwell Green were not from the local area, did not live locally and would not remain at the school for more

161

than a few years. For them, activities connected to Indian ethnicity were not perceived as threatening as they were for some English parents. On the contrary, they were viewed as celebrations of the school's multicultural ethos, promoting harmony and understanding between ethnic groups and, moreover, as interesting and exciting cosmopolitan opportunities to learn about another culture.

In conclusion, some English parents struggled with teachers over whether resistance to participating in Indian activities constituted racism. For teachers, while cross-*religious* participation was wrong, cross-ethnic participation was a positive act of cross-cultural celebration and integration. No wonder, then, that they saw English parents unhappy about their child's involvement as racist.

For some English parents, however, I suggest that things looked very different. Participation in both cross-religious and cross-ethnic activities was perceived as threatening against a background of change personally experienced during their lifetimes. This threat may have loomed even greater if parents saw 'English' and 'Indian' as mutually exclusive opposites. They may have felt that by participating in an Indian dance, their child's very identity as English was being undermined. For them, it is wrong to push other-ethnicity practices onto children, and their complaints constitute not racism but positive efforts to protect their child's ethnic identity.

6.3   Implications for Schools

6.3.1   Racism versus homophobia

It is gratifying to see schools like Woodwell Green taking racism seriously. However, this chapter has shown that by promoting tolerance of different ethnic and religious groups, schools can leave other kinds of intolerance, particularly homophobia, to flourish. This means that some children, especially boys who cannot or will not conform to locally prevalent ideas of masculinity as toughness and heterosexuality, suffer insults and teasing from peers, and feel unable to seek support from adults at school in dealing with these, and with concerns they may have about their own sexuality.

One barrier to primary schools dealing with homophobia is the view that it is inappropriate to talk to young children about sexuality. Many quite young children at Woodwell Green clearly understood what the words 'gay' and 'lesbian' meant, challenging this view. But more fundamentally, it is possible to discuss homosexuality without referring explicitly to sexual activity, by focusing instead on love and relationships.

Resistance to discussing sexuality with children is likely to arise in any British primary school, and in many schools elsewhere too. I argued in this chapter that schools situated in multicultural (especially multi-religious) areas might find it particularly difficult to address homophobia, because of the injunction to respect (i.e. not challenge) religious beliefs and practices. This injunction promotes moral relativism by placing topics about which some religious groups hold strong views (such as homosexuality) beyond discussion. The idea that the beliefs and practices of religions and cultures should be respected and not challenged was also observed in Southall, an area of west London quite close to Woodwell (Baumann 1996). Baumann (1996) criticises this notion of respect on the grounds that it ignores diversity of opinion within cultures or religions, and hardens differences between them. These problems with the notion of respect raise the question of whether we can conceive of respect in an alternative form, which allows more space for dialogue and dissent both within and between particular groups. This might make it easier for schools to raise controversial issues like homophobia, without sacrificing their anti-racism agenda.

If an alternative notion of respect could be found, then it should not be difficult for schools to develop an anti-homophobia position. The very values upon which anti-racism is based, tolerance and justice, are equally applicable to the case of homophobia. In both cases, we are dealing with prejudice against a minority by the majority. Perhaps schools can broach the issue of homophobia by emphasising this common ground and building on the underlying logic of anti-racism.

6.3.2 Controversies in defining racism

We have already seen that school members saw racism as a particularly serious type of harm. With so much at stake, it is no wonder that they sometimes disagreed about what constituted racism. One difference concerned the basis of racism. Contrary to traditional definitions focusing on race alone, the head teacher saw insults based on race, religion and language as racist. Most children agreed that religion-based insults were racist, but they disagreed with the head teacher when it came to language. Accent-based teasing between children was quite common but not usually labelled as racist, perhaps because differences in accent did not map onto ethnic, religious or racial differences and, as such, were too far removed from children's existing definitions and from tensions in wider society. One can imagine this situation being quite different somewhere where language differences are associated with pre-existing differences and/or tensions in a community, such as Quebec.

What this analysis suggests is that definitions of racism vary to make sense of the meaningful differences in local communities and national contexts. Schools need to be aware that these definitions change, and teachers should ensure that their own definitions keep pace with the communities in which they work. It is clearly unhelpful, for example, to define racism with reference to ethnic differences in a community where the main source of tension is between two religious groups of the same ethnicity.

My analyses of differing and changing concepts of racism, and of the silence surrounding homophobia, raise interesting questions about whether children's experiences of harm are influenced by definitions of harm and prioritisation between different types of harm. For example, would a child at Woodwell Green be more hurt by an insult based on skin colour than one based on language, *because* they saw only the first as racist? I am certainly not suggesting that children will not be harmed by (for example) a homophobic insult just because adults at school do not explicitly flag homophobia. But it is possible that the kind of harm will be different. It may even be worse when it is not addressed by adults, because children may interpret this lack of interest as suggesting that the insult is deserved.

Most racism between children at primary school takes the form of verbal abuse, which is relatively easy to identify and hence deal with. However, children as young as 9 years old understood racism not only as name-calling but also as discrimination, usually by adults, and they used this understanding to interpret events in their own lives. Teachers should be ready for children's understanding of racism to embrace new forms. Accusations of discrimination directed towards adults at schools are difficult for schools to deal with, but I would argue that this makes it all the more important for adults at school to discuss the issue and consider how to respond to such an accusation should it take place, and how to support children as they construct more sophisticated concepts of racism and learn when to apply them.

The most heated disagreements over definitions of racism occurred between some teachers and English parents regarding children's participation in other-ethnic activities. I suggested that this disagreement arose because teachers viewed cross-ethnic participation as cosmopolitan and promoting inter-group harmony, while some English parents experienced it as threatening, undermining their child's ethnic identity and confirming their own concerns about local change. If this analysis is correct, then a possible solution could be to recruit worried parents, along with parents of other ethnic groups, to the cause of an explicitly bidirectional programme of cross-ethnic participation. For example, parents could organise a club that teaches children traditional Indian and English dancing or cooking. By making the process of cross-ethnic participation intentionally reciprocal, English parents may experience their children's own participation in Indian activities as less threatening.

Notes

1. 'United' refers to the famous English football (soccer) team Manchester United. Tomb Raider is a computer game.
2. These references to 'gay' as an insult were spontaneous in the sense that I did not ask children specifically about homophobic insults; rather, children referred to these insults when explaining why they did not like particular peers or describing specific arguments to me.
3. This is a reference to violent clashes between white and Asian youths in Bradford in 2001.
4. This poster is described earlier in the chapter.
5. No child mentioned the word 'race', but when children referred to skin colour or, less typically, other physical attributes (such as hair colour), I categorised these as referring to race.
6. I am obviously not claiming to have captured all instances of racism that occurred during my research. Since I am interested here with how members of Woodwell Green defined racism, rather than in the quantity of racism *per se*, I have included only those instances that I heard called 'racism' by a member of the school community. In addition, in an effort to focus on children's perceptions of racism, I have excluded cases of racism that were carried out by and/or directed towards an adult.
7. 'Indian' was the word children used to refer usually to Punjabi, but sometimes also to other South Asian languages such as Urdu. See also Chapter 4 for more on the value of 'speaking Indian' at the school.
8. Harpreet was referring to a recent British TV talent show, in which the three finalists were David Sneddon, Sinéad Quinn (both white) and Lemar Obika (black).
9. These are intricate patterns painted on the skin, particularly hands, with henna.
10. A bindi is a small decoration (typically a red dot) applied on the forehead.
11. I argued in Chapter 4 that this may make it particularly difficult for English children to make friends with Indian children and with children of other ethnic groups who participate in 'Indian' activities, like 'speaking Indian' and dancing to Indian music.

7

Guilty or Not Guilty
Interactive Struggles for Meaning

The previous chapters have examined a range of morally significant situations children experience at school and the values they bring to bear on them, including reciprocity or justice, loyalty, hierarchy and harm avoidance. We have seen that harm avoidance, the value emphasised by the school, is just one of many values that children grapple with in the complex moral events that make up their everyday playground lives. This chapter takes as its starting point the increased societal pressure, documented in Chapter 1, for adults at school to intervene in children's peer relations to prevent them from harming one another. What exactly are adults dealing with, what form does adult intervention usually take, and what are the implications for children's peer relations and moral experiences?[1]

7.1 Children's Willingness to Tell Tales

The first point to note is that the children in my research seemed to have largely accepted adults' increased involvement in their peer relations, in that they were much more willing than previous generations to take their problems to teachers. The head teacher, Mr Gardner, told me that at the start of his career, he might have been approached by one or two children in an hour-long lunch break. This had gradually transformed into a continuous stream of complaints. Similar shifts seem to have occurred elsewhere too. For instance, Evaldsson (2002) notes that

Children's Moral Lives: An Ethnographic and Psychological Approach, First Edition. Ruth Woods.
© 2013 John Wiley & Sons, Ltd. Published 2013 by John Wiley & Sons, Ltd.

Table 7.1 Number of children of different ages against 'telling tales' in hypothetical scenario

Year group (and age in years)	Total number of children	Number (and %) of children claiming boy should **not** tell father
1–2 (5–7)	40	6 (15%)
3–4 (7–9)	40	4 (10%)
5–6 (9–11)	53	13 (25%)

teachers attending a Swedish after-school programme usually intervened in children's conflicts, reflecting their 'professional ambition to stop the disruptive nature of conflicts' (p. 204). In contrast, García-Sánchez (2011) describes tale-telling as socially frowned upon in a small Spanish town, perhaps indicating that attitudes in Spain have changed less than in some other countries (see Chapter 1 for more on differences between countries in the trend towards intervention).

There is evidence that before this recent shift, children were less ready to tell adults about the wrongdoings of a peer. Piaget (1932) told Swiss children a story in which a father goes out, leaving his two sons behind, one of whom then does 'something silly'. When the father returns, he asks the other boy to tell him everything that the brother had done. Piaget asked children what the boy ought to do. He found that most younger children (aged 6 and 7 years) said that the boy should tell his father everything, while most older children (aged over 8 years) said that the boy should tell his father nothing or lie to protect his brother. I presented a similar story to 133 children at Woodwell Green, in interviews (years 1 to 4, aged 5 to 9 years) and questionnaires (years 5 and 6, aged 9 to 11 years). My findings are presented in Table 7.1.

As Table 7.1 indicates, the younger children at Woodwell Green resemble the younger children questioned by Piaget, with only a few stating that the boy should not tell his father. However, at Woodwell Green, this was also true of the older children, whose willingness to tell tales contrasts sharply with the responses of the older children in Piaget's research. A χ^2 test of association did not find a significant relationship between year group and Woodwell Green children's answers. What this finding suggests is that the children of Woodwell Green were more willing than those in Piaget's research to tell adults about the misdemeanours of other children.

During my research, I witnessed almost every child I got to know well at Woodwell Green 'tell tales' on peers, sometimes their best friends.

167

I did hear some children (usually boys) criticising peers who 'told tales' (also known at Woodwell Green as 'grassing' or 'skanking'), but invariably saw these same children complaining to adults about their peers on other occasions. So whilst some children did still condemn the notion of telling adults about the wrongdoing of another child, overall they seemed more willing to involve adults than previous generations.

7.1.1   Telling tales for fun

Another form of evidence that children at Woodwell Green were willing to take their problems to teachers is that some of them actually did so as an innovative form of teasing in which a child would complain to an adult about a peer, not over a genuine grievance but as a move in an ongoing playful interaction. Here are two examples:

1. During wet play, Sandeep tells me that Amandeep punched him. By the twinkle in his eye I can tell that he is playing with Amandeep. 'Don't punch, Amandeep,' I say. Amandeep's face crinkles into an expression of protest, but when he sees Sandeep's face he smiles and says, 'I didn't!'
2. In the playground, I see two year 3 boys fighting. One is laughing as he strangles the other, and the two wheel from side to side as the one being strangled struggles to get free. He calls to me, 'Miss, tell him to stop!' 'It's only a game,' the other one says. 'No it's not!' exclaims the first one. I tell his attacker to stop a few times, and eventually he lets go. The strangled boy flops to the bench, but almost immediately starts grinning. 'Ha ha!' he mocks, pointing at his assailant, who starts moving towards him, but he jumps up and darts away.

My suspicion that children were using me, and other adults, as a tool for playful aggression was confirmed in an interview with Robbie (year 4). I often saw Robbie on the playground with his classmate Soraj. In interviews, both named the other as someone they liked. However, when I saw them on the playground, usually one would run up to me to complain that the other was hitting, kicking or swearing at them, and ask me to tell them off, while the other chased and tried to strike the one telling me. I was therefore surprised, when I asked Robbie in an interview whom he usually argued with at school, that he did not mention Soraj. I went on to query this:

RW: Do you ever argue with Soraj?
ROBBIE: [pauses] No.
RW: What about when you're always coming up to me and complaining about each other?

ROBBIE: No Miss, we're just playing games.
RW: Why does Soraj always tell tales to a teacher then?
ROBBIE: Miss we play a game where you have to tell teachers and stuff.
RW: Oh, it's all part of the game?
ROBBIE: Yeah.

Robbie patiently explained to me that he and Soraj 'play a game where you have to tell teachers and stuff'. Thus, what I had interpreted as a genuine complaint was seen by Robbie as a fun game.[2] I do not know how aware adults were that they were pawns in playful disputes like these. However, even if they did realise, they were in a difficult position because the moral imperative to take children's problems seriously made it hard to ignore complaints even if they believed them to be playful.

7.1.2   Teachers' responses to tales

Teachers could not possibly deal effectively with all of the requests children made for intervention. So they had to make a decision about which to act upon. This is a difficult call given their obligation to protect children from harm. In interviews, I asked four teachers at the school, 'How do you discourage children from telling you trivial problems?' This question uncovered a range of strategies, such as telling children to sort the problem out themselves and providing them with a space and time in the classroom to do so; asking the child, 'Do I really need to know about this?' and telling children to write a note to the teacher if they have a problem with a peer, which the teacher read and responded to at the end of the week. Teachers who used each method felt that they were effective in reducing the torrent of complaints. They also lectured the children on the matter; here is an example, taken from a year 4 classroom of 8- and 9-year-olds:

> Mohamed raises his hand and Miss Chahal chooses him to speak. He starts to say that someone hit him on the shoulder but Miss Chahal gives a huge sigh, turns away from the class, looks at the floor, and turns back. 'Why did I do that? What did Mr Gardner say to you yesterday?' she asks. Harpreet puts her hand up: 'Don't tell tales because you're wasting learning time.' Miss Chahal agrees.

Having employed strategies such as this, teachers were left with a (somewhat) more manageable caseload of disputes to resolve. How did they go about this? Teachers invariably began by trying to find out 'what really happened'. In doing so, they had to grapple with strategies that the children used to blame each other. Research has shown that children and adults use a variety of strategies to assign accountability to particular people and to exonerate others (Bandura 1999; Edwards 1997; Fine 1986). Two strategies that were very common amongst Woodwell Green children were to claim that a harmful act was accidental (a way of displacing responsibility from the agent) or that the harmful act was a justified retaliation to a preceding act (a way of presenting the act as justified). These were often deployed in contradictory ways by different parties to assign blame to one another in playground disputes.

7.2   Children Constructing Accountability

7.2.1   'It was by accident': The role of intention in allocating blame

When assigning blame for a harmful action, adults and older children in numerous studies have been shown to consider intention a very important factor (Nobes et al. 2009; Shultz et al. 1986; Zelazo et al. 1996). Similarly, older children and adults at Woodwell Green took intention into account by being more lenient with a child who harmed accidentally than with one who intended harm. The distinction between intended and accidental harm frequently came up in children's playground disputes, and was often contested. Here is an example from my fieldnotes, describing a group of friends in year 3 (all boys except for Kay, all aged 7 or 8 years):

> Leo runs up and tells me that Reece is crying. So I go with him to where Reece is sitting on the ground in tears, clutching his leg. Kay, Mudit and Sohil are there too, and Hafiz joins us soon afterwards. I crouch beside Reece and ask what happened. He says that he was walking along with Mudit, when Sohil grabbed his leg and twisted it round. Sohil, who is hanging around nearby looking miserable, says quickly and quietly that it was an accident and that he's sorry. But Reece insists that it was on purpose, and adds that Leo pushed him over too. Sohil explains, by way of defence, that Leo had invented a game to creep up on people, but Reece tearfully denies this. Leo says that he meant to get Mudit, but he missed and knocked Reece over instead. Kay, who is sitting beside Reece rubbing her hand on his back, says despairingly, 'Why does Reece always end up upset?' Then Mudit and Leo start play fighting, smacking each other and pretending to be hurt. Hafiz joins in, and then Sohil, and they rough and tumble in front of Reece, who soon starts to laugh. After a few minutes, he turns to me and smiles, 'You can go now Miss Woods.'

This dispute revolved around how harmful actions by Sohil and Leo were interpreted by members of the group. The alleged victim, Reece, described Sohil's action as 'on purpose', whereas Sohil himself claimed that it was accidental. The children did not explicitly use the distinction between intentional and accidental harm in reference to Leo's knocking Reece over, but it was implied in Reece's accusation that Leo *pushed* him over (implying intention), and in Leo's defence that he *knocked* Reece over in the process of playing a game with someone else (implying accidental harm).

Factors influencing children's attributions of intention
Why did children so often disagree about intention in their disputes? One possibility is that they vary somewhat in their overall tendency to attribute intention to others' harmful acts. Kay's wearied question in the extract presented earlier, 'Why does Reece always end up upset?', recalls my argument in Chapter 2, that some children are more sensitive than others, more prone to being upset by playful aggression. It seems likely that this argument can be extended to accidental harm as well.

Another possibility is that children were influenced by their role in the event, as protagonist or victim. Almost all accusations of intended harm I witnessed at Woodwell Green were made by the child who had been hurt, and similarly, almost all claims that the harm was accidental were made by the child who carried out the harmful act. Here are two examples, described to me by year 6 boys (aged 10 or 11 years) during individual interviews about a hypothetical scenario in which one child hits another during a football match:

RW: Have you ever been in a situation like this?
OWEN: No, but I know someone who has.
RW: What happened?
OWEN: Well, this boy, say Ben. He got really into the game, say Hamzah is this other boy.[3] Ben starts, he doesn't mean to foul but he catches people's legs by accident. But Hamzah got mad and one day Ben tripped Hamzah up in a puddle, accidentally, and Hamzah got up and hit Ben in the face, and Ben started crying and went to sit on the bench.
RW: Did he tell the teacher?
OWEN: Um, no he didn't.
RW: Why didn't he?
OWEN: Um, probably, Hamzah would probably beat Ben up.
RW: What makes you think that Ben tripped Hamzah accidentally?

171

OWEN: Because he was um going after the ball, he went for the front, and um when he, when Hamzah passed the ball, it was too late to tackle.

RW: Have you ever been in a situation like this?

MANSUKH: Um, two boys started a fight by playing football. Like one boy was tackling the other boy and the other boy fell over and he started pushing the boy who tripped him over and they started having a fight, and everyone started going around.

RW: What happened then?

MANSUKH: Then all the teachers came rushing over and Mr Maalin [playground supervisor] came, some of the dinner ladies came and pulled one of them away, and then Mr Maalin came and pulled the other one away.

RW: Were the boys friends before the fight?

MANSUKH: Yes. The first boy tripped him um by accident. But I don't think the boy who got tripped over thought that it was a accident, looked like he thought it was on purpose.

RW: Did they stop being friends then?

MANSUKH: They weren't friends, and the next day they came back and went oh hi how you doing!

Owen and Mansukh both described cases where a boy tripped another boy, who interpreted the act as intentional, and thus reacted aggressively. These boys' attributions of intention seemed to be related to their role in the situation. Similarly, Wainryb and Langley (2003, cited in Smetana 2006) also found that American children were more likely to view harm as intentional when they were victims than when they were protagonists.

Children's interpretations of intention also drew on features of the act itself. In the interview quoted earlier, Owen drew on specific sources of information to aid his interpretation of Ben's act as accidental (at least in the retelling of the event; of course this evidence does not necessarily mean that Owen used these cues at the time the event took place). He explained that his interpretation of Ben's act as accidental was based on the precise way in which Ben tackled Hamzah. He also suggested that Ben was often clumsy ('he doesn't mean to foul but he catches people's legs by accident'), implying that this was a typical behaviour for him.

I saw several other cases where children used cues to help them to interpret an act as intended or accidental. One important cue was the way in which the protagonist reacted to the harmful act. In one case, Roshni (year 3) told me that she had a fight with another girl because the girl was swinging Roshni around and then she let go. I suggested that it was probably an accident, but Roshni replied that she knew it was on purpose because after it happened, the girl laughed at her. Here is another example:

A year 3 girl approaches me in the playground and complains that 'a year 6 boy pushed me'. I get her to take me to him. It turns out to be Zak [year 5], who is playing football. I call him over, and he says grinning slightly, 'Miss I pushed her by accident.' 'But you laughed!' the girl says. He smiles disarmingly, 'Yeah Miss well I...' he breaks off, obviously itching to get back to the game, which is continuing around us. I tell him to apologise to her, which he does readily, then he rejoins the game.

In both these cases, victims used protagonists' amused reactions as evidence that they had intended the harm they caused. In addition to cues like this, another factor that children used to judge intention was their prior relationship with the protagonist. In particular, several children seemed to automatically interpret as intentional the harmful actions of peers who they believed disliked them. Here are two examples:

1. I am watching some year 4 children playing a heated game of football [soccer], boys versus girls. The ball hits Zena in the face. I didn't see who kicked it but it looked to me like an accident. Zena stands still with her hands over her face. Mohamed runs over and tries to pull her hands away, but she twists her hands free and turns angrily away from him. She walks over to me, and I hug her. She cries just a little, and I check that she is not injured. Harpreet and Maria come over to ask if she is okay, and Zena confirms that she is. 'Who did it?' Maria asks sharply. 'It was Amar, I hate him!' Zena replies. 'I thought it was Amar,' Maria replies, and she marches over to him. 'I don't think it was on purpose,' I say to Zena. 'Yes it was,' she replies with conviction. 'How do you know?' I ask. 'Because I hate Amar and he hates me,' she says.

2. Year 4 boy Amandeep comes up and asks me if his face is red. I tell him that it is on one side. 'You know Finlay in year 3?' I tell him I don't but ask him to continue anyway. 'He kicked the ball at me.' I sympathise, and remind him that it will soon fade. 'I expect it was an accident,' I add. 'No-o-o,' he says adamantly, stretching the word across several syllables for emphasis. 'How do you know?' I ask. 'Miss he hates me,' he replies.

Like children interpreting playful aggression, these children tended to assume that when a peer with whom they had a negative relationship harmed them, it must be intentional, even if other characteristics of the act suggested accidental harm. Taking prior relationship and other factors, including cues from the event (such as whether the protagonist laughs), the role of the child (protagonist, victim or onlooker) and children's general sensitivity into account, it is no wonder that intention was often an important and contested aspect of playground disputes.

Another factor that may have encouraged children to interpret intention differently from one another is the dichotomous form of the 'on purpose–by accident' distinction that children typically used to refer to intention. This opposition suggests a rather crude view of intention as either present or absent, which may not always accurately represent children's experience. On the basis of interviews with American children about transgressions they had experienced, Wainryb et al. (2005) argue that 'the realm of experiences in which moral life gets played out is made up largely of not-quite-intentional and not-quite-unintentional harm' (p. 82). It is indeed easy to imagine actions that do not readily fit the description as either 'on purpose' or 'by accident'.

For instance, one child might kick the football, aiming to score a goal, and it bounces off the goalpost and hits a nearby non-player in the face. Another child might kick the ball from one end of the pitch to the other, aiming to pass to their friend who is unrealistically far away, and the ball instead veers off the pitch and hits a non-player in the face. Both acts would probably be classed as accidental, but is the first act not more accidental than the second? The dichotomous use of 'by accident' and 'on purpose' does not allow for degrees of intention, and hence may encourage children to take a more oppositional stance to one another in disputes than they would were there a more sophisticated vocabulary available for this topic.

The importance of age

Another factor that probably contributes to children's attributions of intent is age. Research has shown that although children as young as 3 years old *can* take intention into account in certain circumstances, in general younger children tend to focus instead on the consequences of a harmful act, coming to focus on intention as they get older (Piaget 1932; see reviews by Zelazo et al. 1996 and Nobes et al. 2009). The children of Woodwell Green were no different. In interviews (with years 1 to 4, aged 5 to 9 years) and questionnaires (with years 5 and 6, aged 9 to 11 years), I presented 137 children with two scenarios, based on those of Piaget (1932), in which intention was pitted against the consequence of an action. These scenarios read as follows:

174

1. Some boys were playing football. Lee tried to kick the ball hard, but he missed and kicked a boy's leg instead. The boy fell down and his leg started bleeding. Matthew tried to kick another boy's leg hard. But the boy jumped out the way and carried on playing.
2. Katie and Sarah were putting away some shiny new cups. Katie dropped a cup by accident and it broke. Sarah dropped a cup on purpose but it didn't break.

Children were asked to decide who was 'more bad', or whether the two protagonists were both the same. Three children did not complete both questions so their results were excluded. The answers given by the remaining 134 children were scored as zero if they blamed the child who harmed accidentally, one if they blamed both children, and two if they blamed the child whose act was intentional. Their scores for the two scenarios were totalled, giving a final score between zero and four. High numbers indicated a child who focused on intention, while a low score reflected an emphasis on consequences.

Children were also asked to explain their answers. Children who gained a low score (i.e. who blamed the protagonist who caused the most damage rather than the one with the worst intentions) usually focused on the outcome in their explanation. A typical explanation for blaming Lee, for example, was 'He kicked that boy's leg, that was bleeding'. In contrast, children who gained higher scores usually focused on the intention in their explanations. For example, a year 3 boy who blamed Matthew explained, 'Because he's trying to kick the boy, but Lee, he didn't wanna kick the boy, but he wanted to get the ball'.

I hypothesised that, as previous research has found, children would focus increasingly on intention as they got older. Mean scores and standard deviations for each year group are shown in Table 7.2. Statistical analyses found that older children gained significantly higher intention scores than younger children.[4] In other words, as previous researchers have found, older children at Woodwell Green tended to focus on intentions, while younger ones generally focused on consequences.

Table 7.2 Children's intention scores broken down by year group

Year group (and age in years)	Number of children	Mean intention score/4 (and standard deviation)
1–2 (5–7)	41	1.78 (1.39)
3–4 (7–9)	41	2.95 (1.26)
5–6 (9–11)	52	3.25 (1.23)

At least some teachers at Woodwell Green were aware that younger children struggled with the concept of intention. When I interviewed two teachers who taught infant classes (Miss Hart teaching year 1 [5- and 6-year-olds] and Mrs Jones teaching reception [4- and 5-year-olds]), both commented spontaneously that their children did not understand the distinction between intentional and accidental harm. They told me that the children would often assume a harmful action was intended, even when they did not know how the action had come about, or when it was clearly accidental (such as knocking into someone while pulling on one's coat). Mrs Jones considered that children's understanding improved as they moved through years 1 and 2.

Thus age was a significant factor in children's interpretations of intention. The fact that younger children were gradually learning to separate harmful acts into intended and accidental, and to consider the former more serious than the latter, created a number of potential complexities for their disputes. One such complexity lay in learning which kinds of actions can be accidental. Consider the following extracts from a year 1 classroom (5- and 6-year-olds):

1. The children are practising a dance in the school hall. While Miss Hart is at the CD player, Bikram complains to me of classmate Zain, 'He pushed me.' 'It was by accident,' Zain says. 'It was on purpose,' counters Bikram. At a loss, I say nothing. Bikram starts to shove into Zain by exaggerating the dance movements. As Miss Hart approaches, Zain complains to her, 'Miss she keeps pushing me!' Miss Hart doesn't say anything, but Bikram stops immediately.
2. Miss Hart is talking to Karan and Zain in the classroom. Karan complains that Zain said 'Shut up' to him. The three talk together, and I hear Miss Hart comment sceptically to Zain, 'Can you say shut up by accident? No you can't really. What do you say to Karan?' Zain says sorry and they walk off.

In the first extract, Zain used the on purpose–by accident distinction appropriately, to refer to the intention behind a push or shove in a dispute with his classmate Bikram. In the second, he used the distinction inappropriately, to refer to the intention behind an act of verbal aggression. These extracts suggest that he was still learning which types of behaviour can plausibly be carried out accidentally. While children are still grappling with this issue, there are likely to be disputes about how and when to apply intention to contested events.

Young children's dealings with intention were also complicated by differences between them in the rate at which they came to focus on intention over outcome. Here is an example from my fieldnotes, describing two year 1 boys in the playground:

> Vikram comes up rubbing his nose. 'He punched me in the nose,' he complains of Gagandeep who is just walking up. 'It was by accident,' says Gagandeep. Vikram shakes his head and repeats what he already said, in a resentful tone. Gagandeep looks close to tears so I ask him what he thinks happened. He says that they were playing Dragonball Z[5] and play fighting, when Vikram jogged his elbow so that Gagandeep hit him by accident. I tell Vikram that it was an accident and to shake hands to show that they're still friends. They do so but both still seem quite forlorn, so I ask them to tell me about their game. Gagandeep starts to tell me that he's the 'baddie' and Vikram is the 'goodie', but Vikram interrupts saying again, 'He hit me in the nose.'

In this extract, Vikram was completely focused on the harm caused to him by Gagandeep's action, repeating it even after they had shaken hands and Gagandeep had attempted to move on. One interpretation of this event is that Gagandeep had already learned to focus on intention, but Vikram remained oriented to consequences. Hence, when I attempted to resolve the dispute by referring to intention, I may have helped Gagandeep to move on, but not provided a framework that made any sense to Vikram, leaving him struggling to let go of the harmful act.

Teachers on intention

There was widespread agreement among teachers that intention was an important and relevant issue in assigning responsibility for harmful acts. In interviews with four teachers, all confirmed that they often made use of the distinction between 'on purpose' and 'by accident' when sorting out problems between children. Their claims are supported by my field-notes, which record many cases where teachers referred to the distinction between intended and accidental harm. For example, Miss Hart told her year 1 class (of 5- and 6-year-olds) that intentionally harmful acts were wrong, during a discussion in a religious education (RE) class:

> Miss Hart reminds the children that the previous week in RE, they wrote down things that would make God, their parents or their teacher feel happy or sad. She asks the children what would make them feel sad. Some children put their hands up. 'Bobby, stand up,' says Miss Hart. He does so, looking fed up. 'Bobby should be able to tell us one of them now,' says Miss Hart. 'What's just made your teacher sad Bobby?' 'Not listening,' he replies. Miss Hart agrees, and asks the children for other

examples. They suggest a range of behaviours, including spitting, being unkind, punching, kicking, swearing, pinching, playing rough, putting your middle finger up, not letting someone play, and stepping on someone's feet. For the latter Miss Hart comments, 'Yes, well deliberately stepping on their feet, doing it on purpose, that would make you feel sad.'

In this extract, Miss Hart tells the children that *intentionally* stepping on someone's feet was a cause for sadness (with the implication that *accidentally* doing so was not). In so doing, she was teaching children that harmful acts do not necessarily cause sadness in and of themselves. In other words, she was teaching them to orient not only to the outcome of a harmful act, but also to the intention underlying it.

In addition to giving lessons like this one on the significance of intention in interpreting harmful acts, teachers also sometimes used the intention–accident distinction in the classroom. This was typically an effort to diffuse classroom tensions and focus children on their work by passing off small aggressive acts as accidental. For example, when a year 3 boy complained that another boy on his table kept kicking him, his teacher Miss Williams replied, 'I'm sure he didn't do it on purpose'. Similarly, when a year 3 girl complained of a peer, 'She elbowed me', Miss Williams' response was simply, 'She didn't mean to', before proceeding with the lesson. It is clear that teachers at Woodwell Green actively taught children to distinguish between intended and accidental harm and to base their judgement of culpability on that distinction. Similarly, when resolving children's disputes, teachers attended to issues of intention and encouraged children to do so also. In other words, teachers actively taught children that intention is key to responsibility.[6]

7.2.2 *'He started it': Provocation and reciprocity*

In addition to intention, another important factor influencing children's interpretations of harm was reciprocity. We have seen in earlier chapters that reciprocity or justice was an important principle for the children of Woodwell Green. It was common for children to justify harmful actions, such as hitting, swearing at or excluding each other, by claiming that they were retaliations to prior harmful actions. For example, when year 4 boy Mohamed complained to his teacher that classmate Amandeep would not let him play his game, Amandeep retorted, 'You never let *me* play!'

Factors influencing children's application of reciprocity

In principle, reciprocity involves a simple, unambiguous two-way exchange: a provocation followed by a proportionate retaliation (see Chapter 3). In practice, it was often more complicated than this, for two main reasons.

Firstly, children often disputed whether a particular act was unprovoked (hence demanding retaliation) or a proportionate response to a previous provocation. Things were complicated further by a third class of harmful action: acts that were responses to previous provocation but were out of proportion, hence constituting a new provocation. Here is a typical example, involving boys in year 4 (8 and 9 years) and year 6 (10 and 11 years):

> The whistle goes for the end of lunch break. The year 4 class I am working with is already filing into the school building, and Anil, Mohamed and Faizel aren't in the line yet. I see Anil and call him over, asking where Mohamed and Faizel are. He tells me nonchalantly that Mohamed and Hasad [year 6 boy] have gone over the field [away from the school building]. I ask why and Anil replies, equally frankly, 'to have a fight.' I say that we'll have to go and get them. So Anil and I start to walk towards the field when Mohamed, Faizel and Hasad appear. Faizel walks slightly separately from the other two, kicking a ball along. Hasad and Mohamed shout at each other, then Hasad heads straight into the building, following the last straggles of children. Mohamed is covered in mud and close to tears. I ask why they had a fight. 'He kept on kicking my ball and swearing at me,' he replies. He goes on to explain that Hasad and his friends kick Mohamed's ball every lunchtime. Reading between the lines, I ask him, 'So he was kicking your ball, and you swore at him, and he started swearing back?' Mohamed agrees and adds that Hasad was swearing at his mother.[7] Faizel catches up with Mohamed, Anil and me and comments, 'Mohamed started it, he [Hasad] only kicked his ball for a joke.' Mohamed contests this as we head up the stairs.

In this incident, Mohamed initially offered me a simple account in which Hasad caused the fight by kicking his ball and swearing at him. When I questioned him further, his story developed into a string of events, in which Hasad repeatedly kicked his ball, Mohamed swore at Hasad, Hasad swore at Mohamed's mother (a more serious offence than swearing directly at a person), and the fight broke out. Thus, according to Mohamed, it was Hasad who triggered the incident by repeatedly kicking Mohamed's ball, and it was also Hasad who escalated the exchange between them by not simply swearing back at Mohamed, but bringing his mother into it. However, Faizel (a friend of Mohamed's) offered a very different interpretation: it was Mohamed who 'started it' because what Mohamed perceived as a provocation (Hasad kicking his ball) was a joke, thus Mohamed's swearing at Hasad was an over-reaction and the main provocation for the fight.

This incident demonstrates how complex is the process of assigning responsibility for initiating a harmful exchange, as children struggled to define what counted as a legitimate retaliation and what qualified as downright unprovoked aggression. Such contested interpretations often provided the grounds for a reciprocal exchange to become a long cycle, as each child perceived the actions of the other as provocations, and their own actions as retaliations.

A second reason that reciprocity was often contested between children was that some children disputed its legitimacy altogether. During two group interviews with girls and three with boys in year 5 (all aged 9 or 10 years), I posed a hypothetical question about reciprocity: 'One day you ask Jenny[8] if you can play her game, and Jenny says no. The next day you're playing a game. Jenny comes up to you and asks to play. What do you say?'

Most of the children who participated in the group interviews asserted that they would exclude the child who excluded them, as an act of reciprocity. For example, explaining why they would exclude the excluder, Farhan commented, 'Because he never let me play so why should I let him play?' and Amrita explained, 'Cos when you asked her yesterday she said no. And then, why should you say yes?'

However, several children argued against reciprocating the act of exclusion. For example, Simran argued that 'If, if, if, if, if you ask someone and they say no, the next day if they ask you, you should say yes because then the next day if you ask them, they'll say yes! Simple as that!' Here Simran turned the reciprocity argument on its head, using it in a future-oriented way to justify inclusion, rather than in a past-oriented way to justify exclusion. In the following discussion, girls in another discussion group considered a range of arguments for and against excluding the excluder and, in doing so, explored the limits of reciprocity:

RW: It's whether you would say, would you, would you let them play or would you not let them play [clarifying explanation of question given by Maria]

MARIA: [interrupting] Yeah, that's what it says.

KIRAN: No because they've just gone and said to them that they can't play.

AYESHA: Yeah.

JOANNE: Exactly.

AYESHA: No, exactly.

NAVNEET: I agree, I agree.

ZENA: I disagree!

AYESHA: I, I agree.

KIRAN: What do you mean you dis?

[brief laughter]

NAVNEET: Miss she said disacree! [laughs]

[brief laughter]

ZENA: No, because, because, if you say no yeah, if you say no yeah, and then, and then again you asked them to play, they're gonna say no again, and then it's gonna keep on going, then you're never gonna [raises voice] make friends with them.

RW: [while Zena speaks] Yeah

AYESHA: No look!

KIRAN: I know they say no and it's my turn now.

MARIA: No Miss, Miss

[Several girls talk at same time, inaudible]

JOANNE: Let her carry on.

NAVNEET: I know, if they say no

RW: [interrupting] So you think you should let them play?

JOANNE: [interrupting] Let her finish! She ain't finished.

ZENA: Yeah, because next time when you go after them they can let you play and you can be friends and then you, if you didn't, if not, it's gonna keep on going yeah, you're gonna end up with like, arguing

NAVNEET: [interrupting] Miss, Miss

KIRAN: [right into microphone] Yes Zena we know.

NAVNEET: Miss I've got a similar one to Zena's, it's like, if someone's playing, yeah

RW: [at same time as Navneet is speaking] No, Kiran don't move it [tape recorder] around okay.

KIRAN: What will happen?

RW: Well cos it's, like, cos I'm only borrowing it, I don't want it to get damaged or anything cos I'll have to pay for it.

KIRAN: [interrupting] Then you have to pay.

RW: Yeah.

NAVNEET: Miss because you know like, it's like, if you're playing and you say no to someone else and the other person says yes, then you could play with them and the next time they might, then the next time that the person that went up to them might say that you can play now because you let us go, like that.

181

KIRAN: [loudly] Yeah, but you, you said to them
JOANNE: [interrupting] Same reason. That's what I [inaudible]
AYESHA: Miss, I'm confused, I don't know who to go with!
KIRAN: [loudly] No I would go with, look, you lot, you lot have just gone up to them, that they can't play, so, it's obvious that I'm going with myself.
MARIA: [interrupting] I'm going with both.
AYESHA: [interrupting Kiran] Yeah me too.
NAVNEET: You're the loudest one Kiran!

[laughter and sounds of agreement]

ZENA: She's got a big mouth! [laughs]
KIRAN: [inaudible] That, they say to you, that you're not allowed to play, [inaudible]
JOANNE: [interrupting] This is meant to be a library, quiet!

[laughter, several talk at once]

NAVNEET: This is meant to be like this.
RW: Maria, what do you think?
MARIA: [while Navneet and I speak together very quietly and inaudibly] Miss I think that, Miss I think if they be rude to you don't be rude to them because it's their nature, never listen to devils, this is the little green man.
KIRAN: Yeah, listen, don't listen to the [inaudible]

[Several girls talking at same time, inaudible]

MARIA: [still with others talking] That's their nature, right, Miss that's their nature and our nature is good nature yeah.

[Several girls talking at same time, inaudible]

MARIA: First is, don't be rude to anyone.

[Several girls talking at same time, inaudible]

MARIA: Don't be rude to anyone, if they be rude to you, don't be rude back.
RW: But what if they keep on being rude to you then?
MARIA: Keep on, just leave them. Don't talk to them. Just ignore them.
KIRAN: Ignore them.
JOANNE: They won't be [inaudible] in argument.
NAVNEET: They're gonna keep annoying you, they're gonna keep annoying you.
JOANNE   [shouts something, inaudible]
MARIA: Just ignore them.

[inaudible shouting]

ZENA: No, you lose your temper, [inaudible]

[Some inaudible talk followed by a dispute about who should speak next. Then Maria returns to the topic.]

MARIA: You know erm, if they being rude to you don't be rude to back, er if they, just ignore them cos er Miss, every, er, if you, sometimes [inaudible] that, if you ignore the other person, then they're not gonna annoy you anyway.

AYESHA: Yeah. And two wrongs don't make a right.

ZENA: Miss but, what, [laughs] but, but Miss erm, you see, you still play with them, because, because then, one day yeah, um, even though you ignore them, you're gonna lose your temper on you, and then you're gonna end up in swearing at them, and then, and starting a fight, and then you're gonna have a letter home.[9]

In this group interview, the girls grappled with several competing arguments concerning reciprocity. Kiran opened the discussion with her claim that the excluder should be excluded 'because they've just gone and said to them that they can't play'. Three girls agreed with this typical response based on reciprocity, before Zena offered a counter-argument, similar to the head teacher's critique of reciprocity: 'If you say no yeah, if you say no yeah, and then, and then again you asked them to play, they're gonna say no again, and then it's gonna keep on going, then you're never gonna make friends with them.' Navneet (who was officially Zena's best friend; see Chapter 5) supported Zena with an argument very similar to Simran's (who attended in the other girls' group interview): 'If you're playing and you say no to someone else and the other person says yes, then you could play with them and the next time they might, then the next time that the person that went up to them might say that you can play now because you let us go, like that.'

Two girls (Ayesha and Maria) declared sympathy with both Kiran's and Zena's arguments. Maria then introduced a new argument, which is explicitly anti-reciprocity: If someone is rude to you, ignore them and do not react. She justified her 'turn the other cheek' argument with reference to the 'devil'-like nature of rude people compared to the good nature of the ignorer. Zena provided a pragmatic challenge that may have been triggered by my question, 'What if they keep on being rude to you?': It is not possible to keep ignoring someone who is consistently rude, because eventually one loses one's temper, reciprocates and gets into trouble.

What these discussions suggest is that although children do often advocate reciprocity, some are critical of it, arguing instead for other principles (such as harm avoidance through turning the other cheek), or for a break in retributions in order to turn a chain of harmful events into a chain of beneficial ones, in an effort to break the cycle of harm. It may be that girls were more open than boys to these alternatives (as seemed to be the case in the group interviews I ran) because boys were orienting to widespread associations between toughness, masculinity and status, such that not retaliating (especially to a physical attack) would be construed by other boys as a sign of weakness (see Chapter 3). In contrast, while girls at Woodwell Green valued toughness (see Chapter 2), they tended to demonstrate status through relationships (see Chapter 5). In other words, reciprocity was entangled with other important values for boys more than it was for girls. Either way, children at Woodwell Green clearly differed in the extent to which they embraced reciprocity as a legitimate value in the playground, and this difference may have informed their disputes in some cases.

Teachers struggling with reciprocity
Official school rules did not consider reciprocity a legitimate principle when assigning responsibility for children's harmful acts in the playground. This was most evident in the head teacher's refusal to accept retaliation as an excuse for physical aggression, and his argument that retaliation created a cycle of violence; 'If I hit him he'll hit me and I'll hit him and it'll never end' (see Chapter 3). Nevertheless, there were signs that teachers found reciprocity hard to ignore completely. For example, in an interview with me, reception teacher Mrs Jones told me that when a child complained to her of being hurt by a peer, she would ask (for instance), 'What happened to make him push you?' Here is another example from a year 6 classroom:

> The children are sitting at their tables. Fadi [Pakistani Muslim boy] starts to cry, and Mrs Walker, the teaching assistant, sharply asks Jade [English, no religion], who sits opposite, 'Why did you kick him?' 'I didn't,' she says. 'Well someone did!' she exclaims. Miss Lock [class teacher] hears the exchange and calls, 'Jade, come here.' When Jade does so, Miss Lock repeats, 'Look at me!' three times, until finally Jade obeys. She asks sternly, 'Did you kick Fadi?' 'Yes but he kicked me first,' she replies. 'Did you kick her first?' Miss Lock asks Fadi, who protests, 'She kicked me first. I told Mrs Walker then she kicked me again.' Miss Lock says to Jade, 'Even if he did kick you first should you kick him back?'

In this extract, Miss Lock sought Jade's confirmation that she kicked Fadi. Jade provided this, but then claimed that Fadi kicked her first, hence provoking (and justifying) her kick. Fadi denied this, leaving Miss Lock in the difficult position of deciding between two competing descriptions of events. Her solution was not to choose between them, but instead to suggest to Jade that her kick was wrong regardless of whether it was provoked (the official school position on physical aggression). Yet her interest in whether Fadi did kick first and the wording of her final question to Jade ('Even if he did kick you first...') suggest that, like Mrs Jones, Miss Lock saw provocation as relevant to the situation. It seems that, like some of the children, teachers may also have felt some ambivalence regarding the legitimacy of reciprocity when accounting for harmful acts.

7.3 High Court Judges: Teachers 'Sorting it Out'

I suggested earlier that when intervening in children's moral lives, teachers considered their first and main responsibility to be working out 'what really happened'. As we have seen, this was a huge challenge because children frequently interpreted events differently from one another, for example in terms of whether a harmful act was seen as intentional (versus accidental) or a reasonable retaliation (versus a provocation). Working out 'what really happened' was further complicated by the possibility of children deceiving teachers.

7.3.1 Deception

It was widely accepted by children and teachers alike at Woodwell Green that children would sometimes deliberately lie, exaggerate or omit information when telling a teacher about a contested event. Deception could concern intention, provocation or other details of the disputed event. For example, when interviewing year 6 boy Owen about the hypothetical scenario in which Hamzah hit Ben during a playground football game, I asked him what he thought was the best way to resolve the dispute.

OWEN: Tell a teacher.
RW: Who would?
OWEN: Ben.
RW: What would the teacher do?
OWEN: Um, she'd probably sort it out but I think there'd be lots of lies.
RW: Who would lie?
OWEN: Hamzah.
RW: How will the teacher sort it out?
OWEN: She'll have to go and tell the head teacher and he'll sort it out, if it's serious. I think the head teacher would be able to get Hamzah to tell the truth.

In this extract, Owen asserted that the protagonist in the story was likely to lie, presumably to protect his own interests. In response to the same question, three of his classmates also suggested that children would lie to the teacher. For example, when I asked Venya what she thought would happen after Jenny hit Priya, she replied, 'Um, one of those [points to children watching in accompanying picture] will go get a dinner lady and the dinner lady will sort it out but they will still be arguing and Jenny would lie and say she didn't hit Priya, but the other children saw it and they would tell'. In response to the same scenario, year 5 girl Kiran suggested that Hamzah might lie about his intention in order to evade trouble:

RW: What would have been the best way to sort this out? Is it the same as what you just said [to previous question, which asked what would happen next], or different?

KIRAN: Er, when, if Ben told a teacher, Hamzah shoulda said I done it by accident, I didn't mean to hit him.

RW: Why would he say that?

KIRAN: To not get in trouble.

RW: Is it true or not true?

KIRAN: Not true. Cos Hamzah doesn't wanna get in trouble.

These are all claims about hypothetical scenarios, but children also told me about deceptions they had actually carried out or witnessed. For example, in an interview about his friendships, year 4 boy Amar told me about a dispute he had had with classmate Faizel. He explained, 'He [Faizel] was beating up Tahir [Amar's younger cousin], because you know Faizel, he was kicking Tahir, I had to punch him on the head. Mrs Thomas [playground supervisor] came over and stopped the fight. You know Amandeep, he pulled Faizel away'. I asked Amar why Amandeep did this. 'To stop the fight,' he replied. 'Who got in trouble?' I asked. 'Farhan was kicking Faizel on the head but he said no I didn't, no I didn't, but he got out of it, so me, Tahir and Faizel got in trouble, but Tahir was lucky he wasn't doing anything.' According to Amar, then, Farhan denied involvement in this fight and successfully evaded reprimand and punishment.

When he was in year 5, Amar's classmate Sandeep also gave me an example of a child lying to deflect blame, this time regarding the intention behind a harmful act. Sandeep told me that his classmate Faizel sometimes kicked the ball at children who were not playing football 'on purpose' and afterwards claimed that it was 'by accident'. Sandeep told me that he knew Faizel did this on purpose because, before he kicked the ball, he would say, 'Watch this!'

Sometimes children's deception involved not outright lying but exaggeration. For instance, during an interview in which I asked which children in his class he liked the most and least, year 4 boy Amandeep told me he did not like Idris, proceeding to recount a time when the two boys fought over possession of a football. 'And then Mr Gardner [head teacher] was coming yeah, cos somebody told Mr Gardner.' Amandeep told me that at this point he ran off and hid but Idris followed him and started to kick him again. Amandeep told me that he pretended to be really hurt, and when Mr Gardner arrived on the scene he said (Amandeep put on an angry voice), '*Idris what are you doing?*' 'He got a detention for that,' he finished with amused satisfaction, going on to tell me that boys often pretend to be more hurt than they really are, in order to get someone in trouble.

All the examples just offered describe cases of children lying to protect themselves from blame and/or to deflect the blame onto someone else. Children also lied or withheld information to protect friends. For example, in an interview in year 4 about his friendships, Zak named Idris as one of his best friends, explaining, 'If there's something you don't want Miss to know you can tell him and he won't tell'. Griffiths (1995) found that white working-class children in northern England also demonstrated loyalty to one another by lying to a teacher on their friend's behalf.

Sometimes, lies to protect others arose when children who had had a dispute resolved it before the teacher had a chance to intervene. We saw an example in Chapter 3, when Zak told me in an interview that warring children waiting to be reprimanded sometimes made pacts with each other to withhold information about rule transgressions from teachers. During an interview in year 5, his classmate Anil offered a specific example of this tactic. He told me that another boy, Ali, 'was trying to get' him and his classmate Pavandeep. The three ended up being sent to the head teacher's office, but while waiting to be seen, Anil and Ali made friends and agreed not to 'tell on' each other. Here are two further examples, both involving year 4 boys:

1. Having sent the rest of the children out for lunch break, Miss Chahal is talking to Zak and two boys from another year 4 class about an earlier incident in which she saw the three fighting. 'What's been going on?' she asks. All three start talking at once. Miss Chahal stops them, saying, 'I want Zak to tell me. I trust Zak.'[10] So Zak talks and the others interject from time to time. Zak says that someone kicked him by accident. 'By accident?' Miss Chahal repeats in a questioning tone. All three go on to claim that they were arguing about the result of the game of football they were playing, but that they were not actually fighting. 'It looked like fighting,' Miss Chahal comments. Then one of the three says that another boy [not present] was trying to pick a fight with him, but that he used to get into trouble for fighting in year 3 so he replied, 'Forget it' to this boy. Miss Chahal says, in an amused and

187

slightly sarcastic tone, 'Oh, you *used* to fight when you were in year 3 but now that you're in year 4 you don't do that babyish stuff anymore.' They all agree vehemently. She sends them out and after they've gone, she and I laugh.

2. It is lunchtime. Miss Chahal and I are still in her classroom; the children have all gone outside. A student teacher comes in and tells Miss Chahal that two boys in her class, Mohamed and Farhan, were supposed to come and see her before lunch about a scuffle the two had on the stairs this morning. Another child reappears in the classroom to get something they forgot, and Miss Chahal asks them to fetch Mohamed and Farhan. The two appear after a few minutes. Miss Chahal calls the student teacher in, and tells the two boys to apologise for not going to see her. Then she asks them what happened. Farhan says that someone leaned on Mohamed who then bumped into him by mistake. 'Oh, by mistake,' says Miss Chahal smiling. 'It's an accident now is it?'

In both these examples, boys who seem to have had some sort of genuine dispute reframed their interpretation of events into something less serious and, thus, less likely to elicit reprimand or punishment from the teacher.

There is evidence, then, that children quite often attempted to deceive teachers about harmful acts in the playground. Teachers did what they could to prevent children from doing this. A year 4 teacher informed me that she told children that the truth will come out anyway through witnesses, and it would be worse for them then if she discovered that they had lied. She also told them to have the courage to tell the truth. Another year 4 teacher told me that she encouraged children to be truthful by saying that they should try to be a bigger person. These strategies all aim to elevate the status of honesty above the rival considerations that might lead a child to lie (such as fear of getting into trouble, loyalty to a peer and distrust of authority).

7.3.2 'Getting to the bottom of it': Teachers' quest for truth

Recognising that children's accounts of what happened in morally significant events frequently differed from one another, teachers usually offered each child involved an opportunity to present their version of events. This approach is beautifully observed in the following story about four children in the school playground, narrated to me by year 4 boy, Hafiz:

These two, Jacob and Callum, be playing a match of football, and um, Jacob hits Samantha, and Samantha says 'Why did you hit me?' and he says 'It was an accident' and she said 'No it wasn't cos you pushed me and kicked me out the way like' and then Callum says to him that 'You did do it' and Jacob pushes Callum and punches him, and Dominic comes, and Dominic says 'Stop the fight', and Jacob says 'Shut up' to him and he says 'Back to you' and the teacher comes and says 'What's the matter?' and all of them start speaking at once, and the, the teacher said that 'First Callum will speak' and then Callum says that 'We were playing a match of football and then Jacob pushed Samantha and kicked her in the mud.' And the teacher says 'Jacob,' and Jacob says, 'It was an accident' and Samantha says, 'No it wasn't' and the teacher says, 'First let Jacob speak,' and Jacob says, 'I'm done,' and then er the teacher says, 'Dominic you can speak now,' and Dominic says that um, that er, that um, 'Jacob pushed her in the mud and he said it was an accident' and Jacob said 'It was an accident' and Samantha shouts out that it wasn't and Jacob shouts out, 'Shut up Samantha'. And then the teacher says, 'Samantha never lies to a teacher,' and then the teacher said, 'Jacob you liar most of the time,' and Jacob just walks away miserably and um he gets a detention, and Samantha, Samantha runs away, and Callum and Dominic start their own game of football, and then Callum wins the match and he says 'Thanks Dominic for playing with me.'

In this story (which is yet another example of the importance of intention in attributing blame), the teacher successfully adjudicated between the children's competing versions of events, reaching a verdict based on their reputations for honesty (a tactic we return to shortly). However, in reality teachers were sometimes less successful. In a complex event involving several children, deception plus differences in interpretation can make for a highly confusing mass of contradictions. Here are two typical examples, the first from a year 4 classroom (8- and 9-year-olds), and the second from a year 3 classroom (7- and 8-year-olds). Both events took place in the classroom, directly after lunch break.

Incident 1

Idris complains to Miss Chahal, 'Zak said I had the lurgy and that no-one should play with me.'[11] Miss Chahal is annoyed about this and asks Zak and Idris more about what happened. But several contradictory claims emerge, and in the end, Miss Chahal asks, 'Who's involved?' She sends Zak and four other boys to Mr Gardner [head teacher]. After a short while, two of the boys return. The other three return a bit later with Mr Gardner at the same moment as I leave the classroom on an errand for Miss Chahal. In the corridor Mr Gardner shakes his head at me. 'Confusing,' he comments wryly.

Incident 2

Miss Williams gathers together Jack, Jordan and Bradley, who were all involved in a fight at lunchtime. In front of the class, she gives each boy the chance to tell his version of events to her. These are offered very rapidly and I cannot keep up, but record what I can. Jack speaks first. 'Jordan and Lewis was beating up Bradley,' he begins, continuing that Bradley said 'I'm gonna beat up Lewis' but that he, Jack, advised him not to. He claims that an adult intervened at this point, but after she had departed there was a fight. According to Jack, Jordan went to hit Bradley, but Jack got in the way so Jordan hit him instead, and 'So I kicked him', Jack explains. Miss Williams wants to know whether Jack kicked Jordan before or after he realised Jordan hadn't meant to hit him, but Jack doesn't give a clear answer to this question.[12]

Next, it is Jordan's turn. He claims that he was trying to break up a fight when Bradley started hitting him. Then, he says, 'Jack kicked me.' 'You hurt him first?' Miss Williams asks. 'Yes,' Jordan replies, continuing, 'So I accidentally punched him.' Finally, Bradley has his say. 'Me and Tyrone were having a fight, Jordan came along and punched me because Tyrone is his best friend.' Bradley says that he, Bradley, then started to hit Jordan.

The boys say lots more that I don't manage to write down. When they have finished, Miss Williams, exasperated, asks them, 'Why are you doing this? You know it's not the answer.' She reminds them that they have been taught strategies to stop themselves from wanting to hurt someone. 'What are you meant to do when you feel angry?' They claim not to know. 'Take ten deep breaths,' Miss Williams says. 'Why are you doing it? Because you're not thinking first.'

She turns to reprimand two children in her class who are talking, and then Jack complains that during lunch break, Bradley put his middle finger up at him, 'said the F word' and insulted his parents. Bradley denies this. Miss Williams asks if anyone else heard. Jane calls out that it's true. Bradley looks at her in disbelief. Jane asserts confidently that she and two other children were walking past the boys on their way to lunch and heard them. Miss Williams trusts this information. She sends first for Mr Gardner [head teacher] to pursue the issue of exactly what happened but he is not available. Then she sends for Miss Brooks [deputy head], who is also unavailable, so she sends for a teacher who is not with a class, to sit in the corridor, call the children involved one at a time to explain what had happened, and write it down. Then she calls up another group of children to sort out a different dispute from lunchtime.

In both these examples, class teachers attempted to resolve disputes that had broken out during lunch break by asking each child who was involved to give their own account of what had happened. In both cases, the result was a bewildering mess of claims and counter-claims. In the second incident in particular my note-taking skill was no match for the speed and complexity with which the boys' accounts unfolded. On both these occasions, the teachers passed the problem onto another teacher (the first choice of both Miss Chahal and Miss Williams being the head), but of course this option was not always available. Teachers had to try to unravel the confusion effectively yet without taking up too much classroom time; after all, they were supposed to be teaching and might, as with Miss Williams, still have other disputes and complaints to resolve. Given these circumstances, it is inevitable that teachers will rely on strategies and heuristics in order to reach a verdict under tight time constraints. Below we explore some of the strategies they employed.

7.3.3 Witnesses

As we just saw with Miss Williams and Jane, to help them to adjudicate between competing claims, teachers relied on witnesses, children who were not directly involved in the incident but who observed what happened. For example, I was discussing the physical aggression scenario with year 5 boy Mohamed. When I asked what he thought would happen next, he suggested, 'That he'll [Hamzah, the boy who hit] get a detention and a letter home, and the teacher'll say [to Ben, the boy who was hit] good you never hit him back'. 'How will she know about the fight?' I asked.[13] 'All these people here, are like proof, and so is Ben,' he replied. It was extremely common for teachers to use 'witnesses' to provide evidence of what happened. Here are three examples from my fieldnotes.

1. Year 4 classroom [8- and 9-year-olds]: Hassan tells Miss Chahal either that Anil hurt him with a pencil or threw a pencil at him [I did not hear his exact wording]. Miss Chahal tries to find out what happened. Mohamed negates Hassan's account, saying, 'No, he [Hassan] took Anil's pencil out of his hand, he was trying to get it back.' Miss Chahal asks Nyarai, who sits next to Hassan, what happened. She says she doesn't know. 'Miss, I saw!' exclaims Farah. Miss Chahal asks her to elaborate. 'He took it on purpose out of his hand and when Anil tried to get it back he poked him by accident,' she says. Paul comments that Hassan used to be in his class at his former school and used to do this kind of thing all the time. He adds that Pavandeep was in that class as well, but Pavandeep doesn't say anything. Hassan continues to protest. 'Hassan why are you saying no when everyone

around is saying yes?' asks Miss Chahal. 'Don't start crying now Hassan,' she adds, for he looks really unhappy.

2. Waiting outside Mr Gardner's office are year 4 boys Faizel, Anil and Yusuf. I stop to chat with Faizel and Anil, and ask what they're doing outside the head teacher's office. They explain that two boys beat up Yusuf in the playground, so a playground supervisor sent Yusuf to explain to Mr Gardner what happened. Anil and Faizel saw the incident so they were also sent as witnesses.

3. Year 6 classroom [10- and 11-year-olds]: The children are lined up ready to go to assembly. Someone switches off the computer monitor, and someone else draws it to Miss Lock's attention, perhaps also telling her that it was Alan. Miss Lock approaches him and asks, 'Why did the monitor go off?' 'Miss I ain't done anything I swear!' he replies. 'That's a very guilty way to react if you haven't done anything,' responds Miss Lock. Alan says that he was resting his hands by the computer. Miss Lock jumps on this, saying, 'I thought you said you didn't do anything.' She turns to a girl who she thought saw what happened, but the girl replies, 'It was Prajit' [who saw], and steps aside. Prajit does an impression of what Alan was doing, tapping with his hands on the side of the monitor. Alan admits this, and Miss Lock reprimands him for lying, telling him he has to stay in for part of playtime. Alan's brow is deeply furrowed and he has a look of being hard done by.

What is common to all these incidents is the teacher's use of other (ideally uninvolved) children to find out what really happened in a contested situation. In an interview, a year 4 teacher confirmed that she sometimes used children as witnesses to help her work out what really happened. She offered a recent example, in which one boy punched another in the face. According to the teacher, the puncher said he did it because the other boy punched first, while the punched boy retorted, 'No I didn't, I just tagged you'.[14] The teacher told me that while she was happy to resolve minor problems by herself, she considered this one serious and referred it to Mr Gardner, the head teacher, who interviewed individually four children as witnesses in order to get 'to the bottom of things'.

Teachers can use witnesses to work out what happened by examining the coherence of different accounts in relation to one another, and by looking for a dominant account to emerge (as it did in extract 1 above). However, deception and differences in interpretation mean that it was sometimes still difficult to work out what happened. In such cases, teachers needed additional strategies, the most significant of which seemed to be character judgements of the children involved.

7.3.4   Trustworthiness: Truth-seeking or taking sides?

In Hafiz's story, included earlier in this chapter, the teacher resolved the dispute by making judgements about the trustworthiness of different children; 'Samantha never lies to a teacher' and 'Jacob you liar most of the time'. Hafiz here identified a key strategy that teachers relied upon to establish what happened: rank children's accounts based on how likely the child is to be honest to the teacher. In separate interviews, two year 4 teachers commented to me that they trusted particular children in their class to tell the truth. I witnessed an example in the playground one lunchtime, when year 4 girls Farah and Anjali made fun of a dance that classmate Sarina was performing with some friends to a Bollywood song. Shortly afterwards, Sarina hit Farah. Sarina claimed that Farah had hit her first, while Farah and Simran (who was a bystander) both claimed that she did not. Sarina countered Farah's and Simran's claims by saying, 'Yeah but they all hate me that lot'. Mrs Thomas, the playground supervisor who was attempting to resolve the dispute, replied gently, 'Simran doesn't tell lies'.

Children's reliability came up not only when evaluating accounts of what happened, but also when assessing the seriousness of a harmful event. In an interview, a teacher of a reception class (4- and 5-year-olds) told me that when responding to a child who is upset, she differentiates between those for whom 'something's really happened' and children who are 'turning on the waterworks'. In other words, teachers considered that some children were prone to over-reacting and exaggerating their suffering at the hands of another. Here is another example, from my fieldnotes:

> Jason [year group unknown] races toward me, whirling round me for protection, panting that another boy is trying to beat him up. This boy races up, lunges across me [as I try to keep them separate] and punches Jason in the stomach; he doubles over, crouches on the floor and bursts into tears. 'Stay here, what's your name and whose class are you in?' I say to the attacker, and he tells me that his name is Jerome, but I don't recall his class. Miss Brooks [deputy head teacher] is walking past and I call her over. She asks what happened and I tell her what I saw. She asks me to confirm some details, then takes Jerome away. I stay with Jason, who tells me his version of what happened. He gradually stops crying and I encourage him to stand up, but he says it's too sore. Then Miss Brooks returns and, within his earshot and whilst giving me a look, says, 'I know Jason quite well and I think he's fine.' We raise him to his feet and he walks off with his friend.

So teachers interpreted children's accounts not only on the basis of what was said in the particular event they sought to unravel, but also on the basis of their reputations, as honest or deceptive. This renders children's reputations very important, because they can influence a teacher's interpretation and hence who gets blamed and punished. For teachers, this was a strategy for reaching the truth in confusing disputes. But some children perceived teachers' differential trust quite differently: as bias and taking sides. Here is an example, from a group interview I conducted with Zak, Faizel, Amar and Mohamed when they were in year 5. The boys had just been telling me about how some teachers were biased against them (see Chapters 3 and 6).

RW: Who would you prefer to tell problems to then, or would you rather just keep them to yourself?

FAIZEL: I would keep it to myself, and if I wanted to I would take it to, to, if it was outside Miss Rao's classroom I would take it to Miss Rao. I like sorting it out by myself and I like going to Miss Brooks [deputy head] but Mrs Samson [their class teacher] always interferes.

RW: So do you think Miss Brooks is better than the others then?

FAIZEL: She's a bit better, but when it's between me and Sam, she sometimes takes Sam's side. And Mrs Samson always takes Joshua's side innit.

MOHAMED: Yeah cos he plays with girls and stuff like that.

RW: Why do you think that Mrs Samson takes Joshua's side?

MOHAMED: Miss thinks that Faizel tells lies and Miss thinks that Joshua tells the truth.

FAIZEL: Yeah, Mrs Samson always says, 'Oh it's never you is it?' She thinks she's right but she isn't, not all the time.

The boys clearly resented their teacher's trust of Joshua, which they perceived as bias. I interviewed Zak and Faizel a couple of weeks later, and the boys again raised this issue. Faizel had just commented that he disliked Joshua, and I asked him why.

ZAK: This what happened yeah, Zena yeah, I don't know if she got hit by Mohamed.

FAIZEL: She didn't yeah, he just touched her shoulder.

ZAK: Miss the thing about girls yeah, you just touch them and they go running to the teacher, and I had my hand up yeah, I was gonna tell her the truth yeah, but she [their teacher] said *put your hand down*. The teacher asked Joshua what happened.

FAIZEL: Miss the thing about Joshua is that Miss trusts him, but he doesn't tell the truth.

ZAK: Mohamed only said, don't ask Joshua yeah cos he's the girls' friend, and Miss sent him to Miss Brooks.

194

Both Zak and Faizel were adamant that their teacher was wrong to place her trust in Joshua. According to Zak, it was Mohamed who was attempting to avoid bias by pointing out that the witness chosen by their teacher was a friend of the victim, and hence could not be expected to provide an independent, truthful account. Yet these efforts resulted only in punishment for Mohamed.

Of course, it is likely that the boys too were biased in their perceptions of Joshua and how their teacher treated him; Zak at least was suspicious of Joshua because he usually played with girls. He mused to me during an interview, 'He can't stop talking with the girls that's around him. He always plays with girls. Why does he always play with girls, why doesn't he play football? Does he like girls?' Zak and his friends may have assumed that Joshua was biased towards the girls because he did not attempt to present himself as a tough male in the form widely respected among boys at Woodwell Green (see Chapter 3). Nevertheless, it is understandable that when they saw a teacher trusting a child who they considered partisan (being 'the girls' friend'), they felt as though the teacher was taking sides rather than acting as an impartial judge. It is also understandable that children, like Zak, who see things this way are likely to become increasingly disillusioned with the school's system of discipline and thus to try to take justice into their own hands, as we saw in Chapter 3.

7.3.5 Resolving disputes

Adults' solutions: Play together or stay away from each other
Once teachers had heard the evidence, weighed competing accounts against each other and reached a decision about what actually happened, they would then reprimand and/or punish children who had broken school rules (see Chapter 1 for more on school punishments, or 'consequences' as they were typically known). They might also attempt to end the dispute by encouraging children to apologise and make friends (see Chapter 4 for an example from Mrs Samson), or issue advice regarding how to prevent the dispute from arising again. Such advice usually took the form, 'Play together nicely, or stay away from each other'. Here is an example, from a year 3 classroom (7- and 8-year-olds) directly after lunch break:

> Miss Williams calls Megan and Nina to the front of the classroom, to resolve a dispute that took place at lunchtime. Nina offers her version of events first. She lists a whole string of girls' names, continuing, 'We were playing had yeah.'[15] I am soon confused, but gather that Megan wanted to play but when

she was chosen in the dipping [a rhyme designed to select one child from a group], she refused to be on [i.e. the person who must try to catch everyone else]. Nina imitates her, whining, 'I don't wanna play,' as she pouts and folds her arms. Nina continues that Megan said she couldn't run because she had a bad tummy, but she, Nina, had seen her running around.

Now Miss Williams elicits Megan's version, which I find even more confusing. She says something about the dipping which I couldn't follow, then claims that she wanted to play with the other girls but that Nina kept running away. Nina interjects with a protesting 'No-o-o!' Megan says that she told Mr Gardner who said that it was something they needed to sort out between them. Miss Williams comments that he has lots of experience of this sort of thing so was probably right. She says that the two seem to fight almost every day, and suggests that they don't play with each other for a while, or if they start to argue to just walk away from each other. Nina replies, 'I do that but she keeps coming up.' She adds that their classmate Jane always used to 'sort it out' for them but they couldn't find her this lunchtime. Miss Williams comments that that sounds very grown up and she asks Jane how she sorts it out. Jane says she asks them what's wrong and they tell her that they've been fighting, she tells them to make friends and they shake hands. Now Nina spontaneously says, 'Sorry' to Megan, and Miss Williams oversees their apologising and shaking hands with each other.

Miss Williams' suggestion that Megan and Nina stay away from each other was typical; during my fieldwork several children commented to me that teachers and playground supervisors solved problems by telling the children either to 'play together (nicely)' or 'stay away from each other'. Such a solution is, clearly, rather crude, especially given how complex children's disputes can be, based as they are on multiple interpretations and responding to several different values and concerns (as we have seen throughout this book). It is understandable that, with little time at their disposal, teachers would provide such a simple solution, but from children's point of view it can be unsatisfactory. Consider the edict to all play together. Where children are struggling with loyalty disputes (like Sarah, Joshua and Joanne, described in Chapter 4), playing together does not necessarily resolve them, and can exacerbate them. This is certainly the view of these two year 6 children. I was interviewing them individually about the hypothetical dilemma in which two children (for these interviews, Katie and Jasmine) both sought to play exclusively with a third child (Sani).

RW: What do you think will happen next?
MOHAN: Mmm, Katie might, Katie might go and tell the teacher that Jasmine, she's like playing with her friend and she don't want to play, and then Jasmine and Katie might get into a big fight.

RW: What would the teacher do?

MOHAN: She might just say, stop fighting, and you should play together, not be angry with each other anything like that.

RW: Will they be able to play together?

MOHAN: Well, Jasmine might be feeling a bit moody like and if they were playing games they'll always make Katie it, like if they're playing had or Hide and Seek she has to count. She won't have any fun.

RW: What do you think will happen next?

ASHA: I think probably cos they're not actually fighting or shouting at each other the teacher probably wouldn't think that something's going wrong there so I think what Sani would do, Sani would run, not the teacher coming to her, she would go to a teacher and say what shall I do, Katie and Jasmine are not friends, they're fighting.

RW: What would the teacher do?

ASHA: The teacher will say that they all play together and they'll pretend they're walking together and start playing but then it'll start again. They'll play together but Katie and Jasmine will be rude to each other when Sani's not hearing.

These children both thought that a teacher would recommend that the children in the scenario should play together, but that this would not resolve their dispute. Some children were more optimistic about the effects of playing together in this scenario, but these voices of dissent suggest that others found it an inadequate solution to their disputes.

Children also had concerns about adults' advice to stay away from each other. Such a solution is problematic if both children want to play the same game (such as football), use the same playground resources, or have the same mutual friends. Here is an example from my fieldnotes:

A year 3 boy comes up to me in the playground and complains, 'I told Jack he can't play and he won't give my ball back.' I suggest that he threaten to tell Mrs Samson if Jack won't return his ball. He does so, then approaches Mrs Samson, and then me again. He has his ball now but says that Jack is still hanging around even though he's told him he can't play. He informs me that he told Mrs Samson this and she said that Jack had done nothing wrong. I suggest that he moves to a different part of the playground, but he replies that they need this location in order to play football. So I suggest that he ignore Jack. He says that he's been told to keep away from Jack, and asks me to tell Jack to go away. I say that Jack won't take any notice of me and I'm not a dinner lady so he'll have to ask someone else. He walks away dissatisfied.

This boy's problem derived from the tension between his need to stay away from Jack (as per advice given by a teacher or playground supervisor) and his desire to stay in the same location as Jack in order to play football. Given his reluctance to move away, and his inability to make Jack leave, the only other option was for an adult to command Jack to leave the area, something he found both Mrs Samson and me unwilling to do. In this case, the edict to stay away from each other did not seem to be doing much to resolve tensions between these two boys.

Children's solutions: Forgetting and humour

How else might children's disputes be resolved, if not by suggesting that they play together or avoid one another? It is enlightening to look at how children go about solving disputes without involving an adult. One solution that children spoke about in interviews with me was, surprisingly, time and inaction. Several children told me that they resolved disputes with friends simply by allowing time to pass and then resuming the friendship as if nothing had happened. We saw one example earlier in this chapter, when year 6 boy Mansukh described a fight he witnessed between two boys. His account finished by explaining how they made friends: 'They weren't friends, and the next day they came back and went oh hi how you doing!' Here are more examples, this time from year 5 children talking about their own experiences of one of the hypothetical scenarios, in which one child told another that a third child was spreading rumours about him or her.

ZAK: Sam tells Ali stuff that I never said, then me and Ali falled out.
RW: Did you make friends?
ZAK: Yeah.
RW: How did you make friends?
ZAK: Miss pretend it happened on a Tuesday, on Wednesday morning we just be friends.
RW: Did you talk about it to make friends or not?
ZAK: We don't talk to each other, on the next day he says Zak, do you wanna know the answer to this question?

SIMRAN: Um, I was um playing yeah, and then Navneet said to Harpreet not to be my friend for some reason. We were playing so nicely yeah.
RW: What happened then?
SIMRAN: And then everybody started not to be my friend. Not everyone.

[We go off topic briefly to talk about a different matter. Then we return to the situation Simran is describing.]

RW: How did you sort it out?
SIMRAN: I didn't sort it out. It was Friday yeah and everyone went home and on Monday everyone started to be my friends.

RW: Were you upset at the weekend?
SIMRAN: No! Perfectly fine! When people don't like me or they don't be
          my friend, I talk to myself.

Having become used to the probing school approach of investigating what happened and then 'sorting it out', I was surprised when, in interviews, children told me that they solved problems in the opposite way: by essentially ignoring and forgetting them. When I interviewed the 30 members of a year 4 class, I asked them about arguments they had had with peers, and many children commented on how they resolved these arguments. Several mentioned apologising to one another or requesting or declaring friendship, but the most popular solution, mentioned by seven children, was just to forget about the dispute.

For example, Simran told me that she sometimes argued with her friend Harpreet. I asked her if it took a long time to make friends again. 'No,' she replied. 'Cos I start making her laugh, and she laughs.' I asked her whether they talked about what had happened or just forgot about it. 'Forget about it. Cos if you talk about it it's just gonna make it more and more and more.' Similarly, Zena told me that when she argued with her friend Maria, by lunchtime that day they were friends again. I asked if they apologised to one another. 'No, we just forget about it,' she explained. 'Say, hi Maria shall I sit here? Yeah, okay then.'

Children's comments suggest that this solution is only effective between children who are good friends. Simran and Zena both referred to disputes with close friends, as did Zak in the interviews quoted above. Farhan and Amandeep were best friends and in their friendship interviews, they both stated that after arguments and fights with one another, they just forgot about it. For example, when I asked how he had resolved a recent fight with Amandeep, Farhan replied, 'Oh we just be'd friends with each other and we ignored what we just done, and we just carry on'.

Another version of this 'forget about it' approach was to use humour to move on from a dispute, again without ever actually 'sorting it out'. We saw one example earlier in this chapter, when year 4 boy Reece accused his friends of intentionally hurting him during a game. This dispute was resolved in the end not by me, struggling to make sense of the competing versions of events, but by Reece's friends, who play fought in front of Reece until he started laughing. Another example was described by Anjali, in an interview in year 4 about her friendships. She told me that she liked classmate Amrita for several reasons, one of which was, 'If you're like upset of something yeah like she'll talk to you, she'll sort things out, not like a grown up sorts things out'. I asked her what the difference was. 'Well, grown ups say like, just stay away from each other. *Just stay away from each other,*' she imitated in a mocking tone. 'But Amrita says, right we'll sort it out. If I had an argument with someone, let's say Harpreet pinched me hard, Amrita gets us to sit down together, and she makes us both laugh. Like, she does the pinching action, including the friendship in it.' According to Anjali, then, Amrita was able to resolve disputes by turning a harmful act into a playful one, thus enabling children to move on from the harm.

Of course, this was not the only solution that children constructed, and it was an approach that would probably not work in more serious disputes or those occurring between longstanding enemies. In such cases, children sometimes took on a more active role. Here are two examples, both referring to children's own experiences of the hypothetical scenarios I posed in individual interviews. The first refers to the same scenario as Zak and Simran, where a child is accused of spreading rumours. The second refers to the scenario in which one child hits another over a game of football.

OWEN: Er, when I was off sick on holiday, this boy said 'Do you like Owen?' to someone else, and he said yeah, and this other boy said I don't.

RW: How did you find out about it?

OWEN: Someone told me.

RW: Did you do anything about it?

OWEN: No I just sorted it out.

RW: How did you sort it out?

OWEN: I said did you say anything about me and he said yeah and I said what did you say and he said, do you like Owen, and he was like, trying to make himself innocent.

RW: How do you mean?

OWEN: By saying, 'No I didn't' and trying to make other people say no I didn't but the other people were honest.

FARHAN: Yeah. It was with Sam and Ali.

RW: What happened?

FARHAN: They were fighting, they were arguing first which one to be in goal cos they both thought they were good, they both saved the same amount of penalties. They were arguing about it, and then Sam went *grrr* and went to hit Ali but Ali moved and kicked Sam. Then Sam fell down and Ali laughed, so then Sam punched Ali, and then he fell down as well, then Sam held him and whacked him in the stomach.

RW: How did it end?

FARHAN: It ended when um Ali got up and so did Sam, and me, Faizel and Amandeep came and just splitted them up, and about half an hour later they just came up and said sorry.
RW: Did anyone tell a teacher?
FARHAN: No, a teacher didn't get involved, they sorted it out themselves.

According to these accounts, children can resolve quite serious disputes without adult intervention by talking and/or apologising to one another. Their solutions remind us that there are alternatives to the typical adult approach of finding out what happened and advising children to stay away from one another or to play together.

7.4   Implications for Schools

7.4.1   Constructing responsibility

The importance of intention and provocation
We have seen in this chapter that children frequently requested teachers to intervene in and resolve morally significant events in the school playground. Teachers typically solicited the accounts of all those involved, and these accounts often conflicted with one another. The process of reaching a verdict about what happened and who was to blame was thus usually a heated, argumentative one.

Two very common sources of disagreement which had implications for culpability concerned whether a harmful act was 'by accident' or 'on purpose', and whether an act was unprovoked or a reasonable retaliation to a prior harmful action ('She started it'). When attempting to unravel playground disputes, children often referred to these distinctions, and indeed, teachers often asked about them explicitly. Their frequent references to intention and provocation indicate that children considered these significant aspects of the event that had roles to play in assigning responsibility.

However, among adults, there seemed to be some ambivalence about the importance of provocation. School rules do not condone retaliation of any type of harm, and in some settings, teachers explicitly stated that a harmful act would be judged on its own merits, regardless of whether it was provoked or not. Thus, the official school line seemed to be that reciprocity was not a relevant principle, at least not when it came to judging harmful actions. Despite this, teachers did often show an interest in who initiated an exchange of harmful behaviours. This interest is not strictly in keeping with the official school position, which is sometimes silent on and sometimes explicitly against reciprocity. Unfortunately I did not explore this issue further with teachers, but my data raised interesting and important questions about teachers' own views of reciprocity. If adults in school do take provocation into account when interpreting harmful acts, should this not be reflected in official school policy?

Children (and adults) tended to refer to intention and provocation as dichotomies: an action was either intended or accidental; unprovoked or retaliatory. Such simple oppositions may not do justice to children's experiences of transgressions. For instance, Wainryb et al. (2005) argue that most of children's transgressions fall somewhere between intended and unintentional. And we have seen in this chapter that in a long-running dispute, describing one harmful act as provocation and one as retaliation rarely does justice to the history of the conflict. So these dichotomies may distort children's experience and prevent sophisticated conversations about their transgressions. Perhaps schools could consider ways to discuss intention and provocation as matters of degree, rather than as merely present or absent.

A final issue worthy of consideration by schools is the role of age in children's ability to apply concepts of intention and reciprocity to harmful acts. We saw evidence that younger children at Woodwell Green (and elsewhere) did not understand the significance of intention in the same way as older children and adults. While this was recognised by the infant teachers I interviewed at Woodwell Green, it might be worth-while for schools to consider the implications of this developmental progression for children's experiences both of harm in the playground and of teachers' resolutions. For example, some young children might need extra help to let go of the outcome of the action in order to con-sider the intention. It would also be interesting to examine whether children's understanding of provocation changed as they moved through the primary school years.

Implications of blame evasion for moral development
When teachers called upon children to narrate their role in morally significant events, it was usually as part of a process of establishing events, allocating blame and administering consequences and solutions. It is not surprising that children frequently responded to this demand with accounts that placed blame as far away from themselves and their friends as possible.

Pasupathi and Wainryb (2010) suggest that narratives that evade one's responsibility for harmful actions might stifle a child's moral development. They argue that moral development might be facilitated via the produc-tion of narratives that attend to the psychological perspectives of both perpetrator and victim in a balanced way, and that acknowledge one's own agency and the effect on the victim. Such narratives are thought to enable a person to recognise that despite being basically good people, they and others on occasion cause harm to others. Such a recognition, they suggest, enables children to move on from wrongdoing and forgive themselves and others.

These suggestions by Pasupathi and Wainryb are recent and we need more research to assess them. In the meantime, however, they raise interesting questions about the kinds of conversations we are encouraging our children to have about moral issues at school. Given the power that teachers have to intervene and punish, we may be pressuring children into producing accounts that are more defensive (of self and friends) than other accounts that they might produce (and perhaps do produce, away from teachers). Since adults now intervene in children's affairs more often than they used to, children are probably producing more defensive narratives about their own behaviour than previous generations did. By failing to acknowledge responsibility for wrongdoing, defensive accounts may, according to Pasupathi and Wainryb (2010), stifle children's moral development. These are important ideas that could be considered by schools in future, as more research emerges on the relationship between narratives and moral development, and on the kinds of narratives that children produce about moral events in different relationships.

7.4.2   Intervening effectively

We saw in Chapter 1 that adults are now under much more pressure to intervene in children's affairs than they used to be. The aim of this intervention is to protect children from their peers where necessary, such as in cases of sustained bullying. This aim is admirable, but it is important to recognise the obstacles that can prevent a teacher's intervention from being effective and beneficial.

Lessons from children
By delving into disputes, probing to find out exactly what happened and discussing the incidents at length, teachers may actually make the dispute worse. Earlier I quoted Simran, who said that she preferred to forget about a dispute than to talk about it, 'Cos if you talk about it it's just gonna make it more and more and more'. While the 'forget about it' solution seemed to work only for children who were good friends, nevertheless in certain situations teachers' efforts to establish the truth may amplify

disputes. This seems particularly likely when teachers sought to resolve disputes between a few children in front of the whole class, adding an audience to the mix.

This amplification can tip the conflict resolution process from resembling a law court to a talk show. The head teacher once recounted to me how he and the deputy head held a meeting with a group of girls who were embroiled in a dispute about possession. He told me that it was 'like something out of Jerry Springer', with the girls dramatically expressing emotions which he and the deputy head struggled to take seriously.[16] Teachers' attention to children's problems may, in such cases, encourage over-dramatisation of their moral lives.

We saw towards the end of this chapter that children are capable of resolving disputes amongst themselves, using a range of strategies, some of which are completely different from those used by adults (such as humour and ignoring). Perhaps for some situations adults might encourage children to resolve the problem themselves, but under adult supervision or following adult-prescribed guidelines, such as a method for ensuring that all voices are heard. We might think of adults as scaffolding children's nascent ability to solve their own problems – a scaffolding process that would need to take into account the fact that children have at their disposal effective methods for conflict resolution that adults do not generally use. This approach would not only avoid the problem of adults exacerbating disputes, but would also give children more opportunities to develop their confidence and ability to resolve peer-group problems themselves.

It is worth bearing in mind that not only may adult intervention sometimes make a problem worse, it may sometimes simply be impossible for an adult to solve a child's problem. Take Paul and Sarah, whose predicaments were described in Chapters 3 and 4 respectively. Recall that Paul found that several teacher interventions did not help his efforts at inclusion, because they did not have any bearing on boys' dominance hierarchies; if anything, a boy might lose status by seeking a teacher's help, if this is seen as demonstrating a lack of toughness. By hitting an aggressive, dominant peer, Paul finally tackled the problem in terms that made a difference and transformed his place in the peer group. It is unpalatable to imagine that Paul's only solution was to resort to violence, but without wider changes in how boys in working-class areas construct hierarchy, it is difficult to see how a teacher could have helped him.

Another example is the case of Paul's classmate Sarah, who remained isolated throughout the school year despite her teacher's best efforts to help her integrate. I argued in Chapter 4 that Sarah's loneliness was partly a consequence of her ethnic identity as English at a school where the largest ethnic group was Indian. Her English identity prevented her from participating in Indian practices popular with the girls in her class, and so it was difficult for her to play with and build up good relationships with them. Again, it is difficult to see how an adult could have helped Sarah without simultaneously addressing larger issues like the way in which English identity was constructed in this multicultural community.

Acknowledging the possibility of bias
We have seen that for teachers, the main task in resolving children's disputes was finding out what happened. One of the strategies they used to help them do this was trusting some children more than others to tell the truth. In other words, teachers made judgements about the kind of person each child was, and used this judgement to help them to interpret specific contested events.

The problem with this strategy is that it can lead to injustice, in two ways. Firstly, it is likely that almost all children are inconsistent (e.g. usually but not always truthful to teacher). Therefore a strategy of always trusting particular children will sometimes lead to errors. Secondly, teachers' judgements about which children are trustworthy may themselves be biased. I spoke to several children who expressed concerns to me that their teachers trusted peers they believed to be deceptive or loyal to others involved in the dispute. I have already discussed in Chapter 3 how easy it is for teachers to be biased against certain children on the basis of their reputations (or those of their families), and/or of stereotypes and prejudices that teachers might hold, however unwillingly (concerning ethnicity, gender and social class, for example). Here I am really just reiterating that point, and adding that teachers can be biased towards, as well as against, particular children. If, as a result, children perceive their teachers to be unjust, those children are likely to disengage from them and the values they seek to implement.

I am not condemning teachers for what seem to be intrinsically human patterns of perception and thought, but rather suggesting that schools might be ready for the tendency towards bias. Schools need to discuss the processes by which teachers reach verdicts, consider how biases can creep into these, and develop safeguards against them.

Teachers at Woodwell Green struggled to meet their obligations to intervene in children's peer relations with very little time in which to do so. No wonder that they used heuristics to aid their interpretations of what happened in disputes, and no wonder the solutions they offered were often too simple to address the specific and complex problems that children faced. Most of my suggested changes would take time to implement, and time to actually carry out. If we are serious about wanting teachers to take more responsibility for children's well-being in the playground, then we have to provide the resources and time for them to do this properly, or employ staff specifically for this purpose.

Notes

1. Teachers bore the main responsibility at Woodwell Green for resolving disputes and meting out consequences such as detentions. However, playground supervisors were also often called upon to adjudicate when disputes broke out in the playground. For simplicity in this chapter, I have focused on the role of teachers in the interpretation process, but some of the arguments apply to playground supervisors as well.

2. Although Robbie did not name Soraj as someone he argues with, Soraj did name Robbie, so perhaps he understood their interactions differently from Robbie. However, his account of their arguments did not mention physical aggression towards Robbie, so it may be that the arguments to which Soraj refers are not the same as the playful chasing and complaining I witnessed and which Robbie talked about.

3. In recounting his tale, Owen substituted the children's real names with the names given to the protagonists in the hypothetical scenario.

4. A one-way ANOVA found statistically significant age differences, $F(2,131)=15.867$, $p<.001$. Bonferroni post-hoc tests found that years 3–4 and 5–6 scored significantly higher than years 1–2 ($p<.001$ in both cases), but that there was no significant difference between years 3–4 and 5–6.

5. This was a Japanese anime TV series and a popular inspiration for children's games at Woodwell Green during my research.

6. According to Piaget (1932) such teaching might help children to focus on intention from a younger age, but it is not essential; he believed that children would inevitably reach the same endpoint via their experiences in the peer group, regardless of what adults were telling them.

   If Piaget is correct, then we would expect that, having passed through the same developmental sequence, adults the world over will all take intention into account when judging actions. There is in fact intriguing evidence that adults in some societies view intention rather differently. Shweder and Much (1991) describe in detail an interview with the Babaji, a Hindu man from the Orissa area of India, whom they asked whether a man should steal a drug to save his wife's life. The Babaji argued that he should not, justifying his answer with reference to the Hindu concept of dharma, which is translated by Shweder and Much as 'religion, duty, obligation, natural law, truth' (p. 206). A crucial part of the Babaji's argument is the claim that because they go against dharma, sinful actions (such as stealing) are wrong no matter what the intention underlying them and will eventually lead to negative consequences. In the words of Shweder and Much (1991, p. 221):

The Babaji believes that certain kinds of actions (for example, stealing, killing) are inherently sinful and other kinds of actions (for example, giving alms, sacrificing) inherently virtuous. Those qualities of sin and virtue belong to the actions themselves; intentionality and circumstances do not create sins or eliminate them. The act is sinful even if it is done unknowingly. In that view circumstances 'out of one's control' are regarded as one's own fault; they are the manifestations of prior sinful actions.

According to this viewpoint, there are many harmful actions that are wrong regardless of intention. If such a viewpoint is common among adults in some societies (and this suggestion would need to be assessed with further research), then these adults' moral development must have proceeded somewhat differently from the classic picture I presented earlier, in which all children come to focus on intention over outcome as they get older. This suggests that the way that teachers (and other adults) refer to intention in children's disputes may be more influential on children's moral development than Piaget believed.

7. Swearing at a peer's parents was considered a very serious insult by children at Woodwell Green. It was also quite common, until the head teacher implemented a policy whereby children caught doing this automatically received 'a letter home' to their parents or guardians.

8. I used this version of the question in the girls' groups. In the boys' groups, James was substituted for Jenny.

9. In other words, the school would write a letter to the child's parents or guardians about the incident.

10. This was one of several attempts by Miss Chahal to build a trusting relationship between herself and Zak. However, these efforts were not very successful, for reasons that are outlined in Chapter 3.

11. 'Lurgy' is a slang term for a fictitious infectious disease, similar to the term 'cooties' in the USA.

12. In asking this question, Miss Williams seems to be orienting both to the intention behind Jordan's hit (Jack should not retaliate to an accidental harm) and to the principle of reciprocity (retaliation to an intended hit being more reasonable than to an accidental one).

13. Clearly, from the wording of my question, I assumed that the teacher to whom Mohamed referred would be female. While almost all teachers at Woodwell Green were indeed women, this was nevertheless an unwarranted assumption.

14. This is another example of children constructing provocation and retaliation differently from one another.

15. 'Had' is a game whereby one child chases and attempts to tag another, who then has to try to tag someone else, and so on.

16. *The Jerry Springer Show* is an American TV talk show in which participants emotively air their (often scandalous) grievances with one another in front of an audience, usually resulting in a brawl.

8

Children's Moral Lives in Cultural Context

I noted in Chapter 1 that adults in the UK and many other Western nations have become increasingly motivated to protect children from harm. This has manifested itself in schools in at least two ways. Firstly, there is an emphasis on harm avoidance as the most important value in children's peer relations. This emphasis was evident in every Woodwell Green classroom in the form of the rule, 'We never hurt each other on the inside or the outside'. We have seen in preceding chapters that teachers lectured about, carried out exercises on, and reprimanded children for various kinds of harm, including physical aggression, exclusion and racism. The latter was considered particularly harmful; unsurprising given the school's setting in a multicultural area, and in a country which was politically highly motivated to promote integration of ethnic minorities whilst respecting cultural differences.

Secondly, adults in school have become more obligated to intervene in children's lives in order to prevent harm from occurring. This obligation extends to intervention in children's peer relations to prevent bullying from taking place. In Chapter 7 we saw that children have responded to this change by seeking out adults to resolve their problems much more often than previous generations. The intervening adult expected contradictory accounts to emerge from children's disputes and saw it as part of their role to adjudicate between these competing accounts. Thus, they tended to act like a judge, listening to narratives from all parties, calling witnesses, reaching a verdict about what happened and who was to blame, and administering punishments.

Children's Moral Lives: An Ethnographic and Psychological Approach, First Edition. Ruth Woods.
© 2013 John Wiley & Sons, Ltd. Published 2013 by John Wiley & Sons, Ltd.

Via these two paths, our cultural preoccupation with harm avoidance has become embedded in the routine practices that cultural psychologists and social intuitionists consider so important in children's moral development (Haidt 2001; Shweder and Much 1991; Shweder et al. 1987). Recall that according to these theories, children acquire cultural values (i.e. values that are widespread and hegemonic in a particular society or social group) via their participation in practices that in some sense express those values (such as through adults' language and emotional reactions). However, although all children at Woodwell Green participated in practices that expressed adult concerns with harm avoidance, they did not seem to be internalising or accepting this value in any straightforward sense, since they continued to harm one another quite often (as we saw in Chapters 3 to 6).

It is not that the children of Woodwell Green did not care about preventing harm. On the contrary, they often oriented to this value. For example, they treated instances of racism very seriously (see Chapters 4 and 6). Domain theory (which I introduced in Chapter 1) is useful here because it argues that even if people agree in principle about a specific value, they may differ in how they apply that value to a real-life event because of differences in (a) how they interpret that event and (b) how highly they prioritise the value in question relative to other values that are relevant to the event (Smetana 2006; Turiel et al. 1987; Wainryb et al. 2005). So although the children of Woodwell Green might agree in principle with their teachers that harm avoidance is right, they might nevertheless harm a peer in practice, as a result of interpreting an event differently from teachers and/or prioritising a different value. Thus, domain theory provides an account of moral experience which can make sense of why, despite recognising the value of harm avoidance promoted by teachers, children at Woodwell Green continued to carry out harmful acts. In the following section, I explore some of the different interpretations and priorities we came across in the preceding chapters.[1]

8.1   Understanding Children's Interpretations and Priorities

8.1.1   *Interpretations*

Assumptions about reality

As domain theory predicts, at Woodwell Green, people's interpretations of events sometimes varied because they made different assumptions about the world (Smetana 2006). For instance, Chapter 2 showed that certain groups within the school interpreted playfully aggressive behaviour differently from one another, such that some saw harm where others did not. Thus, while children sometimes used racist insults during lighthearted banter with friends, their teachers were troubled by these insults and exhorted children not to use them even in jest. This difference may relate to teachers' and children's contrasting background assumptions about the nature of friendship (with children considering playful aggression an important part of friendship) and/or racism (with adults struggling to see racism as anything but harmful, so seriously did they take it).

We saw in Chapter 6 that members of the school community also differed in how they defined racism, meaning that some saw language-based teasing as racist, while others saw it as, again, lighthearted and harmless playful aggression. Chapter 6 also described how teachers sometimes involved children in activities such as dancing to Bollywood songs, which they saw as harmless celebrations of diversity. However, some English parents interpreted such participation as harmful to their children's own sense of ethnic identity. Some English children may also have felt some discomfort in participating in other-ethnicity practices. I suggested in Chapter 4 that Sarah struggled to make friends partly because her English identity made her reluctant to join in the 'Indian' practices popular with the girls in her class. These contrasting interpretations of what it means to engage in other-ethnicity practices had important implications for whether Sarah's classmates were seen as excluding Sarah or simply carrying out the activities they enjoyed.

As well as disagreeing about whether certain actions were harmful, school members might agree that harm had taken place but interpret the meaning of that harm differently. Some may consider it a legitimate means to an end that they consider valuable. Others might not value that end, or if they do, they might not accept a harmful act as a legitimate way to reach it. For example, some children (especially boys) seemed to consider some harm legitimate as a means of demonstrating and producing toughness, whereas teachers tended to evaluate all harm negatively. We saw another example in Chapter 4, where a whole class of children united to exclude a peer, deliberately harming him as a way of punishing his racist insults. Their teacher, meanwhile, was unequivocal (at least to the children themselves) that their harmful actions were unacceptable, whatever the reason for them.

Relationship to protagonists
A person's interpretation of an event is influenced not only by their background assumptions, but also by their relationship to, and prior perceptions of, those involved (Hymel et al. 1990). For example, children tend to judge

their own misdemeanours more leniently than those of other people (Wainryb et al. 2005), and are more willing to consider extenuating circumstances if a transgressor is a friend (Smetana 2006). Perhaps the most obvious example of this phenomenon was described in Chapter 7, where children interpreted harmful acts of which they were the victims as intentional when the acts were committed by a peer who they believed disliked them, even if all other evidence suggested that the act was accidental.

In Chapters 3 and 7 I suggested that aggressive boys and their teachers might be caught in a cycle in which both were interpreting each other's behaviour negatively because of a pre-existing antagonistic relationship between them. Aggressive boys believed that their teachers were biased. These perceptions probably meant that they were prone to interpret in a negative light anything their teachers did. Meanwhile, they and other children told me that their teachers were suspicious of them, and sometimes blamed them for wrongdoings that they did not commit because of the boys' reputation as troublemakers.

We also saw in Chapter 7 that at least in the narratives they gave to teachers, children's interpretations of disputes altered radically depending on whether they had subsequently made friends with each other or not. In these examples, it is plausible that having made friends, the children involved considered that they had not harmed anyone whilst the adults, viewing the same situation, believed that they did.[2]

These examples illustrate that members of the school community often judged the same event differently to one another because of differences in how they interpreted that event, differences that arose because of contrasting background assumptions, or because of the prior relationship between those involved. Sometimes, these differences occurred between adults and children, helping to explain why it was that children did not wholeheartedly embrace adults' edict that they avoid harming one another.

8.1.2 Priorities

What children value in their peer relations
Domain theorists argue that real-life moral events frequently invoke more than one value, and these may conflict with each other. Consequently, people involved in the event are forced to prioritise between those values they see as relevant (Turiel et al. 1987). In support of this claim, this book has shown that in addition to harm avoidance, the children grappled with a host of other values and obligations in their peer relations. Those that seemed to come up most often were status, reciprocity or justice, loyalty and toughness.[3]

211

Status and hierarchy were issues that affected every child at Woodwell Green, as we saw in Chapters 3, 4 and 5. Boys sought to establish themselves within a hierarchy largely based on their willingness and ability to stand up for themselves against other boys in physically aggressive encounters. Girls' hierarchies were based more on their relationships (with status being gained via friendship with popular peers). Both boys and girls also produced status through their proficiency in locally significant practices, such as 'speaking Indian', football and banter.

Only children of high status were able to make and enforce decisions in the peer group. For instance, high-status Faizel's decisions about who could play football were respected, while low-status Pavandeep faced constant challenges to his decisions when he was owner of the ball (see Chapter 4). High-status children also commanded prestige and privilege, and their affairs were treated as important by peers. For example, when high-status girls argued with each other, they expected their friends to get involved and demonstrate allegiance by breaking up with the girl they had argued with (see Chapter 5). The same was not usually true when lower-status girls argued.

Justice (fairness, reciprocity) was important to both boys and girls at Woodwell Green. Many boys (and some girls) considered it fair to reciprocate if they were hit (Chapter 3) or excluded (see Chapter 7). Girls expected the loyalty of best friends to be reciprocated (Chapter 5), and children also applied ideas of fairness to racism (as discrimination) and teachers' treatment of children when resolving disputes (Chapters 3, 6 and 7). Official school policy did not allow for the principle of justice in children's peer relations (claiming that a reciprocating hit was as serious as an initiating hit). However, there were signs that teachers did orient somewhat to this value when arbitrating disputes and judging harmful acts (see Chapter 7).

Loyalty was also a pervasive concern at the school. It took various forms, such as supporting one's class in football matches and refusing to 'tell tales' on a friend. Chapter 5 described two forms of loyalty that seemed particularly important to many girls at the school: the obligation to be available to one's best friend, and the obligation to demonstrate support for one's friend by sharing her enemies. The chapter demonstrated how difficult it was for a girl to evade these obligations, even if she herself did not subscribe to the values underlying them. For instance, although several girls told me that they tried not to 'get involved' when their friends argued with each other (and thus attempted not to demonstrate loyalty to one friend by severing friendship with her enemy), I only witnessed one girl who ever managed to evade this obligation (Simran), and this only because of strenuous efforts on her part.

Finally, we saw in Chapters 2 and 3 that toughness was an important value to the children, especially boys. Children who could not demonstrate toughness appropriately (whether through skilful banter or a refusal to be physically intimidated) were marginalised by their peers (consider the experiences of Maria as she slowly learned how to banter), and those who were toughest of all tended to be influential and respected (although not necessarily well liked).

Are these values important to children growing up in other circumstances? There is evidence that status, justice and loyalty are perennial concerns for children from diverse backgrounds, although their precise form might vary between settings (Adler and Adler 1998; Davies 1982; Evaldsson 2007; Fry 2006; Griffiths 1995; Hey 1997; Savin-Williams 1976; Smetana et al. 2003). Toughness, on the other hand, is likely to be a particularly significant value for children growing up in somewhat hostile settings, such as poor communities where unemployment, crime and violence are rife (Connolly 1998; Evans 2006; Ferguson 2000; Swain 2003). It makes sense that in such circumstances, people are likely to value toughness or resilience, the ability to hold one's own in hostile interactions, assert one's will and recover rapidly from harm.

The picture this book has painted is of children actively negotiating their way through a complex moral landscape laden with multiple values. No wonder, then, that they did not always conform to adults' exhortations that they avoid harming each other. Instead, they struggled to reconcile teachers' demands with their other concerns, which included loyalty, status, toughness and reciprocity. For example, aggressive boys wrestled with harm avoidance, status, toughness and reciprocity (see Chapter 3), while many girls struggled with harm avoidance, freedom, loyalty and status (see Chapter 5). How did children decide which of these multiple values to prioritise?

Interactions between values

I suggest that a child's decision about which value to prioritise in a specific situation is informed by interactions between the values that that child sees as relevant to the situation. Some values will complement and support one another, while others will compete with and undermine one another.

For example, we saw in Chapter 3 that when a boy hit him in the playground, Zak wrestled with several relevant values: harm avoidance, status, toughness and reciprocity. In this scenario, status, toughness and reciprocity all reinforce one another in promoting a retaliatory hit, while only harm avoidance advocates a different course of action (walk away and/or tell a teacher). Respect for authority would also support the obligation to prevent harm, since the latter obligation comes from authority figures (teachers).

As another example, we saw in Chapter 5 that if popular Zena did not want to play with her best friend Navneet one lunchtime, wishing perhaps instead to play with a high-status peer such as Simran or Anjali, she would wrestle with harm avoidance, freedom, loyalty and status (manifested through the number and status of her friends). In this scenario, harm avoidance and loyalty would push her towards playing with Navneet, while concerns with freedom and status would encourage her in the opposite direction.

A child's decision about how to act in a specific event would not of course be determined simply by the numerical balance between conflicting and complementary values. For one thing, children differed in the relative importance they assigned to each value. So it is possible that all the boys in Zak's and Faizel's class grappled with the same set of values with respect to physical aggression, but nevertheless prioritised those values differently, leading some, like Zak and Faizel, to be physically aggressive, and others, like Pavandeep and Sandeep, not to be.

Why were specific values more important to some children than to others? The significance of a value to a particular child is likely to result partially from his or her success in demonstrating that value. For instance, a child who is of high status may care more about hierarchy than a child lower down. However, the relationship between accomplishment and significance is probably a complex one. Some lower-status children might still care a great deal about status (for example, Paul was unhappy with his low status in Chapter 3, and Pavandeep found it difficult to manage football games when he was ball owner in Chapter 4), but find themselves unable or unwilling to carry out the behaviours associated with high status.

Another factor that may influence the importance of each value to a particular child is his or her recent experiences. For example, if Navneet was upset about receiving a bad mark for her schoolwork that morning, Zena might be more oriented to harm avoidance than usual and decide to play with her.

One set of recent experiences concerns the child's relationship with other people who represent for that child specific values. For example, if Zak has recently been unfairly (in his view, at least) reprimanded by his teacher, he may be particularly likely to eschew the value of harm avoidance she demands of him, and thus to hit back. So in prioritising between values, children's relationships with the other people who demand those values of them are likely to be relevant.

Prioritisation as a social process

The values that children grappled with were experienced at least partly as obligations demanded of them by other people in their lives. The most obvious example was harm avoidance, which teachers (and, likely, other adults, both in and out of school too) demanded of children. In contrast, school staff rarely required that children demonstrate loyalty, toughness or status, and their attitude towards reciprocity in the peer group was ambivalent.

However, children held each other to account for all of these values, punishing those who did not orient to them and meet their associated obligations. In the case of loyalty, children who refused to be available to their best friends were criticised and penalised (consider Maria's and Navneet's reactions to Zena's disloyalty in Chapter 5). Children who refused to sever friendships with a friend's enemy were also prone to punishment (Zena and Simran both commented that if they made friends with Harpreet's enemy, Harpreet would withdraw her friendship from them).

Similarly, children who failed to demonstrate toughness (such as Maria in her early days at Woodwell Green, and Harpreet on occasion; see Chapter 2) also attracted criticism from peers. This was particularly true for boys who did not conform to locally prevalent views of masculinity in terms of toughness, aggression, heterosexuality and physical activity. Thus, boys who played with girls instead of playing football (such as Sohaib and Joshua) or who refused to fight with aggressive peers (such as Pavandeep and Sandeep) were teased, insulted and criticised (see Chapters 3, 6 and 7). The fact that children sanctioned peers who did not meet the norm of toughness suggests that the norm was experienced as obligatory, and the gender difference in sanctions suggests that the strongest obligations were felt between boys.

Children also applied sanctions to peers who did not act in a way appropriate to their position in the hierarchy. For example, when Paul first came to the school and was very low status, several of his classmates criticised him for acting in a domineering way (see Chapter 3). Paul's 'bossiness' was only accepted after he hit an aggressive peer, thus improving his status in the hierarchy. Meanwhile Pavandeep experienced the reverse problem: as ball owner, he was automatically assigned a dominant role in playground football games but was criticised by his peers because he behaved submissively within that role (Chapter 4).

Finally, children also expected peers to behave fairly. Many explicitly affirmed the rightness of hitting or excluding someone who had done the same to them. They reciprocated positive acts as well as negative (Chapter 3), criticised peers who were perceived to be unfair (for example, cheating in football), and were scathing in their criticism of teachers whom they considered biased against specific children (see Chapters 3 and 7).

Teachers and peers were not the only people who demanded obligations of children. Family members, including siblings, cousins and parents, also had expectations. Consequently, every child was obligated to several other people, and these obligations could, as we saw above, support or undermine one another. For instance, many working-class parents promote toughness in their children, a value that would be in line with what children in a working-class community expected of one another, but in tension with what teachers required of children (Evans 2006).

If children usually experience values as embedded in specific relationships with people who are important to them, then decisions about which value to prioritise are decisions that are informed by, and have implications for, those relationships. Perhaps the best example in this book is the predicament of aggressive boys who feel disenfranchised from school values partly because they distrust the teachers who demand those values of them (see Chapter 3). The converse may also be true, of course; a child may be particularly committed to a value expressed in an obligation to a person he or she cares deeply for.

Children constructing virtues

Children did not usually come across competing values in discrete, one-off events that could be resolved and moved on from. Rather, they often struggled with the same competing values repeatedly over time. For example, if Zak decided on one occasion not to hit a peer, this would not resolve the tension he experienced between the values of reciprocity, status, toughness, harm avoidance and respect for authority. The next time someone challenged his status on the playground or attacked him without adequate provocation (in his eyes), the same dilemma would arise again.

By repeatedly confronting clashes between particular values, and resolving them (temporarily) by prioritising them in a particular way, children may build up habitual moral dispositions or virtues (skills enabling a person to readily perceive particular moral values in the events around them, and to respond appropriately to them; Haidt and Joseph 2004, 2008). This process of construction might be supported via children's developing sense of self-identity, whereby they come to see themselves (and have others see them) as a particular type of person.

For instance, if Maria repeatedly prioritises loyalty over independence in her interactions with Zena, she may develop the virtue of loyalty ever more strongly. At the same time, she might begin to think of herself as a loyal person, hence further perpetuating the cycle of virtue development. In time, Maria might come to embody loyalty to such an extent that it becomes increasingly difficult for her to contemplate acting differently in her encounters with Zena. Once developed, virtues need not only be expressed in these selfsame struggles but could generalise to other situations. For instance, Maria might place an increasing emphasis on loyalty in her friendships with other children also.

So children might develop particular virtues not only by observing and imitating people around them or by exposure to moral narratives (as Haidt suggests in his social intuitionist theory), but also through repeated struggles between competing values, in which they come to prioritise the same values over and over again. This is a route by which children might come to embody not only the virtues that are strongly promoted by most adults around them, but also virtues that are denigrated or ignored by them.

The result of children's repeated engagement with multiple values instantiated in specific relationships is that they will experience some values and obligations as compelling, and others as relatively inaccessible. This sense of constraint may increase as they build up habitual prioritisations and develop a sense of identity around specific values. So, although teachers often framed children's decisions to disobey school rules (such as by harming a peer) as a choice freely made by children (see Chapter 1), this is not necessarily how children experience their decisions. Instead, they may feel unable to act in any other way.[4]

8.2 Constructing Responsibility: The Importance of Power and Narrative

This book has demonstrated that in addition to struggling with multiple, competing values embedded in relationships with significant others, another important dimension of children's moral lives is their experience of accountability and responsibility. In this section I explore the processes by which children held each other responsible for moral transgressions on the playground, beginning with their preoccupation with intention and provocation, turning then to the narratives they produce for their teachers and, finally, to the relationship between hierarchy and responsibility.

8.2.1   Intention and provocation

Discursive psychologists have identified various linguistic strategies that adults use to hold each other responsible for transgressions. These include attributions of intention and claims about who initiated a dispute (Edwards 1997). We saw in Chapter 7 that the children of Woodwell Green frequently employed both of these strategies. They assigned intention by using the phrase 'on purpose' as opposed to 'by accident'. They assigned provocation with phrases like 'he started it', the implication being that the one who initiated a harmful exchange is more culpable than the one who reacted. Children often mentioned provocation in their accounts even though official school policy did not acknowledge its relevance. However, teachers did nevertheless show signs of orienting to provocation and reciprocity in their analysis of disputes. Perhaps children were on some level aware of this difference between policy and practice.

In constructing accountability, children frequently referred to intention and provocation, both of which were usually described rather simplistically as present or absent. This opposition does not allow for the gradations of intention that children might experience (Wainryb et al. 2005), nor for the complex history of many disputes, in which each act is construed simultaneously as retaliation and new provocation. Insofar as children come to frame actions in terms of such simple oppositions, they may be losing opportunities for a more sophisticated discussion of who is to blame for moral events.

In claiming that children use language strategically to apportion blame, I am not claiming (as most discursive psychologists probably would; see Edwards 1997) that children's use of linguistic devices is purely a strategic matter that does not reveal anything about their perception of the world. It seems much more likely that what children say about a morally significant event is related in complex ways to how they interpret that event. There is obviously the possibility that children might deliberately and self-consciously lie such that their interpretation and account differ sharply from one another (for instance, Faizel intentionally kicking the ball at a peer and then claiming it was accidental; see Chapter 7). Another possibility is that the language children use to narrate moral events influences (either immediately or over time) their interpretation of such events. For example, the use of the 'by accident' versus 'on purpose' opposition might lead children to interpret intention in an increasingly oversimplified manner.

8.2.2   Children's narratives to adults

Children's experiences of accountability were culturally informed in that they frequently sought adults' help to adjudicate and resolve their disputes. We saw in Chapter 7 that when telling an adjudicating adult what happened, children often held others responsible for transgressions while presenting themselves as (relatively) blameless. This is hardly surprising, given that teachers have the power to blame and punish those they see as doing wrong, and given that children had to counter any accusations made by their opponents, from whom the teacher would also elicit an account. I suggested in Chapter 7 that because of teachers' interventions, children may be more likely than in the past to produce defensive narratives that are geared towards evading responsibility for transgressions. It is possible that for other audiences (such as a sympathetic friend), children might produce less defensive narratives.

What are the implications of these narratives for children's moral experience and development? Pasupathi and Wainryb (2010) argue that the way in which people construct narratives about their own harmful or unjust actions has implications for moral development, via their understanding of themselves (and others) as agents responsible for their actions. They suggest that narratives that attend to the psychological perspectives of both perpetrator and victim in a balanced way, that include the effect on the victim, and that acknowledge the narrator's agency, are most likely to enhance moral development by enabling a sophisticated and realistic understanding of self and others as morally flawed. They suggest that this understanding enables forgiveness and repair of relationships damaged by harmful acts.

Pasupathi and Wainryb (2010) argue that defensive, self-protective narratives do not usually meet these criteria because they fail to acknowledge the responsibility of the narrator. If they are correct, then such narratives stand in the way of children's understanding of their own culpability and imperfection, making it harder for them to forgive and move on from their transgressions, and those of other people.

While these claims need to be assessed with further research, they raise interesting questions about the kinds of narratives that teachers encourage children to produce in the course of resolving playground disputes. It is possible that if children resolved disputes themselves, without the spectre of punishment by adults, they would produce a less defensive narrative that encourages a sense of agency and responsibility. However, children's narratives to one another may, at times, be just as defensive as those offered to adults, since we have seen that children hold each other to account for the values that are important to them. It may be that such narratives differ from those directed to teachers more in the values they orient to than in the tendency to self-protection. Furthermore, we saw in Chapter 7 that children sometimes resolve disputes without producing narratives about what happened at all, instead forgetting about it or using humour to move on. Do such solutions prevent children from developing a more mature moral outlook via their experience of taking responsibility for harmful acts? Or perhaps they too enable the forgiveness that Pasupathi and Wainryb (2010) consider so important, but via a different route? Again, more research is required to clarify which narratives tend to be used by children in their various relationships, and what effect these narratives have on their moral outlook.

8.2.3   Dominance and subordination

Children constructed accountability not only through the way they described transgressions, but also through their hierarchies. Hierarchies and thus power differences are ubiquitous among children (Adler and Adler 1998; Hey 1997; Savin-Williams 1976). At Woodwell Green, children's relationships with one another frequently included elements of dominance, submission and/or struggle (in the case of children who are challenging or competing for their own position in the hierarchy, such as Manpreet and Holly in Chapter 4 and Paul in Chapter 3). Children's positions in the hierarchy had implications for their experiences of agency and responsibility for transgressions.

In Chapter 4 we saw that decisions about who was included in a group were not usually shared among all group members. Instead, one child made such decisions on behalf of the whole group. That child was either placed in this role because he or she 'owned' the game in some way (such as the boy who owned the ball in football games) or was the dominant leader of the group. We saw also that dominance was only achieved via the acknowledgement and submission of other group members. An excellent example was the way in which girls at the after-school club allowed Manpreet to lead them by accepting her decisions and handing over game ownership to her. The only one to resist Manpreet's domination was Holly, who faced a constant power struggle with Manpreet as a result. Another example was Pavandeep's predicament: as owner of the ball he was meant to be in charge of deciding who could play, but he was unsuccessful in this role precisely because some peers did not accept his dominance and challenged his decisions.

We also saw evidence of power relations in Chapter 5, which revealed that dominant girls who had argued with each other (such as Anjali and Harpreet) dictated their friends' gang membership. Here too, these assertions of power were only possible because other girls submitted to them, allowing themselves to be positioned for one dominant girl and against the other, in spite of their stated preference to 'stay out of it'.

All these examples concern acts of inclusion and exclusion. Of course, children exerted power over one another in other ways as well (such as in deciding which game to play and who gets which role in the game; see Chapter 4). In other words, relatively dominant children routinely made decisions on behalf of a group, and relatively submissive children routinely allowed them to without (openly) challenging their decision or their authority.

What are the implications of children's contrasting experiences of dominance and submission during moral events? One implication concerns children's sense of agency and control over their own decisions and actions. We saw above that according to Pasupathi and Wainryb (2010), carrying out harmful actions can actually promote a child's moral development if they acknowledge their own agency in those actions. According to this argument, dominant children are more likely to learn the moral lessons identified by Pasupathi and Wainryb (2010) than submissive children are. If dominant children recognise their dominance, they should be able to see themselves as agents of their own actions, including harmful ones. In contrast, submissive children may experience themselves as relatively powerless and lacking in agency when a dominant peer makes unilateral decisions on their behalf, rendering them unable to take responsibility for transgressions in which they are complicit.

In addition, we saw in Chapters 4 and 5 that while submissive children may not hold themselves responsible for what their group leader does, victims of group leader's transgressions may blame all group members. More research is needed to understand in more detail how children's perspective informs their allocation of responsibility, and what, if any, implications there are for relationships between children with different perspectives (e.g. between victim and submissive group members). It would also be useful to know whether and how adults' judgements of culpability are informed by their awareness of hierarchical relationships between children. For example, do adults reinforce submissive children's abdication of responsibility by also only blaming group leaders for transgressive acts?

Another implication concerns opposition, resistance and subversion. Wainryb (2006) argues that people in subordinate positions frequently oppose and resist their subordination, acts that she suggests might play an important role in moral development. We saw tentative evidence of subversive acts in Chapter 4, where the girls who usually played with Manpreet rejected her leadership for a while to form a dance group with Manpreet's rival, Holly. We also saw evidence in Chapter 5, when having sided with dominant Harpreet, Zena and Navneet secretly made friends with Harpreet's enemy, Anjali.

But the clearest evidence of subversion came not from power relations between children but from those between teachers and children. We saw in Chapter 3 that some aggressive boys developed tense, distrustful relationships with their teachers, in which teachers were continually reprimanding the boys for their investment in physical aggression and toughness, while the boys suspected that their teachers were biased against them. The boys were subversive in that they were very vocal in their criticisms of their teachers to me, and were often rebellious and disruptive in the classroom (Woods 2008).

I suggested in Chapter 3 that their poor relationships with teachers might encourage the boys to invest further in the values that their teachers condemned (status and reciprocity manifested as physical aggression). In addition, alienated from school values and their guardians, these boys might develop an increased sense of solidarity towards one another. Moreover, insofar as they are rebellious, they may also develop virtues of courage and resilience. So experiences of subordination do seem to contain opportunities for moral development in particular directions.

Of course, dominance and submission are a function of specific relationships, so that a child who dominates over one peer may be submissive to another. In addition, children who were usually dominant in their peer relations (such as Zak and Faizel) were unavoidably subordinate in relation to their teachers (albeit still able to challenge and exert power over their teachers in some ways, for example by causing disruption in the classroom or making fun of the teacher). Children's contrasting experiences of dominance and submission may have their own particular implications for moral development.

8.3 Children's Moral Lives: Complex, Constrained, Cultural and Unique

We have seen that children do not passively accept hegemonic moral values (such as harm avoidance). A child's response to their obligations (including the obligation not to harm, promoted by teachers) in a specific situation is informed by their interpretation of the situation, the values they see as relevant and the interactions between them, their relationships with the people who demand these values, recent events, the child's self-identity and their habitual responses (or virtues). Both their willingness to act and their interpretation of events will also be informed by the extent to which they see themselves as responsible for their actions, which will in itself depend on their dominance relative to others involved in the situation, the language used to describe it, and the audience of the child's claims about culpability.

So while all children at Woodwell Green encountered loyalty, status, justice, harm avoidance and toughness, they did not respond in the same way. This is because for each child, these values were embedded in a unique network of relationships and animated by a singular history of experience and sense of identity. Consequently, children varied in which obligations they found most accessible and compelling, with some finding it much easier than others to conform to the hegemonic value of harm avoidance. Thus children's moral lives are social and cultural, as cultural psychologists and social intuitionists have claimed, while also being unique and deeply personal.

Notes

1. Domain theorists argue that all people, regardless of their cultural background, basically subscribe to the same set of moral values (comprising welfare, justice and rights), and disagreements between them arise only because they interpret events and prioritise between competing values differently. Although I agree with domain theorists that people differ in their interpretations and priorities, I do not agree that all disagreements can necessarily be explained in this way. In other words, I am open to the possibility that people may not all subscribe to the same values, hence some disagreements may arise due to people upholding different values to one another, values that may go beyond welfare, justice and rights.

2. This statement says nothing, of course, about whether one or the other was actually correct. This book only touches on the interesting question of whether and how a person's experiences and definitions of harm are influenced by the definitions and claims of the people around them; see Chapter 6 on homophobia.

3. Domain theorists note that, in judging a complex event, people often encounter not only moral values, but also non-moral concerns. Although I do not subscribe to domain theory's definition of what counts as moral (and non-moral), I agree that people's actions are informed by considerations that most would agree are not moral values, such as self-interest or fear. Nevertheless, here I focus on values that might be considered moral.

4. Stating that children do not freely choose their moral values or actions does not imply that children's morality is determined by their culture, the people around them or any other external force. I would argue instead that a child's orientation to his or her obligations is *self-organised*. This means that children do of course learn from the people, practices and narratives around them. However, the effect of (for example) a particular practice on a specific child is given not in the practice itself but in the child. What that child learns from the practice is a function of his or her cognitive, emotional, social and physical organisation. My position here draws on autopoietic theory (Maturana and Varela 1979; von Uexküll 1931/1982); see Woods (2010) for a more detailed exposition.

References

Aboud, F., Mendelson, M. and Purdy, K. 2003. Cross-race peer relations and friendship quality. *International Journal of Behavioral Development* 27, 165–173.

Adamczyk, A. and Pitt, C. 2009. Shaping attitudes about homosexuality: The role of religion and cultural context. *Social Science Research* 38, 338–351.

Adler, P. and Adler, P. 1998. *Peer Power: Preadolescent Culture and Identity.* Rutgers University Press.

Amit-Talai, V. 1995. The waltz of sociability: Intimacy, dislocation and friendship in a Quebec high school. In *Youth Cultures: A Cross-cultural Perspective*, ed. V. Amit-Talai and H. Wulff. Routledge, pp. 144–165.

Asher, S., Parkhurst, J., Hymel, S. and Williams, G. 1990. Peer rejection and loneliness in childhood. In *Peer Rejection in Childhood*, ed. S. Asher and J. Coie. Cambridge University Press, pp. 253–273.

Astor, R. 1994. Children's moral reasoning about family and peer violence: The role of provocation and retribution. *Child Development* 65(4), 1054–1067.

Astor, R. 1998. Moral reasoning about school violence: Informational assumptions about harm within school subcontexts. *Educational Psychologist* 33, 207–221.

Ayoub, M. and Barnett, S. 1965. Ritualized verbal insult in white high school culture. *Journal of American Folklore* 78, 337–344.

Baerveldt, C., Van Duijn, M., Vermeij, L. and Van Hemert, D. 2004. Ethnic boundaries and personal choice: Assessing the influence of individual inclinations to choose intra-ethnic relationships on pupils' networks. *Social Networks* 26, 55–74.

Bandura, A. 1999. Moral disengagement in the perpetration of inhumanities. *Personality and Social Psychology Review* 3, 193–209.

Children's Moral Lives: An Ethnographic and Psychological Approach, First Edition. Ruth Woods.
© 2013 John Wiley & Sons, Ltd. Published 2013 by John Wiley & Sons, Ltd.

Baumann, G. 1996. *Contesting Culture: Discourses of Identity in Multi-ethnic London.* Cambridge University Press.

Benenson, J. 1994. Ages four to six years: Changes in the structures of play networks of girls and boys. *Merrill-Palmer Quarterly* 40, 478–487.

Bhatti, G. 1999. *Asian Children at Home and at School.* Routledge.

Blasi, A. 1987. Comment: The psychological definitions of morality. In *The Emergence of Morality in Young Children,* ed. J. Kagan and S. Lamb. University of Chicago Press, pp. 83–90.

Blatchford, P. 1989. *Playtime in the Primary School: Problems and Improvements.* Routledge.

Blatchford, P. 1993. Bullying in the playground. In *Understanding and Managing Bullying,* ed. D. Tattum. Heinemann, pp. 105–118.

Blatchford, P. 1998. *Social Life in School: Pupils' Experience of Breaktime and Recess from 7 to 16 Years.* Falmer Press.

Blatchford, P. and Sumpner, C. 1998. What do we know about breaktime? Results from a national survey of breaktime and lunchtime in primary and secondary schools [1]. *British Educational Research Journal* 24, 79–94.

Boulton, M. 1992. Participation in playground activities at middle school. *Educational Research* 34, 167–182.

Boulton, M. 1993a. Aggressive fighting in British middle school children. *Educational Studies* 19, 19–39.

Boulton, M. 1993b. Children's abilities to distinguish between playful and aggressive fighting: A developmental perspective. *British Journal of Developmental Psychology* 11(3), 249–263.

Boulton, M. 1994. Understanding and preventing bullying in the junior school playground. In *School Bullying: Insights and Perspectives,* ed. P. Smith and S. Sharp. Routledge, pp. 132–159.

Boulton, M. and Smith, P. 1996. Liking and peer perceptions among Asian and white British children. *Journal of Social and Personal Relationships* 13, 163–177.

Brown, L. 1998. *Raising Their Voices: The Politics of Girls' Anger.* Harvard University Press.

Burman, E. 2008. *Deconstructing Developmental Psychology,* 2nd edn. Routledge.

Connell, R. 1989. Cool guys, swots and wimps: The interplay of masculinity and education. *Oxford Review of Education* 15, 291–303.

Connolly, P. 1998. *Racism, Gender Identities and Young Children: Social Relations in a Multi-ethnic, Inner City Primary School.* Routledge.

Connolly, P. and Keenan, M. 2002. Racist harassment in the white hinterlands: Minority ethnic children and parents' experiences of schooling in Northern Ireland. *British Journal of Sociology of Education* 23, 341–355.

Corsaro, W. 1985. *Friendship and Peer Culture in the Early Years.* Ablex.

Crick, N.R. and Dodge, K.A. 1994. A review and reformulation of social information-processing mechanisms in children's social adjustment. *Psychological Bulletin* 115, 74–101.

Crick, N.R. and Rose, A. 2000. Toward a gender-balanced approach to the study of social-emotional development: A look at relational aggression. In *Toward a Feminist Developmental Psychology*, ed. P. Miller and E. Scholnick. Routledge, pp. 153–168.

Davey, A. and Mullin, P. 1982. Inter-ethnic friendship in British primary schools. *Educational Research* 24, 83–92.

Davies, B. 1982. *Life in the Classroom and Playground: The Accounts of Primary School Children*. Routledge and Kegan Paul.

Davis, P. and Florian, L. 2004. *Teaching Strategies and Approaches for Pupils with Special Educational Needs: A Scoping Study*. HMSO.

DCSF 2010. Religious education in English schools: Non-statutory guidance. https://www.education.gov.uk/publications/eOrderingDownload/DCSF-00114-2010.pdf, accessed 15 February 2013.

Dennis, R. 1996. Racism. In *The Social Science Encyclopedia*, 2nd edn, ed. A. Kuper and J. Kuper. Routledge, pp. 715–717.

DfES 2004. *Every Child Matters: Change for Children in Schools*. London: DfES.

Dodge, K.A. and Coie, J.D. 1987. Social-information-processing factors in reactive and proactive aggression in children's peer groups. *Journal of Personality and Social Psychology* 53, 1146–1158.

Eder, D. 1985. The cycle of popularity: Interpersonal relations among female adolescents. *Sociology of Education* 58(3), 154–165.

Edwards, C. 1987. Culture and the construction of moral values: A comparative ethnography of moral encounters in two cultural settings. In *The Emergence of Morality in Young Children*, ed. J. Kagan and S. Lamb. University of Chicago Press, pp. 123–151.

Edwards, D. 1997. *Discourse and Cognition*. Sage.

Epstein, D. and Johnson, R. 1998. *Schooling Sexualities*. Open University Press.

Eslea, M. and Mukhtar, K. 2000. Bullying and racism among Asian schoolchildren in Britain. *Educational Research* 42, 207–217.

Espelage, D. and Swearer, S. (eds) 2010. *Bullying in North American Schools*, 2nd edn. Routledge.

Evaldsson, A.C. 2002. Boys' gossip telling: Staging identities and indexing (unacceptable) masculine behavior. *Text* 22(2), 199–225.

Evaldsson, A.C. 2004. Shifting moral stances: Morality and gender in same-sex and cross-sex game interaction. *Research on Language and Social Interaction* 37(3), 331–363.

Evaldsson, A.C. 2007. Accounting for friendship: Moral ordering and category membership in preadolescent girls' relational talk. *Research on Language and Social Interaction* 40(4), 377–404.

Evans, G. 2006. *Educational Failure and Working Class White Children in Britain*. Palgrave Macmillan.

Evans, J. 1989. *Children at Play: Life in the School Playground*. Deakin University Press.

References

Ferguson, A. 2000. *Bad Boys: Public Schools in the Making of Black Masculinity.* University of Michigan Press.

Fine, G. 1986. The social organization of adolescent gossip: The rhetoric of moral evaluation. In *Children's Worlds and Children's Language,* ed. J. Cook-Gumperz, W. Corsaro and J. Streeck. Mouton de Gruyter, pp. 405–423.

Fry, D. 1988. Intercommunity differences in aggression among Zapotec children. *Child Development* 59(4), 1008–1019.

Fry, D. 2006. Reciprocity: The foundation stone of morality. In *Handbook of Moral Development,* ed. M. Killen and J. Smetana. Lawrence Erlbaum, pp. 399–422.

García-Sánchez, I. 2011. Language socialization and exclusion. In *The Handbook of Language Socialization,* ed. A. Duranti, E. Ochs and B. Schieffelin. John Wiley & Sons, pp. 391–419.

Gill, T. 2007. *No Fear: Growing Up in a Risk Averse Society.* Calouste Gulbenkian Foundation.

Goodwin, M. 2002. Exclusion in girls' peer group: Ethnographic analysis of language practices on the playground. *Human Development* 45, 392–415.

Goodwin, M. and Kyratzis, A. 2011. Peer language socialization. In *The Handbook of Language Socialization,* ed. A. Duranti, E. Ochs and B. Schieffelin. John Wiley & Sons, pp. 365–390.

Goodwin, M.H. 2006. *The Hidden Life of Girls: Games of Stance, Status, and Exclusion.* Blackwell.

Griffiths, V. 1995. *Adolescent Girls and Their Friends: A Feminist Ethnography.* Avebury.

Haidt, J. 2001. The emotional dog and its rational tail: A social intuitionist approach to moral judgement. *Psychological Review* 108, 814–834.

Haidt, J. and Graham, J. 2007. When morality opposes justice: Conservatives have moral intuitions that liberals may not recognize. *Social Justice Research* 20, 98–116.

Haidt, J. and Joseph, C. 2004. Intuitive ethics: How innately prepared intuitions generate culturally variable virtues. *Daedalus* 133(4), 55–66.

Haidt, J. and Joseph, C. 2008. The moral mind: How five sets of innate moral intuitions guide the development of many culture-specific virtues, and perhaps even modules. In *The Innate Mind, Volume 3: Foundations and the Future,* ed. P. Carruthers, S. Laurence and S. Stich. Oxford University Press, pp. 367–391.

Haidt, J., Koller, S. and Dias, M. 1993. Affect, culture, and morality, or is it wrong to eat your dog? *Journal of Personality and Social Psychology* 65(4), 613–628.

Hallinan, M. and Teixeira, R. 1987. Opportunities and constraints: Black–white differences in the formation of interracial friendships. *Child Development* 58, 1358–1371.

Hartup, W. 1983. Peer relations. In *Carmichael's Manual of Child Psychology, Volume 4: Socialization, Personality, and Social Development,* 4th edn, ed. P.H. Mussen. John Wiley & Sons, pp. 103–196.

References

Hey, V. 1997. *The Company She Keeps: An Ethnography of Girls' Friendship.* Open University Press.

HMSO 2003. *Every Child Matters.* Government Green Paper.

Hooghe, M., Claes, E., Harell, A., Quintelier, E. and Dejaeghere, Y. 2010. Anti-gay sentiment among adolescents in Belgium and Canada: A comparative investigation into the role of gender and religion. *Journal of Homosexuality* 57(3), 384–400.

Horn, S. 2003. Adolescents' reasoning about exclusion from social groups. *Developmental Psychology* 39(1), 71–84.

Hymel, S., Wagner, E. and Butler, L. 1990. Reputational bias: View from the peer group. In *Peer Rejection in Childhood*, ed. S. Asher and J. Coie. Cambridge University Press, pp. 156–185.

Killen, M., Margie, N. and Sinno, S. 2006. Morality in the context of intergroup relations. In *Handbook of Moral Development*, ed. M. Killen and J. Smetana. Lawrence Erlbaum, pp. 155–183.

Kobayashi, A. and Ray, B. 2000. Civil risk and landscapes of marginality in Canada: A pluralist approach to social justice. *Canadian Geographer* 44(4), 401–417.

Kyriacou, C. 1986. *Effective Teaching in Schools.* Simon and Schuster Education.

Kyriacou, C. 1997. *Effective Teaching in Schools: Theory and Practice*, 2nd edn. Stanley Thornes.

Kyriacou, C. 2009. *Effective Teaching in Schools: Theory and Practice*, 3rd edn. Nelson Thornes.

Lefever, H. 1981. 'Playing the dozens': A mechanism for social control. *Phylon* 42(1), 73–85.

Maccoby, E.E. 1990. Gender and relationships: A developmental account. *American Psychologist* 45(4), 513–520.

Maturana, H. and Varela, F. 1979. *Autopoiesis and Cognition: The Realization of the Living.* Kluwer.

McKown, C. 2004. Age and ethnic variations in children's thinking about the nature of racism. *Applied Developmental Psychology* 25, 597–617.

Miller, J. 2006. Insights into moral development from cultural psychology. In *Handbook of Moral Development*, ed. M. Killen and J. Smetana. Lawrence Erlbaum, pp. 375–398.

Mooij, T. 1993. Working towards understanding and prevention in the Netherlands. In *Understanding and Managing Bullying*, ed. D. Tattum. Heinemann, pp. 31–44.

Nobes, G., Panagiotaki, G. and Pawson, C. 2009. The influence of negligence, intention, and outcome on children's moral judgements. *Journal of Experimental Child Psychology* 104, 382–397.

Nucci, L. 1981. Conceptions of personal issues: A domain distinct from moral or societal concepts. *Child Development* 52(1), 114–121.

Nucci, L. and Nucci, M. 1982. Children's responses to moral and social conventional transgressions in free-play settings. *Child Development* 53(5), 1337–1342.

Ofsted 1993. *Achieving Good Behaviour in Schools*. HMSO.

Olson, R., Cadge, W. and Harrison, J. 2006. Religion and public opinion about same-sex marriage. *Social Science Quarterly* 87, 340–360.

Olweus, D. 1991. Bully/victim problems among schoolchildren: Basic facts and effects of a school-based intervention programme. In *The Development and Treatment of Childhood Aggression*, ed. D. Pepler and K. Rubin. Lawrence Erlbaum, pp. 411–448.

Parker-Jenkins, M. 1999. *Sparing the Rod: Schools, Discipline and Children's Rights*. Trentham Books.

Pasupathi, M. and Wainryb, C. 2010. Developing moral agency through narrative. *Human Development* 53, 55–80.

Pellegrini, A. 2003. Perceptions and functions of play and real fighting in early adolescence. *Child Development* 74(5), 1522–1533.

Pellegrini, A. and Blatchford, P. 2000. *The Child at School: Interactions with Peers and Teachers*. Arnold.

Piaget, J. 1932. *The Moral Judgement of the Child*. Routledge and Kegan Paul.

Power, T. 2000. *Play and Exploration in Children and Animals*. Lawrence Erlbaum.

QCA 2004. *Religious education: The non-statutory national framework*. http://webarchive. nationalarchives.gov.uk/20090903160937/http:/qca.org.uk/libraryAssets/ media/9817_re_national_framework_04.pdf, accessed 15 February 2013.

Renold, E. 2002. Presumed innocence: (Hetero)sexual, heterosexist and homophobic harassment among primary school girls and boys. *Childhood* 9(4), 415–434.

Robinson, K. 2005. Doing anti-homophobia and anti-heterosexism in early childhood education: Moving beyond the immobilising impacts of 'risks', 'hears' and 'silences'. Can we afford not to? *Contemporary Issues in Early Childhood* 6(2), 175–188.

Roland, E. 1993. Bullying: A developing tradition of research and management. In *Understanding and Managing Bullying*, ed. D. Tattum. Heinemann, pp. 15–30.

Romera Felix, E., Del Rey Alamillo, R. and Ortega Ruiz, R. 2011. Prevalence and differentiating aspects related to gender with regard to the bullying phenomenon in poor countries. *Psicothema* 23(4), 624–629.

Savin-Williams, R. 1976. An ethological study of dominance formation and maintenance in a group of human adolescents. *Child Development* 47, 972–979.

Sharp, S. and Smith, P. 1993. Tackling bullying: The Sheffield project. In *Understanding and Managing Bullying*, ed. D. Tattum. Heinemann, pp. 45–56.

Shaw, M. 1973. Changes in sociometric choices following forced integration of an elementary school. *Journal of Social Issues* 29, 143–157.

Shultz, T., Wright, K. and Schleifer, M. 1986. Assignment of moral responsibility and punishment. *Child Development* 57, 177–184.

Shweder, R. and Much, N. 1991. Determinations of meaning: Discourse and moral socialization. In *Thinking Through Cultures: Expeditions in Cultural Psychology*, ed. R. Shweder. Harvard University Press, pp. 186–240.

References

Shweder, R., Mahapatra, M. and Miller, J. 1987. Culture and moral development. In *The Emergence of Morality in Young Children*, ed. J. Kagan and S. Lamb. University of Chicago Press, pp. 1–83.

Shweder, R., Much, N., Mahapatra, M. and Park, L. 1997. The 'big three' of morality (autonomy, community, divinity) and the 'big three' explanations of suffering. In *Morality and Health*, ed. A. Brandt and P. Rozin. Routledge, pp. 119–169.

Sluckin, A. 1981. *Growing Up in the Playground: The Social Development of Children*. Routledge and Kegan Paul.

Smetana, J. 1981. Preschool children's conceptions of moral and social rules. *Child Development* 52(4), 1333–1336.

Smetana, J. 2006. Social-cognitive domain theory: Consistencies and variations in children's moral and social judgements. In *Handbook of Moral Development*, ed. M. Killen and J. Smetana. Lawrence Erlbaum, pp. 119–153.

Smetana, J., Campione-Barr, N. and Yell, N. 2003. Children's moral and affective judgements regarding provocation and retaliation. *Merrill-Palmer Quarterly* 49(2), 209–236.

Song, M., Smetana, J. and Kim, S. 1987. Korean children's conceptions of moral and conventional transgressions. *Developmental Psychology* 23(4), 577.

Spiel, C. and Strohmeier, D. 2011. National strategy for violence prevention in the Austrian public school system: Development and implementation. *International Journal of Behavioral Development* 35(5), 412–418.

Svahn, J. and Evaldsson, A.C. 2011. 'You could just ignore me': Situating peer exclusion within the contingencies of girls' everyday interactional practices. *Childhood* 18(4), 491–508.

Swain, J. 2003. How young schoolboys become somebody: The role of the body in the construction of masculinity. *British Journal of Sociology of Education* 24, 299–314.

Swain, J. 2004. The resources and strategies that 10–11-year-old boys use to construct masculinities in the school setting. *British Educational Research Journal* 30, 167–185.

Tattum, D. 1993. What is bullying? In *Understanding and Managing Bullying*, ed. D. Tattum. Heinemann, pp. 3–14.

Theobald, M. and Danby, S. in press. 'Well, now I'm upset': Moral and social orders in the playground. In *Morality in practice: Exploring Childhood, Parenthood and Schooling in Everyday Life*, ed. J. Cromdal and M. Tholander. Equinox.

Tholander, M. and Aronsson, K. 2002. Teasing as serious business: Collaborative staging and response work. *Text* 22(4), 559–595.

Thorne, B. 1993. *Gender Play: Girls and Boys in School*. Open University Press.

Toren, C. 1990. *Making Sense of Hierarchy: Cognition as Social Process in Fiji*. Athlone Press.

Troyna, B. and Hatcher, R. 1992. *Racism in Children's Lives: A Study of Mainly-White Primary Schools*. Routledge.

231

References

Turiel, E. 2006. Thought, emotions, and social interactional processes in moral development. In *Handbook of Moral Development*, ed. M. Killen and J. Smetana. Lawrence Erlbaum, pp. 7–35.

Turiel, E. 2008. Thought about actions in social domains: Morality, social conventions, and social interactions. *Cognitive Development* 23, 136–154.

Turiel, E., Killen, M. and Helwig, C. 1987. Morality: Its structures, functions, and vagaries. In *The Emergence of Morality in Young Children*, ed. J. Kagan and S. Lamb. University of Chicago Press, pp. 155–243.

Van Maanen, J. 1996. Ethnography. In *The Social Science Encyclopedia*, 2nd edn, ed. A. Kuper and J. Kuper. Routledge, pp. 263–265.

Verkuyten, M. and Thijs, J. 2002. Racist victimization among children in the Netherlands: The effect of ethnic group and school. *Ethnic and Racial Studies* 25, 310–331.

von Uexküll, J. 1931/1982. The theory of meaning. *Semiotica* 42, 25–82.

Wainryb, C. 2006. Moral development in culture: Diversity, tolerance, and justice. In *Handbook of Moral Development*, ed. M. Killen and J. Smetana. Lawrence Erlbaum, pp. 211–240.

Wainryb, C., Brehl, B. and Matwin, S. 2005. Being hurt and hurting others: Children's narrative accounts and moral judgements of their own interpersonal conflicts. *Monographs of the Society for Research in Child Development*.

Whiting, B. and Whiting, J. 1975. *Children of Six Cultures: A Psycho-cultural Analysis*. Harvard University Press.

Willis, P.E. 1977. *Learning to Labour: How Working Class Kids Get Working Class Jobs*. Saxon House.

Woods, J. 2005. *A Study of Intersubjectivity in Children's Meaning-making at a Multicultural London Primary School*. PhD thesis. Department of Human Sciences, Brunel University.

Woods, R. 2007. Children constructing 'Englishness' and other ethnic identities at a multicultural London primary school. In *Approaches to Englishness: Differences, Diversity and Identities*, ed. C. Hart. Midrash Publishing, pp. 172–182.

Woods, R. 2008. When rewards and sanctions fail: A case study of a primary school rule-breaker. *International Journal of Qualitative Studies in Education* 21(2), 181–196.

Woods, R. 2009. The use of aggression in primary school boys' decisions about inclusion in and exclusion from playground football games. *British Journal of Educational Psychology* 79(2), 223–238.

Woods, R. 2010. A critique of the concept of accuracy in social information processing models of children's peer relations. *Theory and Psychology* 20(1), 5–27.

Wulff, H. 1995. Inter-racial friendship: Consuming youth styles, ethnicity and teenage femininity in south London. In *Youth Cultures: A Cross-cultural Perspective*, ed. V. Amit-Talai and H. Wulff. Routledge. pp. 63–80.

Zelazo, P., Helwig, C. and Lau, A. 1996. Intention, act, and outcome in behavioral prediction and moral judgement. *Child Development* 67, 2478–2492.

Appendix
Children's Ethnicity, Religion and Gender

The ethnicity, religion and gender of all children mentioned in the book are recorded in tables A.1–A.3. This information is taken from school records. See Chapter 1 for a rationale for this appendix, along with a discussion of the socially constructed nature of ethnic and religious identity.

Children's Moral Lives: An Ethnographic and Psychological Approach, First Edition. Ruth Woods.
© 2013 John Wiley & Sons, Ltd. Published 2013 by John Wiley & Sons, Ltd.

Table A.1 Ethnicity, religion and gender of children with pseudonyms beginning with A to H

Child's pseudonym	Ethnicity	Religion	Gender
Abdi	Somali	Muslim	boy
Adam	English	Christian	boy
Akash	Indian	Hindu	boy
Alan	English	Christian	boy
Ali	Somali	Muslim	boy
Amandeep	Indian	Sikh	boy
Amar	Pakistani	Muslim	boy
Amira	unknown	unknown	girl
Amrita	Indian	Sikh	girl
Anil	mixed	Sikh	boy
Anjali	other	Christian	girl
Asha	Somali	Muslim	girl
Ayaan	Somali	Muslim	boy
Ayesha	Pakistani	Muslim	girl
Bikram	Afghanistani	Sikh	girl
Bobby	English	Christian	boy
Bradley	English	none	boy
Daniel	Scottish	Christian	boy
Erickah	Black African	Christian	girl
Ethan	White Western European	Christian	boy
Fadi	Pakistani	Muslim	boy
Faizel	Pakistani	Muslim	boy
Farah	Pakistani	Muslim	girl
Farhan	Pakistani	Muslim	boy
Finlay	unknown	unknown	boy
Gagandeep	Indian	Sikh	boy
Hafiz	Pakistani	Muslim	boy
Harpreet	Indian	Sikh	girl
Hasad	unknown	unknown	boy
Hassan	Pakistani	Muslim	boy
Holly	English	Christian	girl

Table A.2 Ethnicity, religion and gender of children with pseudonyms beginning with I to M

Child's pseudonym	Ethnicity	Religion	Gender
Idris	Arab	Muslim	boy
Jack	unknown	unknown	boy
Jade	English	none	girl
Jagpal	Indian	Sikh	boy
James	unknown	unknown	boy
Jane	Mixed	Christian	girl
Jaskaran	Indian	Sikh	boy
Jasmeen	Indian	Sikh	girl
Jason	unknown	unknown	boy
Jerome	unknown	unknown	boy
Joanne	English	no religion	girl
Jordan	Mixed	Christian	boy
Joshua	English	none	boy
Karan	Indian	Hindu	boy
Kay	other	unclassified	girl
Kiran	Indian	Sikh	girl
Larry	Mixed	unknown	boy
Laura	English	Christian	girl
Leanne	Mixed	none	girl
Leo	Indian	Christian	boy
Leon	other	Christian	boy
Lewis	English	none	boy
Louise	Indian	Christian	girl
Mahdi	Bangladeshi	Muslim	boy
Mandeer	Indian	Sikh	boy
Manpreet	Indian	Sikh	girl
Mansukh	Indian	Sikh	boy
Maria	Pakistani	Christian	girl
Megan	Welsh	Christian	girl
Michael	unknown	unknown	boy
Mohamed	Pakistani	Muslim	boy
Mohan	Indian	Sikh	boy
Mudit	Indian	Hindu	boy

Appendix

Table A.3 Ethnicity, religion and gender of children with pseudonyms beginning with N to Z

Child's pseudonym	Ethnicity	Religion	Gender
Nadia	unknown	unknown	girl
Navjot	Indian	Sikh	girl
Navneet	Indian	Sikh	girl
Nayna	Indian	Sikh	girl
Nina	Indian	Hindu	girl
Nita	Indian	Sikh	girl
Nyarai	unknown	unknown	girl
Owen	Mixed	Christian	boy
Paul	English	Christian	boy
Paula	Black mixed heritage	Christian	girl
Pavandeep	Afghanistani	Sikh	boy
Prajit	Indian	Sikh	boy
Priyanka	unknown	unknown	girl
Rachel	mixed	none	girl
Reece	other	Christian	boy
Robbie	English	Christian	boy
Roshni	unknown	unknown	girl
Sam	English	none	boy
Sandeep	Indian	Sikh	boy
Sarah	English	Christian	girl
Sarina	Indian	Hindu	girl
Simran	Indian	Sikh	girl
Sohaib	Pakistani	Muslim	boy
Sohil	Indian	Christian	boy
Sophie	English	unknown	girl
Soraj	Indian	Sikh	boy
Tyrone	other Black background	Christian	boy
Venya	Indian	Hindu	girl
Vikram	Indian	Sikh	boy
Yusuf	Pakistani	Muslim	boy
Zain	Arab	Muslim	boy
Zak	Somali	Muslim	boy
Zena	Black Caribbean	Christian	girl
Zohraiz	Iranian	Muslim	boy

Index

Accountability, 81–92,
 108–109, 217
 and intention, 170–178, 201–202,
 218
 and moral development, 202–203,
 218, 219
 and narrative, 201–203, 219
 and provocation, 178–185,
 201–202
 see also Hierarchy
Adults, 14
 and concerns about harm to
 children, 2–4, 21, 38–39,
 45, 47, 208–209
 giving moral lessons, 47–48, 75–78,
 112–113, 145–146
 intervention in children's lives, 96,
 168–170, 208
 finding out what happened,
 185–195 (*see also* Truth)
 historical change, 1–5,
 166–168
 resolving disputes,
 195–198
Arguments, *see* Disputes

Banter, *see* Playful aggression
Boys, *see* Gender
Bullying, 3–4, 148, *see also* Harm

Child abuse, 4
Cultural psychology, 5, 7, 11, 24, 209
Culture
 cross-cultural differences, 43, 50, 213
 and moral development, 5–9, 209

Deception, *see* Truth
Disputes
 about exclusivity, 97, 118, 137
 about game rules, 60
 about intention, 170, 176, 177
 about reciprocity, 178–180
 adults' solutions, 187–198, 203
 between boys and girls, 33–36
 between children and adults, 222
 children's solutions, 198–201, 204
 and gang formation, 127–134
 physical fights, 42, 43, 69, 186
 and teasing, 33, 39, 40
Domain theory, 7, 8, 11, 24, 209–211
Dominance, *see* Hierarchy

Children's Moral Lives: An Ethnographic and Psychological Approach, First Edition. Ruth Woods.
© 2013 John Wiley & Sons, Ltd. Published 2013 by John Wiley & Sons, Ltd.

Ethnicity, 14–15, 43
  and friendship, 99–102
  and identity, 99–101, 158–162,
    164, 210
  see also Multiculturalism; Racism
Ethnography, *see* Participant
  observation
Every Child Matters, *see*
  Government policy
Exclusion, 68, 116
  adult representations of, 76–79, 95,
    105–108
  children's views on, 78–79, 102–104
  and ethnic identity, 99–102,
    107, 210
  for game maintenance and success,
    92–95, 106
  and hierarchy, 80–92, 108–109
  and moral development, 90–92,
    108, 109
  as reciprocity, 104–105
Exclusivity, 110, 118

Fairness, *see* Justice
Femininity, *see* Gender
Fights, *see* Disputes; Physical
  aggression
Football, *see* Games
Freedom, 112–114, 122, 123, 125,
  138–140, 213, 214
Friendship
  contingency friendships, 122–125
  and loyalty, 114–127
  resolving disputes in, 198–200

Games, 30, 32, 99, 129, 141, 142, 147
  chasing games, 110, 142
  dances, 32, 86–87, 100
  football, 34, 59, 80, 92–95, 137,
    197–198
  role-play games, 89–90, 177
Gender, 99
  differences between boys and girls,
    33–38, 136–138, 141

  norms of femininity, 36–37, 44,
    120–122, 213
  norms of masculinity, 36–37,
    64–66, 146–147, 194–195,
    213, 215
Girls, *see* Gender
Government policy, 3, 4, 18
  Every Child Matters, 4
  on homophobia, 148
  on racism, 145

Harm, 3–4, 16–17, 47, 208, 210–211
  adult obligations to prevent, 2–5,
    25, 38–39, 208
  adults' lessons about, 45, 47–48,
    75–76, 177, 178
  disputes about what counts as,
    31–39, 210
  ranking of different types of, 145,
    150, 164
  see also Exclusion; Physical
    aggression; Possessiveness
Hierarchy, 5, 211–212, 214
  effects on moral development,
    90–92, 109, 220–222
  and efficacy, 48, 81–90, 108–109,
    130–134, 141–142, 220–221
  and physical aggression, 63–70,
    81–84, 137
  and popularity, 121, 125, 126, 214
Homophobia
  children's experiences of,
    146–149, 164
  government policy on, 148
  school's position on, 146–149, 162
  tensions with multiculturalism,
    148–150, 163
Hypothetical scenarios, 9, 167,
  198, 200
  about exclusion, 78–79, 81–84,
    90–91, 93
  about intention, 174–175
  about physical aggression, 51–52,
    54–56, 185, 200

about possessiveness, 98, 113, 116, 119, 138
about reciprocity, 180

Intention, 201–202, 218
   adults' views on, 174, 177–178
   children's claims about, 170–177
   in moral development, 206–207
Interpretations
   and assumptions about reality, 209–210
   and bias, 61–63, 72, 194, 205–206
   differences in, 31–39, 45, 129, 170–185, 188–191, 209–211
   and relationship to protagonists, 171–174, 187–188, 210–211

Justice, 8, 50, 201–202, 212, 216
   adult–child clashes over, 60–63, 71
   adults' concerns with, 58, 184–185
   children's concerns with, 49–63, 93, 104–105, 158, 179–184

Language
   accent, 29, 43, 154
   and racism, 153–154
   rhetorical use of, 203, 218
   speaking 'Indian,' 29, 99–102, 154
   see also Narrative
Loneliness, 123–125, 140
Loyalty, 5, 114, 187, 212, 215
   as availability, 98, 108, 114–127, 140–141
   gender differences in, 136–138, 141
   as shared enemies, 127–136, 141–142
   and solidarity, 2, 222
   see also Possessiveness

Masculinity, *see* Gender
Moral development, 216–217
   and accountability, 218
   and culture, 5–10, 209
   and exclusion, 90–92, 108, 109

and hierarchy, 90–92, 109, 220–221
   and intention, 174–177
   and narrative, 7, 202–203, 217, 219–220
   and social interaction, 7
Morality
   cross-cultural differences in, 50
   definitions of, 11–13
   development of (*see* Moral development)
   theories of (*see* Cultural psychology; Domain theory; Social intuitionist theory)
Multiculturalism, 14–16, 144, 208
   and respect, 148–149, 160–162
   school's view of, 144–145, 158–159
   tensions with homophobia, 148–149, 162–163
   see also Ethnicity; Racism

Narrative, 203
   and accountability, 201–203, 217
   and moral development, 7, 202, 217, 219
   see also Language

Participant observation, 10, 18, 20
Physical aggression, 47
   and hierarchy, 63–70, 81–84, 137
   and justice, 49–63, 71–72
   and norms of masculinity, 64–68, 137
Playful aggression
   differences in interpretation of, 31–39, 44, 209–210
   physical, 25, 27, 34, 43–44
   and toughness, 39–41
   verbal, 25, 31–33, 43, 44
   see also Toughness
Playground supervisors, *see* Adults
Popularity, 68, 118–121, 125
Possessiveness, 119, 126, 130–134
   adults' views on, 112, 139
   children's views on, 113
   and loyalty, 140–141

Power, *see* Hierarchy
Prioritising between values, 149,
 213–216, 223
 and development of virtues,
 216–217
 domain theory on, 209
 between freedom and loyalty, 125
 between harm and justice, 53–56, 71
 obligations in relationships,
 215–216
 between types of harm, 145
 when conducting research, 21

Racism, 38–39, 210
 children's experiences of, 105,
 154–158, 164
 definitions of, 150–162
 and English parents, 158–162, 164
 government policy on, 148
 school's position on, 144–146, 162
 see also Ethnicity; Multiculturalism
Reciprocity, *see* Justice
Reputation, 62, 63, 67, 193–195
Respect between children, *see*
 Hierarchy
Respect for religious belief, 148–150,
 160–161, *see also*
 Multiculturalism
Rough and tumble play, *see* Playful
 aggression

School, 13
 discipline methods, 17–18, 38, 54, 57
 rules, 16–18, 25, 47–48, 75, 208

Social class, 16, 43–44, 70, 216
Social interaction and moral
 development, 7
Social interactionist theory, *see*
 Domain theory
Social intuitionist theory, 5–7, 11–12,
 24, 209, 216–217
Social status, *see* Hierarchy
Solidarity, *see* Loyalty
Submission, *see* Hierarchy

Teachers, *see* Adults
Teasing, *see* Playful aggression
Telling tales, 1–2
 children's willingness to, 166–169,
 208
Theories, *see* Cultural psychology;
 Domain theory; Social
 intuitionist theory
Toughness, 39–43, 45, 64–68, 210,
 215
 and social class, 43–44, 215
 see also Physical aggression; Playful
 aggression
Trust, 9, 61–63, 72, 188, 193–195,
 205
Truth
 adult construction of, 188–191,
 203–206
 and deception, 185–188

Virtues, 6, 216–217

Welfare, *see* Harm